India *A Culinary Journey*

India *A Culinary Journey*

Prem Souri Kishore

HIPPOCRENE BOOKS, INC.
New York

Book and cover design by Wanda España/Wee Design Group and K&P Publishing

Front cover photo: Ganges River scene © istockphoto.com/Jeremy Edwards. //
        Indian meal ©istockphoto.com/travellinglight.
Back cover photos: Vegetables, Mumbai chat vendor, Kashmiri girl courtesy of
        Prem Kishore.

For more information, address:
HIPPOCRENE BOOKS, INC.
171 Madison Avenue
New York, NY 10016
www.hippocrenebooks.com

Library of Congress Cataloging-in-Publication Data

Kishore, Prem.
  India : a culinary journey / Prem Souri Kishore.
    p. cm.
  ISBN-13: 978-0-7818-1263-4 (hbk.)
  ISBN-10: 0-7818-1263-1 (hbk.)
  ISBN-13: 978-0-7818-1386-0 (pbk.)
  1. Cooking, Indic. 2. Food--India. 3. Cookbooks. 4. India--Social life
and customs. I. Title.
  TX724.5.I4K58 2011
  641.5954--dc23
                        2011041308

Printed in the United States of America.

Contents

Dedication

To ANURADHA

For inspiring me daily with her brave passionate spirit, wit, sparkle, and radiance

To SANGEETHA

For bringing music and sunshine into my life

To BOBBY

My first fine rapture and firm anchor

Map of India

Foreword by Stephen Huyler

Right now. Drop everything else and enter the entrancing worlds of this book. Prem Kishore will transport you to the heart of India in all its diversity. The pages of *India: A Culinary Journey* are redolent with pungent spices, savory smells, simmering flavors, sticky sweetness.

Drawing you into the sensory world of her childhood and the foods that defined it, Prem invites you to come home with her, to experience the delights and complexities of what it means to grow up in a traditional Indian household. Rarely seen by outsiders, the kitchen is the pulse of every Indian family: both a sacred space where food is first offered to the gods before it may be consumed, and a center of constant activity from early morning until the last moments before slumber.

As I read *India: A Culinary Journey,* I sit at the feet of a masterful storyteller, spellbound as she spins her tales of the kitchens and courtyards of her childhood, of storage rooms brimming with sacks of rice, lentils, grains, of jars of pickles warming in the courtyard sun, of chilies drying on rooftops, of women sharing in the daily grinding of grains and spices, and of the myriad scents and flavors of household cooking that permeate everything.

Prem Kishore's memories of India are a rich blend of spices. She seamlessly balances stories and recipes that encompass the breadth of India: from south to north, pure vegetarian to varied fish and meat dishes, Hindu, Muslim, Christian and Parsi. *India: A Culinary Journey* is truly a tribute to the complex masala of Indian cultures.

I want to stop at every paragraph and read it aloud to my friends, to be able to finally share with fellow Americans what it is truly like to be in an Indian home. Nothing, no experience in an Indian restaurant can hold a candle to it. Indian restaurant food never approximates the subtleties of flavor, scent, texture, and diversity of Indian home cooking. Prem's descriptions make me want to fly right back to India. Luckily this book is jammed with marvelous recipes—accessible ingredients and clear instructions sprinkled with cooking tips garnered from generations of advice passed down from mother to daughter. I want to try them all! The several I have already cooked created sumptuous dishes that all my friends praise.

I'm not adding this book to my library. It won't be stacked among my dozens of favorite cookbooks. I need *India: A Culinary Journey* right at hand.

Like Mom's *Fannie Farmer*, it's future will be well-thumbed and dog-eared, its pages soiled with thumbprints and splattered with bits of recipes, and its cover almost unrecognizable through years of loving use. It soon will be a known part of my family.

—Stephen P. Huyler,
author of *Daughters of India: Art and Identity*

Preface

For my aunt Beulah Souri's hundredth birthday, my cousins from all over the U.S. and the UK arrived at the sprawling house of her son Mahadev in Olympia, Washington, to celebrate her presence with us. Food was our spectacular gift to one another. Twelve of us gathered in the huge embracing kitchen on the waterfront of Puget Sound and cut, diced, gutted, sliced, stewed, pureed, boiled, steamed, and fried, presenting feast after feast for days, swapping stories, reminiscing, singing, dancing, and raising a toast to the history of our family and to our cherished foods of the past and the present. Food was the great connector, the strong fabric, illuminating our family history and traditions.

Every Indian has a food story. What if a billion Indians blogged about food! Think of the incredible storytelling, the must-try recipes, the geographical, cultural, and culinary takes on the varied regions, the sheer range of material, and a whole vocabulary of taste from twenty-nine states and 4,635 communities who speak eighteen official languages and thousands of dialects. Each Indian state has its own language, rituals, and food culture and each region is passionate about the best way to make a signature dish. Food from one region is strikingly different in taste and flavor from those of other regions. The reason being that until railways were built in 1911, there was little contact between the states and food was integral to the identity of a particular state.

With a population comprised of Hindus, Muslims, Sikhs, Christians, Jains, Buddhists, Parsis, Jews, and a multitude of tribal societies, the foods of each region inherited a legacy not only of a myriad of flavors but of a myriad of faiths. And that is why food plays an important role in religious festivals, with specific foods acquiring special significance.

The strongest influence on Indian cuisine has been the *Ayurveda*, the ancient treatise (second millennium BCE) on regulated healthy living and the properties of food. The principle is very simple. The right kind of food helps one achieve optimum health.

A great culinary upheaval came with the surge of invaders, explorers, and traders from Persia, Mongolia, Europe, and the Middle East who brought about a flourishing spice trade and exposed Indian cuisine to outside influences. By the fifteenth century, food in India began to resonate with history, tradition, community, and continuity melding together many cultures.

It is not easy to define Indian cuisine. So much depends on climate, landscape, produce, religions, customs, beliefs, incomes, and imagination. Whether it is an epic *biryani* recipe for 800 people—requiring 100 pounds of meat, 25 pounds of rice, 4 pounds of spices, 10 pounds of clarified butter, and 200 eggs—or a *karela* (bitter gourd) slit halfway, stuffed with spices and vegetables and deep fried, the diversity and range of Indian food reflects multilayered narratives. Food tells us about who we are.

India: A Culinary Journey introduces some of the country's best-known dishes and signature techniques, and draws upon the rich, treasured memories of my grandparents, parents, husband, children, relatives, and friends. The book explores a vibrant food culture, often shaped by the myths and legends connected to each locale. Though every state in India is not represented, as that would be an enormous agenda, what the book does offer is a glimpse of specific landscapes, a sense of the local food scenes, an exploration of the bewildering bounty of foods, and an understanding of the people of India.

Food and Family

My Personal Cooking Gurus

When he was not traveling on business, my father, Jeevanah Souri, would suddenly make forays into the kitchen with keen epicurean expertise and introduce me to anything from quail, partridge, and goat's brains to trotters. There would be a flurry of activity, intense flavors, and energized cooking. My father's food sparked a strange excitement and curiosity in me. Instead of being squeamish, I watched intently as he plucked feathers from a dead chicken, gently washed the liver and brain of a goat, pried apart the claws of a crab, or scaled a fish. It was always a nuanced performance by my father and I enjoyed the inspired meals. But I did not cook.

Even at the time of my marriage, I had not cooked a single dish. I spent my childhood in my grandmother's home in Bangalore, South India. Just when Grandmother, Grace Charles, entrusted me to cut an onion, I moved to my parents' home in Chennai, then known as Madras. There I never went into the kitchen as we had a fulltime cook. My mother, Mabel Souri, suffered from severe bouts of asthma and was banned from the kitchen, which was filled with smoke from the wood fire and the fumes of the kerosene oil stove. So there was no learning the art of cooking at my mother's knee. Instead, my mother introduced me to a world of books, and I was possessed. Once I discovered the joys of reading, I devoured books hungrily—and never entered the kitchen. Nor did I eat food unless it was accompanied by a book propped up on the table.

When my cousins from the Souri family, Rajkumar, Mahadev, Hemalatha, Sheela, Ahalya, and Pratap, and my aunts and uncles arrived on vacations, my mother would cook in the same style as my father—a feverish frenzy— challenging the fumes of the stove and oven to overcome her. And perhaps it was her brave joyous spirit that made her strong during those times, as she helped my father whip up platters of fried fish, juicy prawns bathed in red hot chili spices, meatball kormas, as well as vegetarian food made with subtle finesse. In the late evening on these occasions, the servant and I would carry vessels of water drawn from the well up the wooden staircase to the sweeping terrace. We poured the water over the blistering, sun-baked concrete terrace to cool it. Then we would bring up the mats, tumblers, and banana leaves; and finally, when the whole family was seated under a moon-filled sky, we would eat with exquisite pleasure the dishes my parents had prepared together. Decades later, my doctor cousin Sheela Thiagarajan, who lives in Yorkshire, England, rang me up to tell me she had yet another dream of all of us feasting on my parents' flavorful servings of fish, crab, cutlets, and chicken curries.

At the university where I studied English literature, motivated by my passion for books, I met a young Punjabi Hindu man who had by a quirky coincidence the same first name as mine: Prem, which means love. Could there be a more auspicious sign for our union? Five years later he asked permission from my family, staunch Andhra Christians, to marry me. My distraught father, who could not accept this intercommunal, interfaith marriage, told him that I would make a terrible wife as I "could not even boil water." My father hoped that my shortcomings as a housekeeper would deter the suitor. Blissfully and determinedly, we got married. But what my father said about my skills in the kitchen was true.

I married into a North Indian Punjabi family who were stunned to know that I did not know how to make a simple *roti* (Indian bread). Daily lessons began. My mother-in-law, Basant Kaur, who was an excellent cook, whipped up gourmet vegetarian dishes—which were the heart of all her menus—and rattled off in Punjabi the various ways of cooking spinach, potatoes, peas, and lentils while teaching me the Hindi names (*saag, aloo mutter, dal, and cholay*). As she cooked with finesse and authority, she shared her life experiences with me as she wove together the various strands of the tragic stories about the Indian Partition, when India and Pakistan separated. She was from Rawalpindi which is now part of Pakistan. She spoke of the early struggles of setting up a home in a Southern state with her husband, and of the eccentricity of an aunt who always traveled with her own knife to cut vegetables whenever she visited someone. I began to mumble the strange new names for dishes (*gobi, piaz, baingan, cholay*) and was shocked to know there were more than a dozen varieties of lentils. In my home we had non-vegetarian dishes three times a day. At my in-laws, it was completely vegetarian, except for a meat dish once a month as a special treat for my husband and his younger brother, Rahul, and sister, Sushil. I had to deal with my nervousness as a new daughter-in-law who had yet to be accepted and my clumsiness in peeling a potato, as well as the confusion of not knowing Punjabi. Add to that the challenge of remembering the various stages of cooking an authentic Punjabi meal. I came up with a foolproof plan. As soon as a dish was cooked, I would tell my mother-in-law that the postman was bringing an important letter and I had to go home for a while—that I had applied for a job and was awaiting replies to my inquiries. My home was a street away. I would sprint down the stairs, down the road, and into my home where I grabbed a pencil and paper, wrote down the recipe as much as I could remember it and raced back. Why did I not take down the recipe in front of my mother-in-law? Looking back I think I did not want to look like an idiot who could not even remember the simple ingredients and the intuitive ways of cooking.

✳ ✳ ✳

Balu, a friend of my husband, was from the state of Kerala and a bachelor living on his own in Chennai. He was a superb cook. Often he turned up on weekends with six of our closest friends and rustled up a fiery Kerala fish curry, a spicy *sambhar* (lentil curry), or an excellent *poriyal* (fried vegetables with grated coconut). The meal was consumed accompanied by much laughter and word games. After a satisfying "Balu dinner" we would walk down the street in late evening to the nearest *chai kadai* (tea shop) for a steaming cup of sweet Iranian tea flavored with cardamom. Before Balu left the house, he would meticulously write down a couple of recipes and stick them with rice paste on the walls of my kitchen—my first collection of recipes.

My father, my mother-in-law, and Balu were my cooking gurus who brought their own standards of culinary excellence and signature dishes and more importantly a passion and exuberance to everyday cooking. And then one day, amidst the romantic fiction of Barbara Cartland and Sidney Sheldon thrillers, in a musty, overcrowded, second-hand bookshop near my home called Easwari Lending Library (still in existence and owned by the same shop owner, Palani), in a dim, claustrophobic back room, I found an old tattered cookbook with North and South Indian recipes. My serious encounter with Indian food had begun.

The Theater of Street Food

We moved to Hyderabad after the birth of our first child, Sangeetha, and I set up house with no help from my mother or mother-in-law. I surprised myself by taking pride in choosing vegetables, a cut of meat, a fine specimen of fish, and planning a meal. I began dicing, chopping, and frying. When my second daughter, Anuradha, was born, Govindamma, a cook gifted by my aunt, arrived from Madras, but I was still helping out in the kitchen. This was a blessed time. I enjoyed the independence of being on my own and was flooded with a strange gratification that my own hands were preparing food for my family. This pleasure was most intense when I rolled the cooked rice smothered with spices into small balls and placed them tenderly into the mouths of my children. What could be more intimate than that?

I remembered my grandmother's cooking as well as my few collected recipes, and I began to try out dishes recommended by family, neighbors, friends, and even strangers. Over the years, my writing career took me to different regions of India. Eating foods from various states gave me new delights and excited curiosity and appreciation of another culture, as I tasted different spices and watched varied methods of cooking.

On a visit to Mumbai, I literally stood open mouthed in front of food stalls on Juhu beach. I had discovered an extraordinary street food community and snack food, foods eaten with fingers, lustily and with sheer gusto. Families and friends eating from the same plate. Imagine a traffic-congested road, swirling dust, fumes from a thousand thundering vehicles, and hundreds of people rushing by, the astonishing fresh fragrance of spices and herbs, the hiss and crackle of leaping flames, the skill of the vendor constructing a pyramid-shaped flour cone stuffed with vegetables, the whiff of a roasted tangy fresh vegetable—it made you delirious with anticipation, impatient for the food to reach your mouth. Food vendors catered to truck drivers, bureaucrats, families, off-duty policemen, university students, the young, the old, and anyone who wanted to snack at any time of the day or night, right on the road. Makeshift stalls pop up everywhere, aromatic aromas and the foods keep coming. You can snack on *samosas* (deep-fried dough stuffed with veggies), *pakoras* (fried fritters), *dahi wadas* (lentil doughnuts in yogurt), patties, mint chutneys, sandwiches filled with potato, onion, cucumber, tomato, spicy mushroom, and loaded with chilies and *paneer (cheese)*, and *kachoris* (flour balls stuffed with lentils and spices). And how do I describe the *pani puri* concoction? There is this fragile tiny *puri* (a form of fried bread). Make a wee hole on the top, spoon in a filling of onions, tamarind, mint, chickpeas, and tomatoes and put the whole thing in your mouth. Bite into a shocking explosion of flavors impossible to define.

Street foods are so inventive that you may find yourself guiltily relishing a sandwich with cabbage, pineapple bits, and oozy jams. Or you can take your pick of a variety of omelets and after that head to another vendor two streets away and feast on prawn fry and tandoori chicken. Other staples of street food include lentil *dosas* (pancakes), vegetable fritters, delicious cobs of roasted corn, and *kebabs*—ground meat smothered in curd wrapped in crusty bread. You can end your snacking with mango *lassi* or fruit *chaats*, lemon juice (*nimbu pani*), or spiced *papad* to complement all the savory dishes you have eaten. The list is endless, enticing you from street to street. It is a wondrous, incredibly delicious celebration of food and you are hopelessly lost in a wealth of flavors. Walking along the beach on Marine Drive, it is like a vendor convention. Everyone crowds around the foods. Pink cotton candy, green chillies sizzling in oil, cool glasses of buttermilk. There is a sense of camaraderie, a mix of intense flavors. Nobody knows who you are or which community you belong to, or how much money you earn. All one cares about is the aromatic food spiked with spices, the tastes, smells, sights, and the irresistible spontaneous thrill of instant cooking.

When my husband was needed to help out in the family business, we returned to Chennai and discovered street food was becoming popular in our own city. Every evening, we waited for our regular vendor to set up his open stall of roasted peanuts on the road near our home. We stood patiently while the vendor assembled his stove and placed a *kadai* (wok) on top. Reaching into a jute bag, he scooped up fistfuls of sand and poured them into the hot *kadai*. He twirled the mix around for a few minutes with a big iron ladle. From another jute bag he took out cups of ground nuts and threw them into the hot sand. In a few minutes the nuts were roasted to perfection. Deftly retrieving them, a visual snap-crackle, he sifted the sand, poured the scalding nuts into newspaper cones, and placed them in our eager hands. The newspapers were in the Tamil language. Often I spotted people sitting under a tree after finishing their hot snacks, smoothing out the wrinkled newspaper and catching up on movie gossip and the news of yesterday or the week before.

On the beautiful 22-mile coastline of the Bay of Bengal, on the Marina beach, as you tryst with your beloved, read a novel, debate on politics, or dream with each oncoming wave, you will see vendors bustle around carrying tins of snacks and imaginative hawker food. I challenge any Madrasi (Chennaiite) living in any corner of the world to forget sitting on the warm sand, listening to the rhythm of the waves, and being satiated with the tender green chillies, fried in a thick batter of chickpea flour, red chilli powder, and cumin, the cool sugarcane juice, or the *sundal* (chickpeas again smothered in handfuls of fragrant coconut, sprinkled with mustard, and spiked with the tang of raw shredded mango). Whatever the time of day or night, I know that a vendor in India is somewhere peeling, slicing, dicing, grilling, cooking, crushing the juice of the sugarcane, or frying some delectable dish like *aloo ki tikki* (mashed potato patties), *pao bhajji* (vegetables mashed with bread), *pakoras* (crispy fritters), omelets, and *kababs*. Yes, the cooking utensils are dodgy, the fumes of diesel dangerous, the sand and pollutants myriad, but its comfort food, easily accessible, and it is the taste of India.

Whether it was street food or a meal in a home, as I traveled, met people from different regions of India, and tasted dishes crowded with flamboyant ingredients or those made with stark lightness and simplicity, I found food was a universal constant.

Railway Food Adventures

How well I remember the train journeys we took. Across India, every day, an estimated 12,000 trains travel through 6,800 stations across 40,000 miles to thousands of destinations on tracks laid down 150 years ago. A train journey is quite simply a feast of food. A fond and vivid memory I carry with me is that of my family traveling, loaded with luggage and a shining stainless steel carrier called a tiffin carrier. This was a container of six steel vessels fitting neatly one into another and kept in place by two stiff steel rods. It was filled with lime rice, tamarind rice, mince meat, and vegetables. By the time the third major station, Katpadi, was reached, the tiffin carrier was empty. We then eagerly anticipated every station we passed. That was where the "platform theatre" would take place. A quiet little station would suddenly be transported into a place of utter bedlam as dozens of vendors swarmed across luggage, people, and porters to reach our hands thrust out through the iron grille of the compartment window. The vendors, ranging from little children to old wizened men, scampered up and down the platform shouting their wares and tempting you with *vadais, idlis, dosais* (rice and dal preparations), *biryani* (meat and rice packets), sliced mangoes, *samosas* (a flour pastry stuffed with meat or vegetables), nuts, oranges, bananas, cold drinks, tea, and hot milk. We gorged on the foods, perhaps because they were from a different region. We were strangers partaking of the foods of another culture, defining a group identity. It was a special thrill. As the train clattered across the tracks, we sank back into our seats, eating blissfully, and sipping hot tea in earthy clay cups, which we threw out of the window recklessly when we were done.

We traveled frequently and knew which station was famous for which food item and eagerly looked forward to tasting the delights of a particular region. This is what I call a taste memory. Maharashtra was famous for caramelized *chikki* (*jaggery* and groundnuts). Jaggery is dehydrated cane juice and has a distinct flavor. Nagpur station offered baskets of juicy oranges, and there were succulent Malgova mangoes in Vijayawada, all of which we snapped up. And who can forget that thick creamy hot milk in Vellore, and the nectar-like bananas in Malur (where tribes of monkeys lived among the rafters of the station)? Friends tell me that candied pumpkin in Agra, salted cucumber in Dehra Dun, lemons in Gudur, guava sweets in Varanasi, *halwah* (a rich sweet) in Puri, and salted cashew nuts in Thanjavur are also regional specialties found at stations on Indian railways.

One of the pleasures of a train journey is the sharing of food with people you have never met before. You discuss politics, cricket, films, and income tax; you play card games, exchange novels and recipes, and share life's stories. As the train chugs on, you see shifting landscapes while you taste foods of the land with total strangers. A personal discovery becomes a shared experience.

Nowadays in India there are a number of luxury trains. If you travel in the $12 million Maharajah's Express with twenty-three luxurious carriages stretching nearly a mile and five-star accommodations with fifty staff plus a paramedic, you will luxuriate in marble showers and rosewater sprays, gaze on a flat screen TV, or scan the landscape through panoramic windows. A five-course dinner may include foie gras, wild mushroom ravioli, local bekti fish in tamarind sauce, cashews, poppy seeds, chicken with sweet corn, and chocolate and decadent Indian desserts. Whether it is the ostentatious or the simple chugging passenger train, Indians have a profoundly personal and touching connection with rail travel.

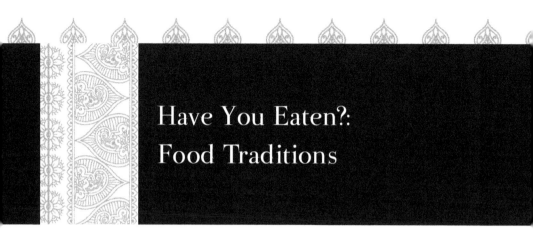

Have You Eaten?: Food Traditions

When an Indian, rich or poor, greets a visitor in a home, the first question is "Have you eaten?" or "Will you eat?". A Sanskrit saying *Athithidevo bhava* (a guest is equal to God) expresses the belief that a guest must always be welcomed with food. Guests bring honor to the host by their mere presence. There was a time when the head of the household stood at the doorstep of his home at meal times and shouted loudly, "Is there someone who is hungry? I invite them into my home." The overwhelming hospitality tradition in India is legendary. Temples and *gurudwaras* feed hundreds and thousands of people every day. In my grandmother's house in Bangalore the wood fire in the kitchen was never put out at night. Some friend or relative, my grandmother said, might find their way to the house and it would be so easy to stoke up the embers and serve hot food. Entertaining guests is the pride of an Indian home, she insisted.

Three meals a day is the norm and each community and family adheres to structured food rituals and family traditions. There is an accepted tradition in which various tastes and textures of the dishes must be served. In Gujarat, the sweet dish is served first. In some regions of Tamil Nadu the sweet is offered as the last item on the menu. In Punjab, many dishes are cooked without much sauce so that they can be scooped up with a piece of *roti*. Mughlai cuisine prides itself on rich, heavy sauces, while in the South the rice eaters need delicately flavored sauces to moisten the rice and make it soft so that it can be shaped into a small ball with the fingers and placed in the mouth. My North Indian Punjabi husband picked up food from the plate using the tips of his fingers, while I, being from South India, used the whole hand much to the hilarity of his family.

One constant edible product used in food all over India is *ghee* or clarified butter. Mention of ghee was made as far back as 8000 BC. Ancient texts inform us that ghee infuses the worshipper with energy and purifies, so it is often poured on deities and used in the lighting of lamps during worship. Milk and ghee are considered sacred and purifying as they come from the holy cow. Ghee is made by converting whole milk into yogurt and then churning it to separate the butter from the liquid. This butter is melted in a heavy-bottomed pan, and when the sediment settles down the clear, fragrant, yellow ghee is separated. Since ghee has the purest form of fat content, it is also a symbol of abundance and fertility and is said to destroy the evil influences of the planets. At birth, the lips of a newborn baby are moistened with a dab of ghee as a symbol of a blessing. When my children were born, special herbal foods made with ghee were given to me, as the clarified butter provides energy and produces good milk for the baby.

We used a lot of ghee in our cooking in those days. Our house was always filled with the rich aromatic flavors of butter being heated in large pans. The ghee was then cooled and stored in jars.

Here in America, I buy ghee in bottles from the Indian grocery store and use it sparingly in seasonings or when making sweets. I am very cautious as I am now overly concerned about the fat content. But who can resist the added delicious flavor? To fatten up skinny children, Indian mothers often use lashings of ghee in boiled lentils to feed them. If there are teenagers studying for an exam, the mother will feed them foods saturated with ghee, almonds, and milk to boost positive energy and thinking. In times past, when a guest left the house, an ambrosial beverage made of ghee, curd, milk, honey, and sugar was offered as goodwill and an energy booster, but these days, with everyone being conscious of diets, this custom has fallen by the wayside.

My grandmother always believed that a dish can never be prepared in a stressful atmosphere because tension, bitterness, and angry thoughts spoil the ingredients. Not just my grandmother, but anyone who cooked in our home always had a *bhajan* (religious song) or a film song on their lips. Food made with happy, good thoughts turns into a larger, richer context of empathy and good will for whomever the food is prepared.

Once the food is prepared in a tranquil manner, it has to be eaten in a calm frame of mind. Eating when you feel grief, anger, greed, or anxiety results in indigestion and disturbs the balance according to *Ayurveda* precepts. My grandmother believed that each morsel had to be chewed thirty-six times if you want the food to be digested well. This was blithely ignored by us. When our large family swapped stories and laughed deliriously during a meal, our grandparents would admonish such excessive talking and gaiety, insisting that it was not beneficial to the digestive system.

Food is not served in courses in India. All the dishes are placed before you right from the start. In many families, couples never ate together, since the duty of the wife was to serve her husband and male relatives. Even now, when I visit some friends, the men and elders are served first. On a hot summer day, my grandmother not only served, but also fanned her husband to keep him cool in the stifling heat. When the meal was done, in traditional families wives ate from the husband's plate of leftovers to express total devotion.

✳ ✳ ✳

The Glass an Inch from Your Lips – The Etiquette of Eating

For a newcomer to India, eating could either be daunting and tricky or an intriguing experience. The first rule: Never eat with your left hand. Food is always eaten with the right hand as the left hand is considered unclean, because most Indians use it to cleanse the body with water after using the toilet. I am often asked by foreigners visiting India—what if you are lefthanded? The answer—use a fork or spoon.

In traditional and conservative homes any water or juice has to be poured into the mouth with head tilted back, directly from the tumbler. The lips cannot touch the rim of the tumbler—an art that requires a little practice and skill. This practice still holds good in many homes in South India. Since saliva is considered polluting, cooks do not taste food while cooking. Pure instinct and mastery of the culinary procedures makes tasting irrelevant. I wonder what the traditionalists think when they see chefs on American TV munching, chewing, and sampling every dish during the cooking process.

When you are served a meal in a traditional household in Tamil Nadu, you partake in almost a ceremony. You may be served in the dining area or even in the kitchen where it is more informal. You sit on a raised plank of wood *(mannai)*, or if the seat is too hard on a straw mat or a thin rug known as a *jamkanam*, which comes in a variety of bright colors and designs. Drinking water is placed on your left in steel tumblers. Juices are offered, like *kanji* (fermented carrots and mustard seeds), *nimbu pani* (lime and water), coconut water, spiced or plain fruit juices, *zeerapani* made with cumin seeds, and the sweet and sour tamarind juice (an excellent digestive). No alcohol is served. Alcohol is generally considered taboo, although some Indians do drink wine with food these days at home and in restaurants.

And then there is the aesthetics of presentation. If you are invited to a palace or a very wealthy home you may be served food on a gold plate accompanied by gold cutlery. More common are silver and stainless steel plates. A popular food platter in most parts of India is the *thali*, a round tray of brass, bell metal, or silver that is very practical and visually appealing. On it are placed an assortment of small metal bowls around the rim to hold individual portions of each dish, like vegetables, chutneys, dals, a meat or fish fry. In the middle of the tray the rotis and rice are served surrounded by diverse pickles and *papads* (dried fried lentil flour pancakes). A dramatic compositon pleasing to the eye as well as the palate.

Our family always looks forward to eating from a banana leaf when we visit India. Instead of steel plates, freshly plucked banana leaves are used as platters. Eating from a banana leaf is considered the purest form of eating, as there is no contamination. The species of the banana plant varies from one community to another. With one look at the leaf, my grandparents could identify the community, the status, the wealth of the family, and the place of origin. So here you are seated on the mat on the ground full of anticipation. The banana leaf is placed before you with the narrow tip of the leaf on the left and the thick end on the right. Although the leaf has been cleaned, the guest always first sprinkles water from a tumbler onto the leaf invoking blessings of the gods. Food items are placed in a specific order. In the lower left corner, a tiny mound of salt is placed. The top and left of the leaf is laden with vegetables, chutneys, fried lentils, and pickles. The top right of the leaf offers hot and sour items. The lower right portion of the leaf will have a container with a sweet dish. In the lower half of the leaf, rice is placed, moistened with *sambar* (the spiced dal dish containing vegetables). Hot ghee is usually poured into the rice to enhance the flavor. Fried items like banana chips and wafers are also placed. Often a separate leaf is placed alongside for meat and seafood dishes. Again everything is presented with care, a dry dish next to one soaking in gravy. When everything is in order, the banana leaf is a magnificent palette of rich colors. And then you mix it all up. After that it is scoops, dabs, and a deft use of the thumb and fingers to take the food up to your mouth. And oh yes, fingers can never go into the mouth. When you finish eating, more rice is placed and this time you mix it with yogurt or buttermilk, cooling down your digestive system. At the end of the meal, you are given a banana.

In a conservative, traditional home, after eating you may wash your hands at a sink or walk outside to a tap and rinse your mouth. Indians are fastidious about hygiene. Water that has been gargled can never be consumed, so you spit it out. In the olden days, belching was often in vogue. The larger the belch, the more the food is appreciated. For the record, I do not indulge in this form of thank you. Leftovers are given to birds, dogs, or insects as they are believed to be messengers of the world of the spirits. You then settle down in the main living room and the hostess offers the *beeda*, a leaf filled with spiced nuts, good for digestion. The children are usually offered fruit.

The After-Dinner Chew

Whether it is called *paan* in North India or *beeda* in the South, no meal is complete without the after-dinner chew. You can chew a betel nut or a betel leaf or a combination of both. The betel nut (also known as the areca nut) is the woody, round nut of the areca palm tree. It becomes soft when sucked for a long time. Its use in India dates back to 400 BC and in a 12th-century treatise, the *Hitopedesa* (Book of Good Counsel), it is said that the "betel nut is bitter, hot, spicy, binding, alkaline, astringent, a foe to the evils of intestine, a fragrance of breath, to the lips a crimson red, a kindler of love flame." Who can resist that? The Kamasutra (an ancient text on courtship rituals) mentions it as necessary for passion and seduction. No religious ceremony, including a wedding, is complete without an auspicious offering to guests of the emerald green heart-shaped betel leaf and nut. No guest departs after a dinner without having a long, satisfying chew. Offering it is a sign of good will. During the Mughal era, accepting the *paan* from the king symbolized a pledge of loyalty and friendship. Sometimes, kings would place a betel nut on the ground and challenge anyone willing to take on the difficult task of picking it up. That would mark a vow of carrying out the deed.

In courts, a betel bearer was always a woman who accompanied the king wherever he went and placed the betel leaf prepared with all its aromatic spices in the king's mouth whenever needed. A special "betel language" existed among lovers in those days. The woman would fold the leaf in a particular shape and present it to the man, who on studying the folded leaf would decode the unspoken message. Perhaps it was an assignation, a confirmation of love, an accusation, or a truce after a lover's quarrel. The *paan* has pleased the palate of so many over the years that hundreds of songs, ribald and passionate, have been written in praise of the *paan*, many of which can be found in Bollywood films.

A leaf and a nut. And yet there is so much romance, history, and tradition wrapped in this tiny package which offers exotic delights. Some say that the Goddess Lakshmi resides in the forepart of the leaf, Lord Shiva on the edges, Lord Vishnu inside the leaf, and Kama the God of love resides everywhere. Yama, the Lord of death, is believed to reside in the stalk which is why the stalk is always snipped off before the leaf is consumed.

The betel leaf and nut, apart from being inseparable from Hindu rituals, is a good digestive and has high calcium content. Anyone can make a simple *paan*. Take a fragrant concoction of the chopped betel nut (*supari*), white lime paste called *choonam* (believed to be made from the shells of oysters, eggs, and mussels), *kattha* (a red paste made from the bark of a tree), aniseed, cloves, fennel seeds, and cardamom, and wrap in an emerald green betel leaf which is four to five inches in length. Fold in a triangular shape and hold the leaf together with a tiny clove. Professional *paan* makers often embellish with silver foil, camphor tobacco, coconut, crushed pearls, or aphrodisiacs.

The Benarasi *paan* is supposedly the ultimate chew and boasts a leaf that is sweet, yellowish-green, delicate, and tender. It is made in the holy city of Benares (Varanasi) and is richly decorated with silver foil and sometimes spiked with intoxicants.

The *paan* ingredients are kept in a special small box inlaid with silver or brass. An elaborate carved scissor-shaped nutcracker is used to snip the cloves and cardamoms. I cherish a beautiful framed ornate betel nutcracker bought at the Raja Kelkar Museum in Pune, Maharashtra state, and gifted to me. Each state in India prides itself in making its own special containers, and they became elaborate works of art and are now collector's items. Many are seen in museum collections. Artists were so inventive in the past that there are even brass betel leaf cases shaped like vintage cars with tiny wheels so that the case could easily be passed around a large gathering.

Eating *paan* is so soothing and addictive that some people eat it right through the day. Little wonder there are hundreds of *paan* shops in cities where people gather to chat, gossip, and relax. Unfortunately many people spit the betel juice on the ground in public roadways, forcing the government to endorse heavy fines.

My favorite memory of *paan* is the summer when I was nine years old. My parents, aunts, and uncles from Chennai swooped down on Bangalore, idyllic for vacations with its coolness and verdant foliage everywhere. Satiated after a long and cherished meal prepared by my grandmother for her children, the elders flung the straw mats under the shade of the mango trees. Ceremoniously, my grandfather brought out the prized *His Masters Voice* gramophone and placed it on the mat. I gazed rapturously at the record label. It was a picture of a dog presumably listening to the sound of his master's voice. I trembled with the delight of anticipation for I knew any moment he would ask me to crank it up. Carefully he placed the circular black record on the turntable and rested his eyes on me. I sprang forward and very gently turned the handle. When the handle became tight, I looked up and nodded; Grandfather placed the shiny needle on the first groove and the deep, sonorous voice of the famed singer Pankaj Mallick singing the song *Ayye Bahare (Spring has come and filled the air)* filled the somnolent, drugged afternoon. This was followed by the elders swapping stories and gossip, while Grandmother carefully brought out the brass container wherein reposed, in various compartments, the *paan* ingredients. As stories, jokes, and laughter drifted around, she adeptly twisted the leaves and inserted the fragrant delights, and passed them to each member of the family. Since I was only nine years old, I looked longingly at the *paan* forbidden to me. Children were not allowed to eat *paan*. It was an adult pleasure like smoking. The leaf and spices and nuts were too overpowering for the delicate stomach of a child. But Grandmother quietly whisked a small nut into my waiting hands, and I rolled it around my mouth as long as I could, savoring the woody flavor and finally make the inevitable crunch. I was one of THEM. Grandmother and the others then stretched out somnolently on the soft mats and swished the handmade fans of bamboo. (The fan handle was a useful tool to spank me when I was too fidgety and also served the purpose of scratching oneself on the back when a bold ant chose to clamber onto a sleeping body.)

Alas! Due to time constrictions, nowadays, many restaurants and households offer fennel seed mixed with shredded dried coconut as an end of meal digestive.

Coconut Blessings and the Evil Eye

When a guest leaves in South India, a coconut is often given as a token of goodwill and blessings. The coconut is an essential element in Hindu worship and is always offered in temples and household worship. On the sea coast, fishermen offer the coconut to the sea to propitiate the gods. In wedding ceremonies the coconut becomes a symbol of fertility and is placed at the top of a pot representing the womb. It is also said that coconuts were used as a substitute for human heads when certain rites in the past demanded human sacrifice. Today when a coconut is part of a ritual, the blessings of the gods are invoked when starting a new venture, be it the purchase of a house or a business.

Turmeric is also auspicious. It is the ginger-like rhizome that is powdered and used as a religious mark on the forehead and often given to guests when they leave. Images of deities are always smeared with turmeric. There is a ceremony in Hindu families where the bride is smeared with turmeric the day before the wedding. Not only is this a blessing but it gives the skin a glow and radiance. In Gujarat, an expectant mother sits on a low stool in the center of a red square marked out on the floor. Relatives and friends sing songs and the sister-in-law smears the forehead of the pregnant woman with turmeric paste and rice. In Tamil Nadu, the root of the turmeric is always given to a married woman guest and brought as a gift to pregnant mothers for removing the "evil eye".

The "evil eye" has always been taken seriously in India. It means someone has "eyed" you with envy, jealousy, or covetousness and may have the power to hurt you. Too much praise by anyone is looked on with suspicion. I remember when giving the milk bottle to my baby girls, my mother would rush to cover the bottle with a cloth to avoid someone putting their evil eye on the milk.

Attending a wedding or a festivity during my childhood was an important occasion. I would be dressed in a silk brocaded skirt and blouse, adorned with gold earrings, necklaces, bangles, a waist belt, and toe rings. My grandmother, on returning home, would mutter that many a guest at the wedding had laid "their evil eye on me." And so to remove the effect, I would be seated and a plate with a small lighted lamp surrounded by salt and chillies would be circled round my face thrice. The salt and chillies were then thrown into the fire. If there was a bad odor with crackling and hissing it meant that the evil spirits had been destroyed and doom would befall the person who cast the evil eye. If there was mere smoke, no one had put the evil eye on me. This was ironic because my grandmother was a staunch Christian and attended church regularly, and my grandfather was one of the elders of the church. When my daughter was diagnosed with a serious illness here in the U.S., many relatives and friends from all over the world were very sure that there was an evil eye on her and insisted that I do the salt and chilli ritual. Indian babies are always marked with a small black dot in the middle of the forehead or near the chin to avert the evil eye. Mirrors are sewn into clothing so that bad energy is reflected back.

Pumpkins and limes also play an important role in fending off the evil eye. In South India, at the entrance of a new house being built a pumpkin with a human figure drawn on it would be hung as an antidote to the evil eye. Decay of the pumpkin meant that the evil eye had been warded off. Shopkeepers hang a lime fruit tied along with chillies in front of their sales counter, as lime is auspicious and chillies deter evil. Lime garlands are put around the aggressive deities, like Durga, Kali, and Mariamma, to cool down their tempers. During the marriage ceremony, the lime is a symbol of fertility and both groom and bride hold the lime for a considerable length of time warding off the evil eye. On new moon day, garlands of limes and two chillies are strung across lintels of homes to ward off evil influence.

The Kitchen: A Sacred Space

The kitchen in an Indian Hindu home is a place endowed with sanctity, and images of deities are placed there for worship. Cleanliness is mandatory. Shoes or slippers are never brought into the kitchen, and you are unwelcome if you did not bathe before entering. This is the place where the woman of the house reigns with a subtle authority. She is the kitchen goddess.

Women begin the day by lighting a fire, stove, or stick of incense in the kitchen and chanting morning prayers. Then the cooking begins. In many homes, the whole family sits on the floor on mats partaking of the meal while the mother prepares hot breads (*rotis*) or rice and serves everyone. It is here she enjoys the company of her friends and relatives, shares joys, troubles, gossip, and secrets. Sometimes a kitchen opens into a courtyard and here the householder bargains with vegetable, bangle, and saree vendors. In olden days, some homes had two kitchens. One kitchen was used for the cooking of non-vegetarian food and the other for vegetarian food.

It was not surprising to find in joint families feisty daughters-in-law running independent kitchens. On our first visit to Hyderabad, we stayed with an uncle of my husband. In this joint household, the daughter-in-law ruled over her own private kitchen while her in-laws cooked in a separate one. So we found ourselves relishing our first cup of tea and biscuits in the parents' kitchen and then moving back for a breakfast of roti and omelets in the daughter-in-law's kitchen. Though I found it vastly amusing, I enjoyed the separate kitchens with their individual ambience.

Although the kitchen is the core and heart of the household where the woman of the house presides, on certain days the kitchen is taboo to her. In orthodox homes a woman was not allowed into the kitchen during her period of menstruation. She was considered impure during those days. Another explanation is that these were days of rest and it was a time for her body to refresh and reenergize. Even now a South Indian friend of mine and her daughter are not allowed to touch any utensil in the home of the grandparents when menstruating. If they did it inadvertently, they would have to take a bath immediately. Some communities in India also continue to follow this old tradition when a young woman reaches puberty.

Traditional Oil Baths

It is in the kitchen that whole vats or *undas* of water are boiled for the regular oil bath. The oil bath day is a significant one. When I was young, most Tamilians in Tamil Nadu State anointed their bodies, including the eyes, with *gingelly* (sesame) oil two days of the week. Wednesdays and Saturdays were set aside for oil baths for men; and Tuesdays and Fridays for women. Oil bath days were days of rest from sex activity too as the body replenished itself. So this was a smart form of family planning. Different states show their preferences by using local oils. Coconut oil is used in Kerala, mustard oil in Bengal and parts of North India, while South Indians favor sesame oil.

Come Deepavalli, the Festival of Lights, usually celebrated in October or November, the oil bath became a spiritual ritual. I would be woken up at four in the morning when it was still dark. The sesame oil was heated in a pan and poured carefully into a vessel. The day before I would have rushed down the street to buy oil from the oil press (*chekku*). This *gingelly* oil had been pressed from sesame oil seeds. The seeds were put into a grinding stone, a pestle and mortar arrangement with two cows tethered to the pestle circling the oil press and crushing the seeds. While avoiding the cows, balancing the brass pitcher of oil and clutching the oily greasy receipt from the owner required skill, I did it, though awed by the huge animals, the thick smell of oil, and the thunderous sound of the creaking wheels.

My hair, long and thick like a banana stem my neighbors always told me, was let loose from the long constricting braids and the oil poured on my center parting, deliciously warm and fluid. The gentle massage began, all over the scalp—soothing, languorous. My hair soaked every drop of goodness. The oil dripped and slid into my eyes, ears, and mouth but I was stoic because I knew it was a Deepavalli ritual. A half hour later, I would be taken into the bathroom where I faced a huge *unda* (brass vessel) of hot water in which floated *neem* leaves and turmeric. The servant woman hitched up her saree and started vigorously washing my hair with the pods of *sheekakai* which had already been boiling with herbs. The hot water removed every trace of grime and oil. My hair was dried and then I lay on a mat while it was spread over a large loosely woven basket. Under the basket was placed a clay plate filled with embers and *sambrani* incense. The smoke swirled through the openings in the basket and coiled gently through my hair. Minutes later, my hair was plaited and twisted with fresh smelling pure white jasmine. I was ready for Deepavalli. It is not the lights, the firecrackers, the new clothes, or the sumptuous food that lingers in my mind from this elaborate and extravagant festival. It is the oil bath.

Grandmother:
A Taste of the Times

Kolams, Coffee, and the Fisherwoman

Oftentimes when I am faced in the morning with an impossible list of things to do, I think back to the times when life with my grandmother was relaxed, unhurried, ritualistic, and reassuring.

Hamsa, the servant woman, arrived at the stroke of 6:00 AM. The sonorous single chime of the grandfather clock coincided with the rattle of the garden gate. I would spring out of bed, rush down and wrest the chains that locked the gate at night. Hamsa would go to the verandah near the kitchen, reach up to a shelf, and pick up a vessel containing rice flour. She then took a long wooden broom and filled a bucket with water. She tucked her saree into her waist in one neat swoop and sprinkled water at the entrance of the kitchen. She then vigorously swept the area and began to draw with alacrity and swiftness, an intricate design with the white rice flour. She took a little rice flour and dropped it on the ground, then a little more, evenly spaced, until there was a diamond-shaped grid of white dots. With deft fingers, she dexterously traced with the rice flour thin white lines between the dots, some straight, some looped, some whorled. The bare, grey, concrete floor became an abstract pattern or a lotus blossom with petals, stamens, and leaves. Sometimes it was a simple line; other times the lines were superimposed with two or three lines forming intricate grids. No lines were left open. If they were, evil spirits could enter the home.

Hamsa was creating the *kolam* the auspicious artwork made of simple rice flour to welcome the morning and Goddess Lakshmi, the harbinger of wealth and prosperity; and what better place to do it than the kitchen front where the food was prepared. She would later draw another design in front of the house to welcome the Goddess. Hamsa did not copy the designs from any book. She had learned the designs from watching her mother and grandmother. If we ran out of rice flour Hamsa was not fazed. She merely took black lentils (*urad dal*), red lentils (*masoor dal*), yellow lentils (*tur dal*), and olive green lentils (moong) and created colorful patterns.

Every day millions of women all over India engage in this ritual with rice flour and water. During the day the *kolam* is trampled, blown away, or simply walked on; but every morning a new one is made, symbolizing that all things are temporary. In rural homes, where the floor is covered with sunburnt cow dung (to keep away insects), white rice flour designs are dramatic against an earthy brown floor. The tradition dates back to 2500 BC when there is mention of *gopis* (milkmaids) drawing *kolams* to forget the pain when their beloved God Krishna goes away. The earliest references to *kolam* drawing in Tamil literary works occur in the sixteenth century. The intricate, precise patterns of the *kolam* are known to be expressive of mathematical ideas. *Kolam* drawing is also listed as one of the sixty-four forms of art in the sage Vatsyayana's *Kamasutra*, the book on the varying dimensions of physical love. Geometric patterns vary from region to region with colored powders used in other regions of India. It is called *Alpana* in Bengal, *Muggulu* in Andhra, *Rangavalli* in Karnataka, *Rangoli* in northern India, and *Pookalam* in Kerala.

On festival days, I would find the whole street covered with *kolams* made by householders who spent many hours drawing complex patterns covering thousands of square feet. Nowadays *kolams* are drawn with the help of perforated trays and stencils. Since I am not adept at drawing a *kolam*, I place a vinyl replica of *kolams* outside my front door in Los Angeles on festive occasions.

Once the *kolams* were done, it was time for the coffee ritual in the kitchen. My grandmother would never dream of allowing anyone to enter the kitchen without bathing. Indeed, no matter how tired she was at night, the kitchen would be thoroughly swept and the cement floor scoured with buckets of water, thus removing cooking odors, oils, and spills. In the morning, she would pull up a plank (*mannai*) near the oven. It was an oblong clay oven a foot and a half high, three feet long, and three feet wide. There were three holes on top for the cooking vessels. Below at floor level there was a small hole in the oven through which the firewood was pushed. Heat was regulated. I would nestle against the curve of her hip watching with fascination the embers slowly begin to glow, leap into flame, and greet the day. Grandmother would take a long iron pipe (*othankol*), place it strategically near the embers and blow gently to keep the flame steady. Sometimes the fire, due to damp wood, would not light; and we would rush out of the kitchen, red-eyed and tearful to take in gulps of fresh air and then tackle the fire again. I always envied my grandfather and uncles, who could on a hot searing day walk around with their chests bared, while Grandmother and the aunts would be wearing thick *cholis* (blouses) and six yards of saree wrapped around them over an under skirt while heavy earrings, chains, bangles, and rings adorned their bodies.

Grandmother took a shiny steel vessel for coffee from the rack against the wall filled with copper, brass, and iron vessels of diverse shapes and sizes. But our collection could not rival the neighbors, who collected cooking vessels as part of their daughter's dowry. This assortment of vessels filled four rooms of their house. Scoured by my grandmother and Hamsa with sand, ashes, and coconut fiber, the vessels shone with a brilliance reflecting my face. The coffee aroma would fill our kitchen and my grandfather would arrive with the morning newspaper tucked under his arm, lured by the fragrance of steaming coffee. He pulled up another *mannai* and began the coffee ritual—slowly, carefully, was it concentration or devotion? It was an act of total focus, as the coffee mixed with milk and sugar was poured into tall steel tumblers, half and half. He took the two tumblers, deftly flicked his wrist, and poured one into the other from a distance of two feet so that the coffee was cooled to the right temperature and arrived in your hands with a frothy welcome. We sipped the coffee contentedly, as my grandfather whipped out the newspaper and read the English headlines loudly with my grandmother inserting a wry comment or two. She prided herself on knowing English taught to her in the missionary schools run by the British in her hometown in Nellore, Andhra Pradesh.

Saturday was *dosa* day. The evening before, the servant girl Ponnamma would have prepared the rice and lentil paste by grinding it on the granite stone, a gargantuan version of the mortar and pestle. I can still hear the deep rumble of stone against stone, the squishy, sloshy sound of rice and lentils ground in what was called wet grinding. Now and then it was my turn to quickly slap some water into the churning white mass. And there was Ponnamma, with her bright orange saree hitched up, her burnished bare legs on either side of the stone, singing a folk song in Kannada or tossing out a riddle to me. She pushed the rice back into the granite bowl when it threatened to overflow, at the same time avoiding having her fingers bruised by the heavy grinding stone. I always feel guilty when I look at the ready-made mix in my kitchen cabinet and whip up *dosa* dough in two seconds! How I miss the drawn-out ritual of the messy but tactile process of grinding.

The *dosa* paste was then left to ferment overnight. The next morning, my grandmother would decide which *dosa* it was going to be: paper-thin ghee *dosa*, or *masala* ones stuffed with vegetables. The batter would be ladled onto a hot griddle or *tava* that had been smeared with oil. The hot griddle would be wiped with a piece of onion making it non-stick, and there appeared the perfect *dosa*, crinkly and lacy at the edges. *Dosas* had to be eaten hot off the *tava* so they were always made one by one while we were seated. My grandmother never flipped the *dosa*; she always cooked it on one side, and it was perfect. Never did I see a raggedy *dosa*, every one of them was a perfect circle as she swirled the batter quickly and evenly. The *dosa* was accompanied by a chutney, a relish made with a little water, lime, coriander, pomegranate seeds, mango, tamarind, tomato, onion, red chilies, roasted *dals*, coconut, garlic—the permutations were endless. On another day, she might spoon on mashed potatoes seasoned with turmeric and mixed with *moong dal*, green chilies, curry leaves, and mustard seeds. Grandmother knew the perfect proportions and would fry the ingredients separately. The whole mixture would be tempered with ghee. A perfect complement to the *dosa.*

We had no sooner finished breakfast than the afternoon meal was planned with meticulous detail. While being satiated with the redolent repast of a noon meal, "What shall I cook for dinner?" was a topic that came up on cue and was discussed eagerly. Even today Indian householders are constantly conjuring up ideas for meals as soon as they awaken. In Los Angeles, when my friend Prema Raj Mohan calls, her first question is "What did you make today?" And off we go into an energized conversation about the items made, the ingredients, a special discovery about a certain flavor, and oftentimes we may even go into a spice-induced euphoria.

But back to my grandmother's home. After breakfast, we went to the storeroom where the rice bins were kept. She would open the bin and take out the required amount using an *ollock,* a small steel measure. I would thrust my right hand into the bin and let the rice flow through my fingers, a pure sensory thrill. The room was cool and dark. It held sacks of rice and dal bought from the paddy fields; rows of jars of mango, lime, and vegetable pickles; tightly sealed tins of oils, ghee, dried wafers, *appalams;* and a shelf with extra-large vessels, pans, and pots to be used when cooking in large quantities for guests.

Some days, suddenly there would be a keening, piercing song. It was the fisherwoman who was at the garden gate singing aloud that she had brought fresh fish from the lake, indeed the banana leaf covering the fish was still dripping cool water. The sounds brought every member of the household out to witness in a few moments an entire drama of wit, rhetoric, retort, anger, and persuasion. First, the wares were displayed and the banana leaves covering the fish whipped deftly off. This was the cue for my grandparents to shake their heads and tut tut in disapproval saying they longed for the good old days when a fish looked like a whale. The fisherwoman would put her hand under her chin, wag her head in horror, and widen her eyes in total disbelief. Her prized fish was underrated? "Why this is fit for a *queen, a maharani* [... looking in admiration at my grandmother] and a *maharaja, a king* [looking flirtatiously at my grandfather]." Grandfather would cut to the chase and ask, "How much?" and then promptly recoil in horror at the outrageous price and then snigger at the audacity of the fisherwoman. Was it for the entire basket, that fancy price? The woman would not deign to reply, but in one graceful swoop, would place the banana leaves back on the fish and rise in one fluid motion to take off. Grandmother would cry out, "Wait, wait, let's talk," to which the seller would reply she had come first to this house as it was an auspicious house of plenty and now her whole day was ruined. Grandfather would mutter that we were the only fools to buy from this woman, as no one in their right senses would tolerate such cunning. Then the woman would embark on a litany of hard times, the poor fish catch, the mechanized boats destroying the livelihood of fishermen who went on catamarans, the morals of today's society, and eventually a compromise was reached, the fisherwoman would be given a tumbler of cool buttermilk, and the fish taken to the kitchen.

Meanwhile the fisherwoman would talk about her husband who had a nasty cold that simply would not leave him. Grandmother would stop in her tracks and give her a recipe for pepper-flavored rice, the perfect remedy for colds. It was called *Miryalu Annam* (pepper rice). "Roast the black peppers and a few curry leaves and powder them," suggested my grandmother. "Then heat ghee and add sesame and cumin seeds to cooked rice and salt to taste. Combine the mixture with the pepper and curry leaves. The cold will vanish before dawn breaks," challenged my grandmother and off the fisherwoman left thanking her profusely.

In some wealthy homes, even if there are a dozen servants, it is the mistress of the house who prepares the main dish. No meal was prepared carelessly. And looking back I find that my grandmother spent almost the whole day in the kitchen because food cooked slowly and it was the central part of her life. My aunt Beulah Souri, who lives in Seattle and is 100 years old, thinks nothing of whipping up a tasty *rice biryani* (a flavorful rice and meat dish spiced with cloves, cardamoms, coriander, onions, tomatoes) even though she is in a wheelchair. Her joy is to cook for family. For my grandmother and aunt, cooking was not a chore but a labor of love.

So Grandmother would then rustle up an appetizing lunch. The dal was cooked and I loved the tempering part where a little oil was heated and curry leaves and mustard seeds were roasted along with a few red chillies. The splutter and sharp, pungent smell was heaven. While Grandmother gutted the fish, I would stay in the sunlit garden amidst a profusion of crotons, jasmine, roses, bougainvillea, butterflies, and fat squirrels, and begin to clean the rice. It was put into a woven straw tray and I would remove the many small stones. I prided myself on finding that elusive tiny stone under a grain of rice. For a final de-husking, I shook the tray, threw the rice in the air in one brisk movement and received it back into the receptacle never dropping a single grain, while the wind blew away the husk.

Fresh vegetables were always grown in the backyard, so there was never a dearth of green plantains, tomatoes, tamarind, cabbage, squash, okra, drumsticks, tomatoes, curry leaves, chillies, coriander, ginger, mango, or coconuts. We even had a cashew tree. The nuts were used for flavor and as a thickening agent. Grandmother would decide the vegetables for the meal after a long detailed discussion with Grandfather, and I would be bidden to bring the particular vegetables and herbs from the garden. The servant girl Ponnamma was expert in cutting greens and onions. It was a skilled art as she flicked her wrist and fingers as the thick leaves fell in tiny fragments in a neat pile. Grandmother would be pleased and tell Ponnamma she would make a good wife as she believed that when prospective families came to evaluate the bride they would question her on her skill at cutting vegetables and greens. I would laugh uproariously at this much to the annoyance of my grandmother.

Of all the various knives used in slicing, chopping, and dicing the *aravamanai* was the one that terrified me. Shaped like a sickle, it was a curved steel blade eight inches long attached to a wooden base. If you were slicing an onion you would have to hold the onion with the first two fingers and thumb of each hand, then move the onion into the blade and push down. The pieces scatter as you dexterously keep slicing. South Indian households have a simple coconut scraper, which is a round, serrated metal disc attached to a wooden board. This method of scraping the coconut requires practiced precision and Grandmother was expert in cutting or grating the coconut which played an important role in garnishing curries.

When the cooking was finished, my grandmother covered the food with a lid and put hot coals on top, to retain the heat. After this, I ran to the kitchen garden and cut huge, lush emerald green banana leaves. Later when studying poetry, I was thrilled to find in Sanskrit poetry that banana stems have been likened to the smooth burnished glowing limbs of a young woman. Sometimes Grandmother asked me to fetch banana blossoms which she cooked with tiny shrimp, a beloved dish of my grandfather. But for now it was the leaf, to be washed thoroughly under the tap, the droplets shaken off and then the leaves laid on the floor in the eating space on the verandah a few inches away from each other. I then unfurled the narrow straw mats and placed them neatly parallel to one another. Some food was kept apart to be used for a surprise guest, or if no one came, the food was to be given to a hungry pet, a wandering cow, goat, dog, or cat, or to the birds. This

Yogurt was always made daily at home. Carefully guarded live culture was mixed into milk that had been boiled and then cooled, and the mixture was then left for a few hours or overnight. Yogurt set easily as the tropical climate of India was perfect. In the U.S. and all around the world, many Indians still make yogurt from a culture kept and guarded zealously over the years. Rashmi, the wife of Sunny Narang, our nephew who lives in Los Angeles, makes superb yogurt from a culture given to her by her mother, Vijayeta, who lives in northern California. Rashmi tells me that this tradition of using the culture has been faithfully followed by her mother for the last thirty years. "I do not think that any South Indian family in the U.S. ever buys store bought yogurt!" she says. The culture from home yogurt is always given by a friend or relative and we keep the tradition alive. "All you need to do," Rashmi says, "is to take half a teaspoon of the home yogurt in the house and mix it with boiled milk that has been cooled. Then you place a tight lid on it and for further sealing, wrap a thick cloth over it and place it in a quiet corner of the kitchen undisturbed for at least four hours. Preferably overnight. The end result is fresh, white, nutritious yogurt." In South Indian households, most women carry out the business of preparing the yogurt culture as the last task in the kitchen in the evening.

invoked blessings. We sat cross-legged on the mat, sprinkled a little water on the banana leaf and shook it out, the culmination of a busy, bustling morning. Food was served—milk-white mounds of cooked rice, purple *brinjal* fry, golden yellow dal, red tomato chutney, crisp *papads* (lentil wafers dried in the sun), a small vessel containing homemade churned yogurt rounded off by a sweet *payasam* (sweet dish made with milk and vermicelli).

We always ate with our fingers. Even when my aunts and uncles arrived for the summer thoroughly Anglicized (which meant short bobbed hair, guitars, the jive, gin and whisky) and asked for forks and knives, Grandmother would sternly rebuke, "Food must be eaten only with the hands. It tastes much better." My grandmother, like any other woman in the kitchen, was empowered in her space. Her power was absolute here. Meanwhile the aunts and uncles frowned disapprovingly whenever she fed me from time to time with choice morsels, a piece of chicken, fish, and rice rolled into a ball and deftly popped into my eager mouth. This tactile sensation of the fingers, food, and mouth remains one of my most bonding memories. This was a tender, outward manifestation of her deep love for me, as she literally fed me with hands that had prepared the food. Later, anchored in tradition, I would feed my own children in this manner when they were young.

Cool water stored in round-bottomed earthenware pots quenched our thirst. The pots were designed over the centuries to stay balanced on the heads that carried water from the wells or to nestle snugly around the curves of a woman's waist. Our water came from the well, was boiled—perhaps after the British missionary influence—and stored in large pots.

Replete, we would shake out the mats, throw away the banana leaves in the dust bin in the backyard, and laze under the shade of the lichi mango and pomegranate trees while the somnolent noonday sun dappled the leaves overhead. We then partook of the fruits, the succulent sweet, fibrous *sapota* fruit, malty in flavor and smooth skinned, or *nungu* (ice apple) in the summer. I particularly liked the *nungus* bought from the vendor, who would come to our garden gate and sing out "*Nungu, Nungu.*" We would all rush out and buy the hard fruit of the *palymrah* tree, often called the celestial tree as every part of it could be used. The shell was almost white, orange-streaked, or black and when it was removed you would find three or four soft as jelly and creamy pieces of fruit resembling translucent ice. The British called them ice apples, and they have an exquisite cold texture and exquisite taste. You could eat them straight away or sprinkle sugar and cardamom on them and slurp. They could also be chopped up and put in a glass of cold coconut water and imbibed. I preferred to eat the fruit with my bare hands.

While my grandparents napped, I read story books, transporting me to meadows filled with daffodils, hawthorn hedges, goblins, boarding schools, bullying prefects, knights, duels, marshmallows, secret passages in a castle, and English characters who inhabited a different world from mine as I lay on a straw mat listening to the cawing of a hungry crow or saw through the corner of my eye the flash of a green parrot in flight before it finally rested on the branches of a pomegranate tree—the pomegranate tree of knowledge, my grandfather told me. He was fascinated by Greek mythology and reminded me that the Goddess Demeter lost her daughter Persephone to the god of the underworld because she ate one seed of the pomegranate fruit. In later history classes I noted that in Mughal paintings, beauteous men and women always held the splendid red flowers of the pomegranate tree. It is a rare kind of fruit with its large, vermilion, tough outer covering revealing a fibrous skin, and inside perfect ruby red seeds covered by a fragile membrane. Crunch on the seeds and the mouth is filled with a delicious sourness tinged with the sweet juice. Grandmother crushed the seeds and gave this to visitors as a delicious drink. Sometimes the seeds were crushed to a fine paste and used as stuffing along with other spices when preparing vegetables. As I write this I remember the Hindi film *Anarkali,* starring Pradeep Kumar and Madhubala. The heroine, a courtesan played by Madhubala, was called Anarkali which means pomegranate bud or flower of the pomegranate. A tragic, haunting song was a background to the copious tears the audience shed when she was buried alive in a wall of bricks by the king who did not want his son to marry her as she was a common courtesan.

Refreshed, at four o'clock my grandmother would bustle into the kitchen, this time for tiffin—the Indian equivalent of teatime. The word was coined by the British and came from an old English dialect. The slang word "tiffing" meant a little sip. In this case tiffin was a snack time after lunch and before dinner. We sipped coffee again and ate her *pakoras* and *bajis* (fritters). We feasted on these sizzlers straight from the frying pan. The accompanying sauce or chutney would be made of tamarind more often than not as it was growing right there in our garden. The tamarind tree is a very graceful tree, with tiny emerald green leaves embracing the tamarind pods. I would clamber up the tree, take the green pod, remove the outer covering, and munch the tender green tamarind even though it set my teeth on edge. For cooking we would collect the brown tamarind fruit pods , remove the seeds, soak the acidic flesh in the water, and squeeze the juice out. This tamarind water was used in the curries or sauces as a souring agent. For the chutney, the tamarind was ground with spices and a little jaggery. Today you can get tamarind paste in containers in stores or as a brick of seedless pulp. They keep indefinitely without refrigeration and if you buy in blocks you can keep it wrapped in a cool place for a year. Simmer the pulp in water and then use a sieve to eliminate the fiber.

Later at twilight, when the lamps were lit, Grandmother would cook the fish and an extra vegetable for the evening. Or she made a "cutlet"—ground meat, pounded and seasoned with green chillies, turmeric, crushed onions, mashed potatoes, and a dash of pepper and then dipped in egg and breadcrumbs and fried in oil. We ate dinner quietly amidst the rich pungent smells of a fine meal.

Satiated, my grandfather sat in the cavernous rattan easy chair, and under the steady light of a kerosene lantern, read to me the poetry of Keats,

Shelley, Shakespeare, and passages from Walter Scott and Charles Dickens. He was a true colonial at heart, and every night made me sing "God Save our Gracious Queen," even though we had gained independence. When my aunts and uncles visited us in the summer, the anthem was stopped judiciously by my grandfather.

Cooking with Grandmother was adventurous, especially if she decided to take me along for buying vegetables, fruits, meats, and oils from the Russell Market. The preceding days we would decide what to wear, as we were bound to meet many friends, and Grandmother would shake out the neem leaves from the folds of one of her sumptuous silk sarees. The leaves deterred mites and insects. She then laid out a brilliant parrot green cotton skirt for me and a bright yellow blouse with puff sleeves. The most exciting part of the journey to the market was the ride in a *jutka*. This was a horse-drawn tiny carriage. Not the Victorian grand one, although we did hire one of those on one occasion and bowled down the streets bursting with pride. But it was too expensive so we settled on the *jutka* for the monthly marketing. If the *jutka* driver ever raised his whip my grandfather would soundly berate him and once he even made us get down. Only when the driver swore he would never use the whip did we get on again. On the return ride, with Grandfather sitting in front next to the driver and Grandmother with me squashed beside her in the back, we clip-clopped our way home, laden with gunny bags of mangoes, jack fruit, lentils, rice, vessels of oil, and fragrant bunches of marigolds, roses, chrysanthemums, asters, jasmine, and lilies bought from the women sitting outside the market with overflowing baskets of flowers. These were memorable outings.

In a Pickle

Once every three months, we hired three strong women to grind the spices. I was often asked to help, as I was tall and gangly and the pole used to pound the spices was a six-foot wooden pole with an iron rim. Garlic, ginger, nutmeg, fennel seeds, dried hot peppers, fenugreek, cardamom, and cinnamon would be put at varying intervals in the big granite stone resembling a huge deep vessel. The women with my grandmother stood around the stone. One of the women would start a slow rhythmic chant as she lifted the pole and brought it down on the spices in the stone vessel. As soon as she dropped it, I would grab it, hoist it up in the air and bring it down never missing a beat and then the other women repeated the movement. My eyes would smart with the red pungent spices and my throat would be raw with the smell of the red chillies, but I would never give up the pole. The pounding continued till the spices were smooth and ready. They would be put in airtight clay jars or small tin boxes while Grandmother told me over and over again that pepper was good for the liver and spleen, ginger was an appetizer and good for a cough, cloves were the perfect remedy for a toothache, cardamom for skin eruptions, garlic was good for the blood, and so on until I was soporific and ready for a hot lunch.

Come summer it was pickle and *appalam* (lentil wafers) time. Though pickles are relished at all meals, they are particularly welcome during the monsoons when the days are dark and the sky smothered with dense clouds. The rain falls in incessant torrents, and you needed that spicy tang of the pickle to add zest to the gloomy days. Pickles can be made from any fruit or vegetable ranging from mangoes, lemons, potatoes, and lotus shoot, to eggplant, carrot, bitter gourd, and chillies. You can preserve in salt alone without the addition of oil and spices. A pickle can also be made from rinds, peels, skins, and seeds. In India there is an amazing variety of fruits and vegetables from which to choose. Ginger, turmeric, and asafetida can be pickled with beans or split peas as they are digestives. Pickles can be prepared in lime juice, tamarind sauce, mango powder, or even pomegranate seeds to give them a special flavor. An accessory to a cooked dish, a pickle adds a fiery taste or a sweetness to any meal. Each pickle recipe reflects the cuisine of a state. Every vegetable, meat, and fruit is used in countless pickle variations along with special spices and oil, mustard, and even vinegar.

Travel around the world, meet Indians, and they will tell you that it is the addition of the pickle to the meal that makes it a special one. Pickles are a godsend when you are faced with a bland, dull rice and lentil dish. The same lime pickle made in the South tastes different from the one prepared in Gujarat—the difference is in the oil base. The Northerners prefer mustard oil while sesame oil is used in the South. Vinegar is used in the north and tamarind or lime juice in the South. Chili powder, turmeric, mustard seeds, and jaggery are popular in the South while the same vegetables are treated to cloves, aniseed, and cardamom in the North.

In my home, a particular week in summer was set aside for the preparation of mango and lime pickles. "Pickles and *appalams*," said Grandmother, "embellish a meal. No meal is complete without it." Since it required a lot of physical work, professional pickle and *appalam* makers were hired. The women from the rural areas went from home to home, sometimes even staying overnight during the season. First, spices were picked clean by the women. They were spread on trays and sunned outdoors. Ginger, chilies, cumin seeds, asafetida, cardamom, cinnamon, cloves, fenugreek seeds, mango powder, and mustard seeds were divided into neat little mounds and coarsely ground or finely pounded. The raw mangoes and limes would be sliced and cubed. Grandmother with her eagle eye would inspect the vegetables and fruits, which had to be of the best quality. Never was second-grade produce used, so it was always the fresh and plump carrots, turnips, and green chilies that were bought. "See that the ladles are dry, the jars sterile, otherwise mold and fungi will appear in the pickle within a few days," she admonished.

Neighbors would saunter in, gossip, discuss clothes, jewels, swap recipes, joke (sometimes verging on the bawdy), watch with interest the goings on, partake of the dal and rice and yogurt my grandmother would have laid out. Everything was discussed from the latest movie and jewelry bought to the philosophical. They too brought their contributions: crisply fried *pakoras,* a sweet dish, or a bunch of bananas. Every home had a different recipe for the same pickle and often unusual combos, like beans and onions, would be made. Some families heated vegetables to a boiling point and then preserved them with salt solution. Others salted, sunned, dried, and bottled the pickle right away to preserve the chewy taste. A year's worth of pickles, *appalams,* and *papads* were then stored in huge ceramic jars, allowed to ferment, and sunned every day.

The *varagulus* (rice wafers) were also much in demand. Mats were put out on the terrace and thin, soft old muslin sarees spread out. The ends of the cloth were weighted down with stones in case an errant breeze came along. Small balls of ground lentils were dried on the cloth and these were the rice wafers (*varagulu*). After a few days, once the wafers were crisp, they were put in jars and stored away to be enjoyed at every meal.

The Mango Daze

They say that the connection between food and memory is an organic one. One bite of a green mango and I am transported to that deep summer afternoon when I bit into my first mango. Again, I just have to hear the word *mango* and I immediately dissolve into a beatific state. Eyes glaze, a lusty smile quivers around the lips, and a torrent of memories come tumbling in a rush, as I remember sharp, intense sensations, and images—luscious, satiny, smooth and velvety—of my favorite fruit of all time: the mango. The mango daze, the mango days. I am delirious at this point. Days or daze—what does it matter?

It is summer in Bangalore and the mango season. It begins with the swing under the mango tree. Kicking off the ground with bare feet, gaining momentum, twining my arms round the knotted gnarly ropes and soaring up into the branches of the mango tree. The trick was to calculate the distance between the swing and the branch laden with luscious mangoes. My fingers grab a firm golden fruit and with a quick strong tug I am on my way swooping down with the fruit firmly held in my hands. After that, it is a time of bliss while the teeth sink into the fruit the color of turmeric. I bite deep into the succulent nectar's soft flesh while the juices spread to every corner of my mouth. They dribble down my cheeks, lips, neck, and hands and I am lost in dizzying joy. Then my teeth hit the seed. I take it out with the mushy pulp and start sucking slowly, languorously, until the seed is bare. Replete in a hypnotic languor, I throw away the seed and take off again to another branch hanging heavy with mangoes. This time a latecomer. A raw mango. That was a different kind of thrill. Eaten raw, dipped in torrid chili powder and stinging salt. Rapture. No doubt about it, the best recipe for a mango dish is a raw mango.

To ripen mangoes quickly, we would put them in a paper bag for a few days, as this speeds up the process, or we immersed them in rice bins. Every day I would be summoned to go to the rice bin and check to see if the mangoes were ripe. I held each one in my hands and squeezed them gently. If too spongy, they were overripe; they had to be solid but soft. Just before dinner the mangoes would be selected by my grandfather and placed in huge copper vessels where they lay floating in cool dark water—fresh, fragrant, and cool to the touch.

At times, my grandmother would tell me to take off my skirt and blouse before I would be given a mango. "The juice might spoil your clothes," she clucked. So there I am, the mango clutched in my throbbing fist, the juice running down my naked body. Satiated, I stand under the tap while the cold water sluices down my limbs and dry clothes await.

My grandparents would order mangoes by the basket months in advance from mango orchards in the heart of Andhra Pradesh, even though the mango trees in our garden were in abundance. Who can resist the Andhra mangoes, with extraordinary color and flavor due to the hot, humid climate? Trains would bear the precious burden and we rushed to the railway station to collect our baskets. The guard ticked off each basket according to his list of customers shoving and pushing around him.

The mango in my opinion is the fruit of all fruits. The myriad shapes— round, oval, paisley, long, narrow, weighing five pounds or as small as a peach. Colors ranging from sunburst yellow to sunset flaming orange, from emerald green to luscious red. The names of mangoes are hypnotic, exotic, splendid, spectacular. I roll them sensuously around my tongue. *Alphonso*, sweet and succulent. *Shahjehan*, revered for its floral aroma. *Suvarna Rekha*, what a beautiful sonorous name. The *Kesar*, small with a green skin even though it is ripe, taking its name from the Hindi word *saffron*. *Rumani* and *Banganapalli*, both oval, large, golden yellow, meaty and firm with the sweetest of flesh. *Chitla,* amazingly sweet, as well as the *Sharifa, Totapari, Dusheri, Sapheda, Malgova* and *Dusseheri.* And the green, raw mango was always called *Polly* mango, because it resembled a parrot's beak, and all parrots were called Polly, right? Another irresistible temptation was the sucking mango, a tiny elongated mango that could be eaten only one way—sucking. A small hole was made on top of the mango and the flesh pressed gently; I sucked up the juice in a swooshing sound and then munched on the soft flesh. A truly messy mango, but delightful. I have been told that when the *Neelam* mango is cut open a bee flies out! In Goa there are thirty varieties grown. Belize, on the other side of the world, also has mangoes. They are called *Slipper, Julie, Thundershock, Bellyful.* Not appetizing names, but who cares?

On special days, like birthdays, and festivals, such as Deepavalli, Christmas, New Year's Day, or a special celebration, we would string mango leaves together and tie the garland on the lintel of the doorway of the house. Mango leaves, like banana leaves, are auspicious; and this way anyone who enters the house is blessed, as well as the occupants.

The earliest mention of the mango which originated in the foothills of the Himalayas is believed to be in the Hindu scriptures dating back to 4000 BC.

It is believed that Buddhist monks took the fruit to Malaysia and South East Asia, where Persian traders relished it so much they took it to Brazil and the West Indies. From there the mango traveled to Florida and then to California in the 1890s.

The mango flower indicated seasons were changing. The mango blossom epitomized romance and is one of the five flowers strung on the bow of the God of Love, Manmatha. Sanskrit literature is filled with references, and poets looked on this fruit as a symbol of prosperity. At festival times, five mango leaves smeared with turmeric are kept in a pot. And the mango tree is often personified as Lakshmi, the Goddess of Wealth. The Mughals were always reproducing it in their designs. It is said that the Empress Nur Jehan, who loved the arts and was an astute politician, asked her court artisans to use the mango shape in a fabric design, which later was called "paisley" by Britishers. Incidentally, paisley today is a classic Indian pattern, but the fabric mills of Britain during the colonization of India reproduced the motif in a French village called "Paisley" and hence the name came into being.

Mangoes are rich in vitamins, potassium, and antioxidants, and contain fiber. One of the condiments used regularly in curries in my kitchen is *amchur* which is mangoes dried and ground into powder. The distinct tart flavor gives the dish an extra spark. Mangoes today are made into sherbets, ice creams, puddings, fruit salads, chutneys, tarts, breads, relishes, and many other mango delights. During times of famine in India, even the mango seed, after a long boil, was eaten. Today, I can order mango salsa, chicken with mango chutney, or a mango-gazpacho where the mango is smothered with jalapeño, corn, garlic, red peppers, basil, cilantro, orange juice, white vinegar, lemon juice, cucumber, and scallions.

But no unique fusion can top the memory of the pristine mango plucked from a tree on a swing.

Sacred Favorites

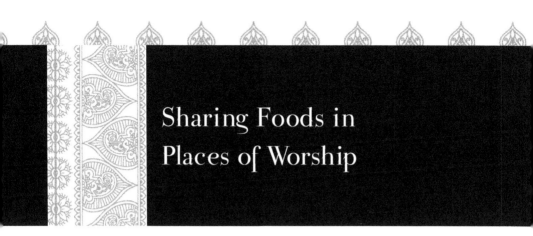

Sharing Foods in Places of Worship

The word *Hindu* refers to a follower of Hinduism and this is the name given to the ancient scriptures of India. Hindus currently constitute 80 percent of the population of India.

There are more than twenty major religious feast days in the Hindu calendar year. Families meet on religious feast days and for worship ceremonies. Feast days, fast days, births, weddings, and religious festivals are celebrated with the preparation and sharing of food. During religious feasts in certain communities, meat, fish, eggs, onions, and garlic are not eaten for a complexity of reasons. And the reason for vegetarianism? One's food shapes personality and anything eaten at the expense of an animal's suffering is taboo as all living things are held sacred. The "Bhagavad Gita" (*Song of the Divine Spirit*) in the *Mahabharata*, says, "From food do all creatures come into being."

In Hindu communities, *prasad*, the food that has been offered to the gods, is given to worshippers after a ritual or *puja*. A *puja* is performed every day in almost every Hindu home. The ceremony is believed to be the pure essence of God that strengthens spirituality and is a blessing. In a typical *puja*, the space where the *puja* is performed is cleaned; and then the deity or deities are bathed in milk, ghee, sugar, and honey. Offerings of sweets, salty snacks, fruits, flowers, and turmeric are placed on a brass/silver/copper tray in front of the deity. Incense is lighted, and lamps filled with ghee. After the ceremony, betel nuts, betel leaves, and cloves are distributed.

Certain foods are prepared as an offering to the gods who it is believed have a favorite dish. Lord Ganesha, the Elephant God, has a sweet tusk and a fondness for sugary dumplings. *Modaka* is a sweet preparation offered to Lord Ganesha, and another favorite of his, the *sundal*, is made of cooked chickpeas garnished with onions, chilies, and lime juice. Lord Hanuman adores lentil puffs; and Lord Krishna is known for his love of buttermilk. When worshiping Lord Rama, *kosumalli* is made with soaked raw lentils, diced cucumber, and coconut with a dash of lemon juice, as well as *panaka*, a pep-me-up drink with jaggery, ginger, and cardamom.

Some foods are associated exclusively with temples, such as the *aravanai* (rice cooked with jaggery) at the Srirangam temple in Tamil Nadu, the *palpayasam* (rice boiled with milk and sugar) at the Guravayoor temple in Kerala, and the *amritakalasam* (balls of jaggery and green gram flour) at Kodaganallur in Karnataka. Lord Ganesha temples in Kerala prepare *unni appams*, fried spongy pancakes made of rice powder, banana, jackfruit, and jaggery. While the Padmanabha Swami temple in Trivandrum is known for its special *aviyal* made of vegetables, coconut, and coconut oil, the Muruga temple gods in the Palani hills of Tamil Nadu are offered sugar, honey, cardamoms, ghee, and fruits. The Vishnu temple in Kanchipuram is legendary for the making of the giant *idli* (steamed rice cake) weighing a kilo and a half and spiced with pepper, ginger, cumin, and asafetida. In the famed Tirupatti temple in Andhra Pradesh as many as 70,000 *laddus* are made in the kitchens every day and offered to worshipers who come from all over the world. *Laddus* are round balls of urad dal, ghee, sugar, cashew nuts, cardamom, and raisins. It is said that the Jagannatha temple in Orissa has over 1,000 cooks who make hundreds of varieties of dishes serving the gods five times a day. The food, which is made of rice, wheat, vegetables, jaggery, and spices, is offered to pilgrims.

The holiest shrine for the Sikhs is the sixteenth-century Golden Temple in Amritsar in Punjab, so called because the dome is covered in gold leaf. The temple rests on a large sacred pool (Pool of Immortality giving Nectar) from which Amritsar received its name. The Sikh religion was founded in 1469 by Guru Nanak who was beloved of both Hindus and Muslims. The Sikh religion believes that we are all one family, propagating the eradication of caste and religious barriers. One of the Sikh concepts is the *langar* (common kitchen) which was established to abolish caste distinction so that a person of any caste could sit next to anyone and be given a meal. In any Sikh temple (*gurudwara*) around the world you can always be sure of being invited to this meal or *langar*. When I visited the resplendent temple I was told that every day 50,000 people are given food prepared on the temple premises. Rich or poor, everyone sat on the floor before a steel plate and tumbler of water. Hundreds of volunteer food servers placed dhal and vegetables on the plates while I cupped my hands and a roti was placed in it. A rich *halva* made from semolina, sugar, and ghee was served. It was an intense sacred experience, as people from all over the world sat on the floor together and shared a common meal.

In my in-laws' home in Los Angeles, I looked forward to the matriarch of the family, Satwant Kaur, distributing the sweet *pershad*, the ritually blessed sweet prepared with devotion by her own hands, which we received reverentially in our upturned hands after prayers.

Restaurants, Home-Cooked Food, and Fasting

It is interesting to find that many South Indian restaurants are named after gods and goddesses, like Annapurna, Sri Krishna, Sri Rama, Lakshmi Vilas, Durga, and Shri Vinayaka. By using the names of the deities not only is the restaurant consecrated, but customers also feel blessed while eating. It is not surprising that they are all vegetarian restaurants. Annapurna (*Anna* means food in Sanskrit) is the Hindu goddess of the provider of food. She is the incarnation of the Hindu Goddess Parvati, the wife of Lord Shiva. In temple art, she is depicted giving food to Lord Shiva who holds a begging bowl (a skull) in his hands as he asks for food that gives energy and enlightenment. I often came across the idol of Annapurna kept in kitchens and on the counters of restaurants.

The first hotels in South India were run by the upper class Brahmin caste people in the nineteenth century. Within Hinduism, there are two main castes: Vaishnavites, who are followers of Lord Vishnu, and Shaivaites, who are devotees of Lord Shiva. The Brahmins in both communities are mostly vegetarians, and there is a larger incidence of non-vegetarians among the Vaishnavites. Many rules evolved regarding purity and pollution guidelines due to the caste system. A person of a superior caste would never eat food cooked by someone of a lower caste. For a long time, non-Brahmins were denied access to vegetarian restaurants until legislation on untouchability was introduced.

* * *

Food from a restaurant can never compete with home-cooked food. In the urban sprawling city of Mumbai, despite office cafeterias, international cuisine, and thousands of restaurants, a survey showed that 250,000 office workers prefer home-cooked meals. There is an extraordinary system of lunch distribution to accommodate this tradition. Each day 6,000 carriers or *dabbawallahs,* (*dabba* means lunch box and *walla* translates to man who carries) pick up coded hot lunch boxes (*tiffin* carriers) and stack them one on top of another. These lunch boxes are collected from homes, the food having been cooked lovingly by mothers, grandmothers, sisters, or aunts, and using bicycles, scooters, and commuter trains, the lunches move at a frenzied speed with clockwork precision and are delivered punctually to the right office worker in the city. After lunch the *tiffins* are returned to the homes on the same route by these men who have an amazing memory and mark the *tiffins* with their own coded signals. This complex network is labor intensive and trustworthy through raging monsoons or political rallies that bring the city to a standstill. The only concession to technology is that you can now sign up for this service through email or text messaging!

✳ ✳ ✳

Despite the Indian passion for food, fasting is deemed necessary by most Hindus. A fast is not only a religious vow seeking divine grace, but the practice also helps in concentration and contemplation, sublimates passion, and overhauls the body system. It is also a mark of respect to a favorite god or a form of penance. Fasts are taken on certain days, depending on the phases of the moon. Shivarathri, Sankranthri, and Rama Navami are the more commonly observed holy days for fasting. The dark phase of the moon calls for abstinence from spices, ghee, and oils, and certain foods. Spices are known to heat the body and exert negative energy during this time. Regular food is replaced by nuts, bananas, fruits, sago, and water chestnuts. During fast days, some eat before moonrise once a day or after sunset. Many Hindus fast on Fridays.

In many parts of India, wives fast frequently in order to purify themselves, ensuring long life and health for the husband. The *Karwa Chouth* festival is an important ritual of fasting which married Hindu women observe in the northern and western parts of India. Sometime in October-November on the fourth day of the new moon married women begin their fast before sunrise, wear festive clothes, and often do not even take a sip of water. Earthen pots are filled with sweets. The fast ends only at night after offering prayers and sighting the new moon through a sieve. Sweets and gifts are then shared. Happily these days men too have taken to fasting to ensure that their wives too have longevity and prosperity.

Fasts or restrictive eating occur on certain days of the lunar month. One need not abstain from food completely but restrict the intake. Some people subsist only on fruits, or rock salt may replace sea salt. Or some only eat food left over from the previous day. Some eat before moonrise or after sunset on a Friday. In some communities when a family mourns the death of a family member, food is cooked in a clay pot with vegetables and rice and there is no consumption of non-vegetarian food or spices for a week or a month. This ensures respect for the dead and an homage by way of abstinence.

Widows in some parts of India have been made to follow strict traditions when their husband passes away. The women bereft of their partner have been forced to give up meat, eggs, lentils, fish, onion, and garlic, and to frequently participate in fasting. Many have been exiled to pilgrimage centers and the holy city of Benares (Varanasi) where they live on food given by worshipers. This might consist of rice, gruel, vegetables, milk, or fruit. In certain families, a widow was not allowed to heat her meager dish of rice and she had to eat it cold, as her food was not allowed to be near the fire which was considered sacred. This is an ugly side of food traditions, but fortunately it is quickly disappearing.

Celebrating Food and Festivals

Indians seem to be in a perpetual state of celebration with music, dancing, rituals, and food traditions forming an integral part of festivals. Celebrations center on seasons, mythological incidents, weddings, or birthdays in the lives of gods and goddesses. Sometimes festivals are organized according to the conjunction of planets and constellations, eclipses, or phases of the moon. Each festival has its own special dishes differing from region to region, and a variety of foods is offered to the gods before being consumed by families, friends, and neighbors. Sweets in particular are a major part of any festival in India. They are eaten at the beginning of a meal, as well as during and after. Since the gods themselves have a sanctified sweet tooth, Indians use the excuse to consume vast quantities. In days gone by, a Bengali friend tells me that before drinking water one must put a small sweet in the mouth. India is one big sweet tooth!

A festival begins with a *puja*, an act of worship. It begins with the deity in the temple being washed in milk, honey, and ghee, and decorated in resplendent silks and jewels. The deity is then offered fruit, flowers, incense, coconut, sugar cubes, and other gifts. Lamps are lighted, worshipers prostrate themselves to the accompaniment of *bhajans* (devotional songs), and food, the medium through which the festival is celebrated, is offered to everyone.

In Chennai we lived in a housing colony of fifty-four apartments. It was a micro India with Hindus, Muslims, Andhras, Christians, and Punjabis living in perfect harmony. Come festival time, the children from a Muslim household would appear with a plate of *biryani* on the day of Eid. Christmas saw my daughters dressed in new silk skirts and blouses, visiting each home with plates of cake and Indian sweets, while Hindu festivals would see us welcoming hordes of children dressed in festive clothes bringing a signature dish from their community. No plate went back empty. Everyone would return the favor with fruit or flowers. There was so much sharing and getting to know each other's culture. It was never forced or structured. It just happened.

Pongal

The Hindu year begins with spring when everything is in bloom. *Sankranti* is the entry of the sun into a new zodiacal sign and the beginning of the new solar month. The date falls between January 12 and 14 in the South when, according to Hindu astronomical calculations, the sun starts on the northern course.

In Tamil Nadu, this harvest festival of thanksgiving is called *Pongal* and marks the beginning of the new year when everyone gives thanks to the gods. The festival is associated with the traditional rice dish of the same name. The festival is also the time to dispense with the old and embrace the new. The whole house is scoured from top to bottom; old clothes and old furniture are thrown into a bonfire as a symbol of beginning anew and the driving out of evil spirits. This spring cleaning was always a boisterous occasion in our family with leaping flames and a merciless minimalizing of household stuff. Some women exchange kitchen vessels. Mothers present their daughters with kitchen utensils, rice, fruits, saffron, and sugarcane. Outside the homes, *kolam* (rice flour designs) are made, and in the center a cow dung ball is placed and decorated with a pumpkin flower. Rice is boiled in milk in a special pot, and as the milk boils over everyone in the house shouts out *"Pongalo Pongal"* ("boiling over") which is deemed auspicious. This newly harvested cooked rice (*pongal*) spiced with herbs, nuts, and raisins is placed on three leaves before the deities in the house, camphor is lighted, and the gods invoked to bless the family. In rural areas, some of the food is offered to cattle and then shared with everyone. In villages, fresh produce from the fields, like pumpkin, tubers, and sugarcane, are laid out ceremoniously, and huts are rethatched.

On the second day, *Surya*, there is much visiting of relatives and friends; and the streets are alive with color and movement as everyone wears new clothes and sets off on a visit with much chatter and laughter. The third day, *Mattu*, sees cattle taken from house to house, with horns lavishly painted and decorated with bells, silken sarees, tassels, and garlands of flowers. They are fed specially cooked rice and participate in a test of valor against the young men in a sport called *jallikattu*. Young men pit their strength and courage against the bulls as they try to mount them and pluck the rupee notes attached to their horns. In the olden days, the *jallikattu* was the time when local rulers selected a husband for their daughters from the participants. In Tamil Nadu this sport has recently been banned.

Gangaur and Holi

In Rajasthan, *Gangaur* is a women's festival celebrated in Spring with worship and prayers to the Goddess Gauri, the benign aspect of Parvati, the consort of Lord Shiva. Carrying burnished brass pots filled with fresh water, flowers, and fruits, married women pray for conjugal happiness while unmarried women pray for a good husband. On the final day of the eighteen-day festival, women fast, wear colorful clothes and jewelry, exchange sweets, and take earthen images of Gangaur in procession to immerse in the nearby lake or tank.

During the month of March in North India when it is spring and fields are rich with yellow mustard flowers and wheat, *Holi*, the boisterous festival of colors, celebrates nature's bounty and the wish for more blessings. People smear colored powder on one another or dyed waters are thrown on anyone passing by. Perhaps daubing colors on one another marks that there is no distinction of class, age, or gender. Various legends are connected with the festival's origin. One of them is the story of Prahalad, a boy-child sent by the gods to deliver the land of Braj from the cruelty of King Hiranyakashyap. The king's sister Holika lured the child into a fire hoping it would consume him. The boy's purity and goodness left him untouched, and the wicked Holika herself perished in the flames. *Holi* gets its name from Holika, and every year images of Holika are burnt in bonfires. *Malpuas*, wheat pancakes dipped in sugar syrup, are popular, as are *pedas* and *burfis*, milk-based sweets.This festival is also an exhilarating event where a number of people indulge in *bhang* (cannabis) drunk in iced drinks or even mixed with vegetables and fried into edible snacks.

Navroz

The Parsis, followers of the Iranian prophet Zarathustra (600 BC) who fled from Persia to escape persecution from the Arabs and arrived on the west coast of India, are passionate about food and there is always a lavish spread of fish, mutton, chicken, fruits, and nuts at any celebration. *Pulaos* are very popular, and chicken curries and fish masalas ending with a sweet *falooda* made from milk, rosewater, and vermicilli are staples at any celebration. On New Years Day (*Navroz*), which is in the month of March, Parsis eat *sevai*, a milk pudding.

Onam

The spring festival of *Onam* celebrates the spirit of the popular demon King Mahabali in Kerala in the form of sports, ritual, and feasting in the month of August or September. Spectacular processions with magnificently adorned elephants, dance and music performances, boat races (a boat can be paddled by 100 people), elaborate designs with rice powder in front of homes, and feasting mark the festival. It is said that some gods, angered at the pride of Mahabali who had extended his kingdom over three worlds, entreated Lord Vishnu for protection. Lord Vishnu disguised himself as Vamana the dwarf and visited the king. Lord Vishnu then asked the king for a favor. He asked for three steps of land from the king. The king granted this small request. Lord Vishnu immediately revealed himself and with two steps covered heaven and earth and won back the whole of Mahabali's kingdom for the gods. Mahabali was sent to the underworld but is allowed to return annually as he had been a generous and good king. At *Onam* time Keralites host grand feasts to welcome the king that include *olan* (potatoes in coconut milk) and *payasam* (rice pudding).

Raksha Bandhan

During the month of August, brothers and sisters reaffirm their affection, faith, and trust in each other. The sister ties an amulet *(rakhi)* made of colored string, beads, and in some cases precious stones on the wrist of her brother. He in turn gives her money and she gifts him with a box of delicious sweets. One of the many legends tells us that this festival originated in the Rajput era when Rajput women tied the amulet on the wrists of their husbands and brothers when they went off onto the battlefield. The amulet would protect them from harm. This tradition was skillfully used by the Maharanai Karmavati, queen of Mewar, who was under threat of attack from her enemy, Bahadur Shah. She sent the Mughal King Humayun a *rakhi* and claimed him as her brother. This obligated him to offer protection, and the significance of the *rakhi* tradition has since been adopted in homes to reflect the bonds of kinship and affection between brother and sister. Nowadays a *rakhi* can also be tied around the wrist of a friend symbolizing loyalty and affection. After a long and difficult work relationship with the director of my organization for many years, things changed and I cherish the day he made me his *rakhi* sister by tying the *rakhi* thread on my wrist.

Ganesh Chaturthi

In September, the birthday of the cheerful elephant-headed Ganesha, the God of wisdom, learning, and remover of obstacles, is celebrated all over India. One story relates that when Lord Shiva was away, his wife Parvati wished to take a bath; and not wanting to be surprised by anyone, she fashioned a child out of clay and breathed life into it, called him Ganesha, and placed the child outside her room. When Lord Shiva tried to enter the room, the child barred him. Enraged, Lord Shiva cut off his head. Parvati was inconsolable, and Lord Shiva asked that someone fetch another head for Ganesha. The first creature found was an elephant. So the head was brought and placed on Ganesha's shoulders.

On this popular festival day, giant idols of the God Ganesha are created with clay or papier mache, taken in procession, and then immersed in the sea. Ganesha loved sugary offerings so they are always placed before the God at the altar in each household. *Modak* is a delicious melt-in-the-mouth rice pudding filled with coconut, thick milk, cream, sugar, and cardamom served for this festival. Mumbai is well known for its range of sweet *laddos* and *halwas* sold by every shopkeeper in the city at this time.

Navaratri or Dussera

In South India, around September and October, the joyous festival of *Dussera* is celebrated as the Nine Nights (*Navaratri*) festival. On each night a different sweet dish is prepared and shared by family and friends. A special altar is made to Goddess Durga featuring dolls collected over the years by the family. The festival glorifies Shakti, the primordial female energy of the universe as manifest in the Goddess Durga, the Eternal Mother. She has a smiling face with ten hands, each holding a different weapon, and a lion resting at her feet. Goddess Durga is as destructive as she is protective, gentle, and benevolent. She was created when the gods needed an all-powerful being to destroy the buffalo-headed demon King Mahishasura. Streets and homes are decorated with lamps and vehicles are adorned with marigold flowers, neem leaves, and other bright flowers. A strict vegetarian diet is observed. People visit one another and exchange gifts, and some eat only fruits for those nine days.

Each house prides itself on putting up an altar (*kolo*) to the Goddess Durga. The altar with several levels is decorated with dolls and images of deities. There is a lot of competition to see who has the best *kolo*, with displays often taking up a whole room. My children and I would visit all the neighbor's homes and admire the splendid impressive displays. On the tenth day the decorated images of the Goddess Durga are immersed in the sea. Moving with the times, creative artists have fashioned Durgas made of glass, dals, shells, plastic bottles, and even wood shavings. Some years ago, the Durgas resembled Lady Diana and Mother Teresa; and in 2007, a Harry Potter scene was created but later taken down at the request of the author of the Harry Potter series.

In Maharashtra and in the Gujarat community, during *Dussera* people dance in sheer abandon the *dandiya raas*. Dancers, using colorful sticks tap one another's sticks gracefully and dexterously in complex rhythms while changing partners and dancing in a circle. The spins and turns, the drum beats, the glittering clothes with embellished mirrorwork, ornate jewelry, and mesmerizing choreography highlight the festival. There are many *dandiya raas* performances, competitions with singers and orchestras brought from India making it an extravagant and spectacular event.

During *Dussera*, it is believed that any project started on the tenth day of the festival is bound to succeed. So people worship the tools that help them make a living. Cars, buses, pens, computers, household articles, plows, and vessels are all decorated with marigolds, jasmine flowers, and even tinsel, while prayers are said invoking the God's blessings.

Sanjhi

In rural parts of Haryana in Punjab, the festival of *Sanjhi* is celebrated in October. *Sanjhi* is the name of the Goddess Mother crafted by women out of cow dung paste and placed in the front wall of the house as a symbol of health and prosperity. The Goddess on the front wall of the house is offered food every day of the nine days of Durga Puja.

Janmashtami

Krishna is the beloved flute-playing, butter-stealing God inspiring hundreds of legends. In Uttar Pradesh where he was raised, as well as all over India, *ras lila,* the re-enactment of his dances with the cowherd girls (*gopis*), is performed with pageantry, music, and rejoicing. When Krishna was a young boy, he and his friends would form human pyramids, standing one on top of another, and steal the butter, milk, and curds that were stored in clay pots on the rafters of the house. Krishna is well-known for his pranks, and all these mischievous deeds are celebrated in song and dance with great hilarity by his worshipers. A sweet made with puffed rice, sugar, and curd called *naivedya* is made to commemorate the birth of Krishna (*Janmashtami*).

Deepavalli

The festival of lights, called *Deepavalli* in the South of India and *Divali* in the North, is perhaps the most widely celebrated festival in India and marks the return of Lord Rama, the hero of the epic *Ramayana*, to Ayodhya after a fourteen-year exile in the forest. The name of the festival is derived from the Sanskrit word *"deepavalli"* which means a row of lamps. Thousands of lights illumine every city and village across India in the month of November. Fireworks are set off to guide Lord Rama home. There is much feasting, card games are played, gifts are exchanged, new clothes are worn, and gold is bought. Residents renovate, paint, remodel, or buy new property, while business houses give every employee a special bonus; and the day is regarded as the beginning of the financial year. It is almost like New Year. This festival is noted for the preparation of every kind of sweet dish. Sweet shops sell or give away sweets to customers. Every household delights in making specific *Deepavalli* sweet preparations, while every woman firmly believes that buying new clothes and jewelry during this time is auspicious.

Eid

Ramadan is the holy month of fasting and lasts for thirty days, corresponding to lunar reckoning and astrological calculations (so Ramadan falls at a different time each year). Muslims fast from sunrise to sunset. It is believed that this is the auspicious month in which the first verses of the *Quoran* were revealed to the Prophet Muhammad. The practice of fasting from sunrise to sunset was initiated to teach Muslims about humility, sharing, discipline, and spiritual reflection. Muslims host *Iftar* evenings when the daily fast is broken with fruits like dates, figs, and olives. The end of the fast is celebrated in the three-day festival of *Eid Ul-fitr*. Every kind of sumptuous *biryani* is prepared in Muslim homes. Special prayers are held at mosques and food and money distributed to the poor.

Christmas

The anniversary of the birth of Jesus Christ is celebrated all over India by Christians. The month of December sees carol singing, church services, decorations, illuminations, special cakes, roasts, pastries, Indian sweets, exchange of gifts, the appearance of Santa Claus, winemaking, and lots of feasting. We did not have pine trees in Chennai so a branch of a mango or neem tree made a unique Christmas tree, and we even ventured into making homemade wine which filled the whole house with the languorous sweetness of the grape.

Coming of Age

There is a celebration that many communities still perform when a girl reaches puberty. It is considered a rite of passage, a joyous one to be remembered over the years. In many a rural area in the South, the girl is taken to the river carrying a boy child on her hip. She is bedecked with flowers and led to the waters for a ritual bath. Then she is fed with fruit and milk. At the end of the meal she tosses a few morsels to the birds and insects. Back home she is adorned with silk sarees and jewels, her hair is decorated with head ornaments and then she is taken to the temple for blessings. In the olden days the girl was taken in an open car through the streets. Returning home, she would eat a mound of rice and lentils saturated in ghee for energy and well being.

When I attained what they call "maturity," my grandmother not only dressed me up every evening and gave me special foods, but hired "nagaswaram" (reed instrument) musicians to play Carnatic, religious music, early in the morning on the verandah of our house. I was mortified as my classmates who lived nearby now knew that I was "mature!" And the neighbors had been alerted that I was now of marriageable age!

The Food Heritage

Ayurveda and Vegetarians: Body, Mind and Spirit

Excavations in archeological sites in northern India reveal that in 2500 BCE grains were harvested and meat and milk were provided by cattle. The economy of India's oldest civilization, the Indus Valley civilization, was based on agriculture and animal husbandry. Farmers cultivated rice and wheat; grew lentils, figs, dates, melons; raised goats, sheep, and cattle; and made alcoholic beverages in clay stills.

Our understanding of this period is derived from a collection of evocative Sanskrit hymns, the four *Vedas* (Divine Knowledge): *Rig Veda*, *Sama Veda*, *Yajur Veda*, and *Atharva Veda*. Rich in lyricism, the *Vedas* are believed to have been composed between 1500 and 1000 BCE. It is said they emanated from Brahma's (the Creator) breath and were revealed orally to *munis* (sages). The *Vedas* passed from generation to generation through memorization and recitation.

Ayurveda is a Sanskrit word derived from *ayus* (life) and *vid* (knowledge). It was written around 600 BC with origins from the *Atharva Veda* (1000 BC) which contains a classification of diseases, healing, the treatment of the sick, and disciplined practices in food consumption. The guidelines of *Ayurveda* state that food influences the body and this in turn affects mental and spiritual health, while ingredients added to a dish not only give a special flavor but have medicinal qualities.

According to *Ayurveda*, the universe is comprised of five elements: earth, air, fire, wind, and water. The right combination of these in each individual determines their constitution. There are three types of constitutions—*Vatha*, *Pita*, and *Kapha*. Each item of food is dominated by one or two of these elements. One has to identify one's individual constitution and avoid foods that are not conducive to spiritual and physical development.

A basic concept of *Ayurvedic* medicine is the temperature of foods. Foods are classified into degrees of heat and cold. Hot fruits and vegetables include figs, dates, nuts, apples, cabbage, onions, garlic, leeks, carrots, and potatoes.

Honey, butter, and cream also heat the body. A hot body tires easily and is susceptible to ear and liver ailments, and one feels thirsty all the time since heat is the property of air and fire. Cold is the property of earth and water. A cold body is prone to weak digestion, colds, and rheumatism. Cold foods consist of yogurt, fish, peaches, pears, prunes, and citrus fruits. Whether you delight in hot or cold foods, nothing should be eaten in excess.

According to *Ayurveda*, food is either *satvic, rajasic,* or *tamasic*. A person who eats s*atvic* food will be alert, intelligent, and a quick thinker. *Satvic* food is easily digested and fresh. Spicy food is consumed by people who do not have the capacity of deep understanding, and the *rajasic* element is dominant in them. A *tamas* person is ignorant and eats only food saturated in dense, heavy oils and spices.

At one time, the cook or host would diligently prepare a dish taking into consideration the individual's age, disposition, the season, the time of day, and the health of the person. In an Indian meal you balance six tastes: salt, sweetness, bitterness, tartness, sourness, and astringency. But there is never a confusion of the taste buds. The sweet taste is nourishing and gives strength; the sour taste (lime, tamarind) stimulates digestion and is good for the heart; the salty taste is good for digestion.

✳✳✳

Worship of the cow increased during the Vedic period around 1500 BCE when literature formulated the religion and philosophy of Hinduism. A strong association between spirituality and vegetarianism slowly became an important aspect of Indian life. The cow became sanctified, and it was forbidden for Hindus to eat the meat of the cow. By the 4th century, killing a cow became a capital offence. The cow provided nutritious milk and plowed and fertilized the fields so it made economic sense to protect the cow. Today everything that comes from the cow is considered useful. In rural areas, the dung of the cow is slapped on floors and walls of huts, and serves as an insecticide and disinfectant. Some people believe that cow urine should be drunk after childbirth and even regularly as it has medicinal qualities.

Buddhism (founded by Siddhartha Gautama) and Jainism (founded by Vardhamana, also known as Mahavira) flourished in India in the 6th century BC. The two religions challenged the caste system, questioned the teachings and rites of the *Vedas*, and were successful in converting people to considering all living things as sacred. But meat eating is not explicitly forbidden by Buddhists.

Followers of Jainism are vegetarians and do not eat meat or fish. Jains believe in rigid food restriction and also do not eat onions or tubers, like radish, carrots, potatoes, ginger, turmeric, and garlic, as they feel insects underground may be killed while the vegetables are uprooted. They do not eat honey as bees would be destroyed and some Jains even wear a mask to avoid inhaling insects. Jain monks and nuns often sweep the ground before them so that they may not step on an insect. During fasts they abstain from curds, ghee, oil, or sweets. The fragile silver foil that often covers sweets is supposed to be beaten into thinness between layers of soft leather so some Jains avoid such sweets. One would imagine Jain cooking devoid of many ingredients would be bland and dull, instead Jain food is tasty and delicious.

With constant invasions, religious beliefs and customs were so intertwined with food habits that in 1857 the ruling British became alarmed at the growing power of the Indians who realized that their culture and religion were being compromised. Muzzleloading rifles were issued to the Indian army with cartridges, one end of which was paper wrapped and had to be bitten off before loading. The paper was coated with grease to make it waterproof. The Hindu soldiers thought that the grease was fat from the sacred cow, while the Muslim soldiers believed that the grease came from the pig which was a taboo food for them. The Indian troops (sepoys) refused to bite the cartridges and thus came about the Sepoy Mutiny, the beginning of the crumbling of the British Empire.

Today the majority of the Indian population is vegetarian. Although Hindus are mostly vegetarian, along the coastal regions of Bengal and Maharashtra fish is eaten due to climate, availability of produce, and geography. Most South Indian Hindus are strict vegetarians. Many Indians believe that excluding meat from the diet purifies the mind. It is commonly believed that vegetarians are sharp, quick in thinking, alert, and in harmony with nature.

So what comprises an Indian vegetarian meal? A vegetarian meal consists of rotis made from wheat which provides carbohydrates, rice, and fresh vegetables. Supplementing this are the high-protein dals (lentils), whole, split, oiled, not oiled, ground into flour, or used in curries, chutneys, steamed cakes, and sprouted salads. Around sixty varieties of lentils can be found in Indian regional cuisine. They come in many colors—black, orange, yellow, brown, white, red, green— and also flaunt different tastes, fragrances, and textures. They can be used as appetizers, the main course, or even desserts. Used for thousands of years, every Indian will have a favorite version of a particular dal and the memory of eating it. I have heard of the kali dal or black dal being cooked for five hours on a very slow fire and served as a Mughal classic.

My husband must have dal every day. It's a comfort food. Even after partaking of an extravagant feast outside the home, he will enter the kitchen on returning home, clatter dishes and pans and look for the homemade dal that I prepare every day. But then even the gods favor the simple legume. In Tirupati, the Balaji Temple is the source for thousands of *laddus* (a sweet dish made of urad dal) made every day for devotees. Since Indians obsess so much about dal, other countries, like Australia, Canada, and the U.S. are exporting dals to India to fulfil the demand for lentils.

The most important lentils are *urad* (black gram), *mung* (green gram), *toor* (red gram), and *chana* (Bengal gram). Anyone inviting you to their home in north India will use the phrase, "Come over for some *dal-chaval*," meaning, "There will always be lentils and rice so come over." A well-prepared dal with the right seasoning and served with rice or rotis and yogurt can rival any gourmet dish.

Invasions and
the Mughal Legacy

In 1525 AD, the Mughals arrived in India from Central Asia. Arabs began their sorties into Sindh, now the southernmost province of Pakistan; loose federations of kingdoms began to take shape. When the Seljuk Turks led by Mahmud Ghazni swept down into India, kingdoms were quickly annexed, and Muslim territories proliferated. The Mughals ruled northern India for three centuries—1526-1858 AD. The Mughals brought with them the religion of Islam, based on the teachings of the Koran. The history of India was changed by this new religion and the existing diet and customs were enhanced with an extravagance of cuisine. The Mughals introduced their favorite dishes and cooking methods that transformed local fare into something rich, tasty, and spectacular.

Mughal manuscripts contain hundreds of illustrations of great platters of food and drink served by attendants to the nobility. The Mughals loved rich celebratory food and left a lasting impression on Indian culinary traditions. Indian food was also enhanced by new cooking methods which included grilled meats, rich gravies, elaborate breads, heavy rich cream, dried fruits, the *tandoor* (standing oven) cuisine, and professional chefs called *halwaii, rikaabdar, bawarchi, maharaj,* and *bhatiara*. In the royal kitchens, meats were cooked in lavish and flamboyant styles. Mughlai cuisine became legendary as rich food was served on elaborate jade platters. It was believed that jade would react with any poison and change color, and hence it was used to protect anyone who attended a banquet. Poisoned food was always in the suspicious minds of emperors like Babur, who was the survivor of many food assassination attempts.

Host and guests would rinse their hands in perfumed silver bowls of water and sit on splendid, embellished crafted carpets. Rich rice pilafs, *tandoor* cuisine where breads are baked in a standing oven, and *biryanis* were often presented on gold and silver platters, garnished with fried onion rings and sautéed pistachios, almonds, and raisins, and the whole covered with edible silver sheets. Dishes had exotic names like *Shah Jahani Biryani,* named after the Mughal emperor Shah Jahan. Some historical evidence, however, tells us that prior to the Mughal invasion there was a dish known as "*Oon Soru*" in the state of Tamil Nadu in the south of India made of meat, ghee, and spices used to feed soldiers. However, it is the Mughlai *biryani* that is still termed a royal dish. Emperor Akbar, who entertained poets, musicians, scholars, and painters, often hosted elaborate, grand meals with thirty dishes, which included a variety of game birds, like the pheasant and waterfowl, as well as varied species of fish, followed by the Mughal custom of relaxing in the landscaped perfumed gardens.

Another delicacy of Mughlai cuisine is the *dumpukht*, an indolent, leisurely style of slow cooking. *Dumpukht* means cooking with steam so flavors are sealed. This form of cooking by the Mughals is mentioned in the literature of AD 1606. A vessel made of clay or metal with a heavy base and narrow neck containing meat, vegetables, and spices was placed on hot charcoals. The clay lid was sealed with a paste of flour and water. The heat was gentle and kept the flavors in, and the narrow neck of the vessel pushed the steam back. Coals were also placed on the lid to distribute heat evenly. The slow cooker produced tender meat flavored with aromatic spices—a truly elaborate and distinctive dish.

It was a long history of Mughal rule extending from the eleventh to the nineteenth century, remembered for not only *kekabs, kulfis, biryanis,* exotic breads, and flavors but magnificent monuments, extravagant palaces, sprawling extensive gardens, a passion for paintings, music, refinements, an opulent style, and the exquisitely proportioned Taj Mahal built by Emperor Shah Jahan in memory of his beloved wife Mumtaz Mahal. An eternal legacy.

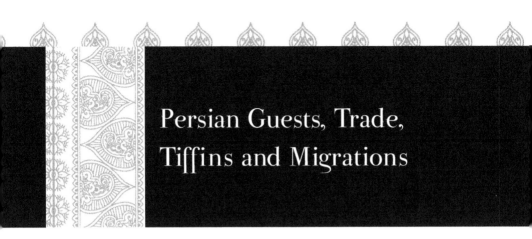

Persian Guests, Trade, Tiffins and Migrations

In the 6th or 7th century BC, one of the oldest religions, Zoroastrianism, was founded in Persia (Iran) by the prophet Zarathustra. The followers of Zoroastrianism, known as Parsis, fled to India to escape religious persecution and arrived in Gujarat on the west coast. The Hindu king at that time did not want any foreigners and sent an emissary with a full glass of milk to say symbolically that India was filled to the brim with people and that he did not want to add to the population. The Parsis added sugar to the glass and sent it back saying they would dissolve like the sugar into the existing population and sweeten the country as well as enhance the Indian culture without changing it. The Parsis were welcomed and soon adopted Gujarati as their *lingua franca*. They did preserve many of their religious and culinary traditions though, Parsi cooking shows signs of Iranian influence as a number of dishes use apricots and nuts and are often linked to origins in the Middle East and even Greece.

Meanwhile, the long coastline of India and the spices found in the country were exciting the imagination of Europe. The Portuguese, the first European powers in India, based themselves with trading stations on the western coast of India around the sixteenth century, bringing Roman Catholicism and a penchant for building ostentatious baroque churches; but they were distracted by the discovery of Brazil and unable to compete with the next wave of colonizers. The Portuguese left India, but not before introducing pork, rich fruit cakes, pies, tomatoes, peppers, potatoes, guavas, cashews, cocoa, and chilies. The French and Dutch also fought for Indian spices but eventually left leaving India to the British. In 1608 the British arrived with the blessing of Queen Elizabeth I at a time when the turbulent Mughal empire was disintegrating and there were internal rivalries. They soon became a sovereign power and India became the glittering jewel in the crown of the British colonial empire. What did the British contribute? After all, they ruled

India for 200 years. The British were quite unaffected by the cornucopia of Indian food and ate mostly British fare cooked by Indian servants, and perhaps considered Indian food to be unhygienic, too spicy, and unpalatable. Here the influence was minimal except perhaps for sitting on chairs at a table and their interest in porridge, puddings, ice cream, fine china, forks, knives, and cakes. The English word *tiffin* (for snacks) was adopted in the Indian culinary vocabulary and words like "curry" became synonymous with Indian cooking. Indeed there is no such thing as "curry" in Indian cuisine. It is perhaps an anglicization of the Tamil word *"kari"* which meant a sauce of vegetables and meat cooked in spices. The British used it to describe any stew or anything fried. In truth, anything cooked by an Indian! Today there are more than 10,000 Indian restaurants in England.

But northwest India and eastern Bengal, where Muslims were most numerous, was given to those who feared for the safety of Islam and wanted a separate state, and so Pakistan was founded. This was not a peaceful transition. The Partition of India became brutal and bloody, with five million refugees crisscrossing from one country to the other. Years later when an uneasy truce was made, Mumbai became an exciting cosmopolitan city welcoming North Indians and Sindhi populations, who were refugees displaced from the North West Frontier. They quickly assimilated into the local culture.

Food became a very interesting mix in India with the embracing of different styles and the introduction of *naan, tandoori chicken, kulchas,* and *kebabs*. On highways, popup kitchen restaurants (*dhabas*) spread rapidly. A *dhaba* is a roadside eatery serving food close to home-cooking at affordable prices. The *dhabas* are long associated with good North Indian food. We were visiting Delhi once and *dhaba* eating was recommended by everyone. So there we were, seated on a rough bench, a few feet from the dusty road, practically within a hairs breadth of being knocked over by a speeding cyclist or a pedestrian rushing by. There was no fancy décor. We had to shout our request for *tandoori* and *naan* over the clatter of dishes, noisy hungry customers, and orders of food taken at high decibel. Just as we were getting frustrated and infuriated the food arrived, the chaotic world around us fell away and all we did was focus on the soft as butter *naan* and the exquisite succulence of the tender chicken smothered with cream and enriched with spices. Food bliss I still remember.

On a recent visit to the south of India, I was happily astonished to find that traditional restaurants that prided themselves on the traditional rice preparation *idli* and *dosa* were competing with North Indian designer-style restaurants that were becoming popular with their new sumptuous flavors. At the same time, we found North India was lured by the oil-free, light, and nutritious cuisine of South India. With urban and rural migration, food habits now tend to be flexible, and there is much more fusion and acceptance of the cuisine of other regions.

Today in any state in India chances are that you may find a young woman or man chopping potatoes, rinsing peppers, dicing onions and tomatoes, and preparing a pasta with Kerala shrimp to be shipped abroad to the United States and then stockpiled on supermarket shelves. Indian regional cuisine is fast becoming international and becoming well-known for gourmet frozen meals that can be eaten in ten minutes. The containers come with instructions, nutritional facts, and even wine pairing suggestions. Vegetables like broccoli, zucchini, red and yellow peppers, asparagus, mushrooms, and kiwi fruit are now grown in India for overseas clients' consumption. Food in upscale Indian restaurants is slowly becoming a little fetish, sometimes a spectacle with a dazzle that makes the dish an eating experience. Traditional *dosas* (rice pancakes) are stuffed with *chow mein* instead of potatoes and spices; the *utthapam* (thicker version of *dosa*) comes crusted with cheese; and railway stations sell veggie burgers. Fancy chicken marinated in squid ink covered with curry leaves or sea bass with a layer of raw mango? The traditional *idli* served in a vegetarian restaurant in Artesia, California, an hour from where I live has sliced the *idli* and fried it in oil so that it resembles french fries! Nowadays with a creative chef you can order chocolate with *rasmalai,* a four-layer cake blended with *halwa*, and ice cream with hot *jelabis* and *gulab jamuns*. Urban Indians are becoming more adventurous in their search for sublime food. Indian food can be contemporary, trendy, casual, traditional, or classic. But the greeting will always be *"Have You Eaten?"*

In An Indian Kitchen

Kitchen Vessels

Each vessel has a specific role in an Indian kitchen, and to people like my grandmother, it is sacrilege to use it otherwise.

The Earthenware Pot

The earthenware pot *(kumbha)*, the receptacle of water or food, is symbolic of the womb, the reproductive power. In Indian mythology, it is associated with mother goddesses and is seen as the receptacle of life. Earthenware pots in a household are filled with water and are embellished with decorations as they are the containers of life.

Water is always cool in the hot summers when stored in huge earthenware pots. Smaller rounded water pots with narrow mouths to avoid spillage were designed to fit the curves of women's waists and to stay balanced on their heads when carrying water from the wells or tanks. All across the countryside, earthenware pots are used for cooking as the unglazed clay allows the ingredients to breathe. In Punjab and Uttar Pradesh, mustard greens and black lentils are prepared in clay pots; in Hyderabad many people favor the *biryani* cooked in a new clay pot. Fish in Goa and Kerala is always cooked in earthenware pots as a lot of tamarind is used. Tamarind is highly acidic and reacts with a steel vessel. Curds or yogurt is served and stored in earthenware pots.

Stone, Copper and Brass Vessels and Utensils

Copper frying vessels, ladles, and kitchen knives have been found in the Indus valley towns of Mohenjodaro and Harappa from around 2500 BCE. Mention is made in the *Rig Vedas* (Hindu Scriptures) in 1000 BCE of myriad utensils such as storage vessels, drinking cups, cooking pots, mortar and pestle, roasting spits, strainers, cauldrons, spoons, leather storage bags for curds, liquor, and water, and deep grinders, many of which still are used today. Regional artists in India have crafted their own designs and ornamentation in metal; and it is said that more often than not, no two kitchen vessels in the same region are similar. Next to clay, metal was considered most beneficial to health as the various minerals in metals were believed to have properties that kept a body healthy.

Porous soft stone vessels were in vogue and were excellent for retaining the flavor of foods for days. The *kalchatti* (stone vessel) was popular as the stone would absorb the oil and gently permeate the food cooking in it.

Copper was commonly used. Artfully designed and ornamented utensils came in different shapes and sizes. When copper became scarce, brass, an alloy of copper and zinc, was used; and even today Moradabad, Mirzapur, Pune, and Ahmadabad have all become centers of brass vessel making. Traditionally in India, brass vessels that were re-tinned regularly were used. Since most foods had a sour ingredient, this was necessary. All the *undas* (brass large vessels for storing water) in my mother's and grandmother's homes were scoured daily with tamarind ash and coconut fiber till they gleamed like molten gold. Other brass items that gleamed on the shelves of the kitchen were sieves, ladles, oil containers, and spoons, as well as measuring cups for rice, oils, flours, and lentils. Brass is excellent for retaining heat and is malleable enough to be crafted into any shape. Traditional Indian foods are best cooked in brass or copper pots and oftentimes a cook in India will place not only a tight lid on top of the vessel to prevent the aromas from escaping, but also a couple of live coals so that there is a gentle warmth coming from the top as well as the bottom of the vessel.

Unfortunately, with the advent of stainless steel, bell metal (seven parts copper and one part tin) and brass are disappearing and the pungent, tasty aromatic flavors that emanated from these metals has been reduced. In Bengal, bell metal utensils noted for their creative artistry and stark elegance are still used for cooking and serving dishes. Today, many people collect the old vessels for their design and shape, and a great many have ended up as collector's items or in museums.

Kadai and Tawa

The *kadai* (a deep cast-iron skillet similar to a wok) is used for deep frying and a *tawa* (a cast-iron flat round skillet) is used for *rotis*. The *tawa*, which can be bought from any Indian grocery store, is perfect for Indian cooking. The traces of iron that seep into the food is good for the body. *Tawas* conduct heat evenly, are slow to heat, and stay hot for a long time. A *tawa* is heavy so you should be careful when using it so that it does not drop on your toes, which happened to me once. It has a concave surface and is made from cast iron, and should be tempered before using: First wash and dry, then rub the surface with a few drops of vegetable oil and heat till hot; sprinkle on one tablespoon salt and some whole wheat flour and wipe gently; cook for a further five minutes; remove from heat and cool; then wash, dry and heat the *tawa* again for another five minutes. It is worth the trouble as you can multitask with this one. Sauté, fry, boil, stew, and whip up a full meal. But the best *kadai* is a well-worn one inherited from your grandmother.

Dekchi

A *dekchi* is a round-bottomed vessel ideal for making curries.

Stainless Steel Vessels

Stainless steel vessels rarely rust and are easy to clean. Easily maintained and long lasting they withstand high temperatures and nowadays vessels of all shapes and sizes are made with a designer look.

Spices and Herbs

In some parts of India, a bride stands on a spice grinding stone when making her marriage vows to make sure that the marriage has a strong foundation. Could the symbolic stone used for grinding spices be the cornerstone of Indian cooking?

Spices have a dramatic history through the centuries, involving intrigue, fights, assassinations, villains, heroes, traders, sailing ships, and explorers. On May 20, 1498, Vasco da Gama stepped on Indian soil and, as legend goes, is believed to have proclaimed, "For Christ! For Spices!"

In India spices are known to have been used by the Indus Valley people 4,500 years ago, and grinding stones have been excavated in Mohenjo Daro and Harappa, now a part of Pakistan. Spices were imported into Egypt from India as early as 1700 BCE for the purpose of embalming mummies. The *Rig Veda* (1500 BCE) mentions mustard, the *Yujar Veda* refers to black pepper, and the *Atharva Veda* has a reference to turmeric. In Valmiki's *Ramayana* (400 BCE), King Dasaratha's body is preserved in spices and balms.

An Indian family prides itself on storing at least fifteen to twenty fresh spices and spice blends, and many blends are close family secrets, handed down from generation to generation. In olden times in large households, an assistant to the chief cook was called the *masaalchi*, and his job was to grind all the spices every day to a smooth, fine consistency. Every home in India has a small grinding stone made of black granite and a stone rolling pin to crush the spices. Every Indian home around the world has one precious spice box in the kitchen. Spice mixtures are wet and dry. The wet mixtures are spices moistened with oil, vinegar, water, or coconut milk to make a paste; while the dry mixtures are powdered. There are hundreds of combinations with varying ingredients. Proportions and balance are the secret. There is a certain order in which spices must be put into the cooking. No spice should dominate, but a calculated and artful blending of different seasonings will create the indefinable, delicate nuances that characterize Indian cooking. For instance, excess turmeric and fenugreek seeds can make a dish bitter.

Subtle or potent, the *masala*—a mixture of ground or whole spices—is the essence of Indian cuisine. By using spices, you can modify, adapt, enhance, and add zest and flavor to a simple dish. They can dramatically transform the same food so that it tastes different from one day to another. For instance, a vegetable cooked with cumin seeds tastes different when cooked with sesame seeds.

Spice blends are known for the area where they originated. Flavors vary from region to region. *Garam masala* is used in North India, *sambar masala* in the south, then there is Delhi's *chaat masala* for snack foods, and Kerala's signature *dal masala*.

Saffron, the costliest spice, is cultivated in Jammu and Kashmir in the north and often included in the trousseau of brides. Ginger is produced in most states. South India produces cardamom, turmeric, pepper, and ginger. Chili peppers (the Portugese brought the chili pepper to India 500 years ago) are cultivated in Orissa, Andhra Pradesh, Maharashtra, Orissa, and Rajasthan. Today, India supplies almost half of the world's spices.

Spices can be used whole or ground, in all varieties of food: meat, fish, poultry, vegetables, and even fruit. But of course all spices are not used together for a dish. A meat dish may require only cloves, peppercorns, bay leaves, cinnamon sticks, cardamom, and a slice of ginger. A vegetable dish may need turmeric, black mustard seeds, and green chilies. Some spices must be roasted first and then added while the dish is being cooked. Roasting ensures that the raw taste of the spices is removed and the spices are easy to digest. A heavy-bottomed pan is ideal for roasting, and spices must be stirred frequently for six or seven minutes (no longer) until the whole kitchen is filled with a heady aroma. The volatile oils in the spices diminish the moment spices are heated so they must be cooked quickly.

Spices should be stored in airtight containers away from strong light and in a cool place. They can also be frozen for six months and will still keep their color. I am of the firm belief that whole spices ground fresh are better than those that come in packaged containers.

While writing this book, I met groups of Indian nurses who had come to the United States to work in hospitals. When I asked them what was the most precious possession they brought from India, they shouted out in unison: "SPICES!"

In India, spices are valued for their antiseptic qualities as well as flavors and aromas. *(The medicinal properties of the spices mentioned below are beliefs of Indian people over the centuries.)*

Amchur (green mango powder): Made from green mango that is peeled, dried, and powdered. Has a sour, tangy taste and gives a sharp bite to dishes. Used more in North India than the South in *samosas* and pickles.

Asafetida *(Heeng)*: Essential part of Indian cooking. It is sold in either a thick wad of a gummy substance or in a powdered form. The gummy variety is the best and should be broken off into fragments. It has an acrid bitter taste and powerful aroma, but improves on cooking and is an excellent digestive. It is always put in dals (lentils) to prevent gas problems. But it has to be used sparingly or it ruins the taste of the dish. Supposed to help the voice and is eaten by singers.

Aniseed: Has a delicate, aromatic taste and can be used in dips and meat dishes. Eliminates bad breath so is a mouth freshener. Its oil relieves arthritis. Offered to guests after a meal in homes and restaurants. Used in Kashmir, Goan dishes, and Chettinad cooking in the South.

Ajwain: Found mainly in Gujarat. Ajwain leaves can be dipped in batter and fried. Before using in dishes, crush with hands to release a powerful aromatic flavor. It is also used in the making of breads, rotis, and *parathas*. When used with beans and lentils it reduces flatulence and acidity.

Basil (*Thulasi* leaf): Known as *tulsi* in Hindi, it is the most sacred plant in Hinduism and is grown either in the front or back yard of most Hindu homes. The householder offers worship every day where the plant grows. In Vishnu temples, the abode of Lord Vishnu, you are given water in which holy basil leaves have been soaked. Basil leaves are also used in ceremonies in temples. But basil is rarely used in Indian cooking as frying destroys the delicate fragrance.

Bay leaf: Introduced by the Mughals, bay leaves give a rich sweet scent to pilafs and can be ground or broken into large fragments and added to other spices. Should be used sparingly and removed from a dish before serving. Boiled with water it is an antiseptic, freshens the breath, is good for gums and eyesight, and is claimed to be an aphrodisiac. The acid from the leaves is used to discourage moths, and in some households bay leaves are placed between clothes.

Cardamom (*Elaichi*): An important ingredient in *garam masala* and adds aroma to *biryanis* and pilafs. Essential in the preparation of sweet dishes, like *kulfi* and any pudding; a digestive; cools the blood; also a preservative. Used in a cooling summer drink. The cardamom in the North, often called the queen of Indian spices, is used in the making of tea. India grows 80 percent of the world's crop. Kashmiri brides wear a silver locket filled with cardamom which they gift to the groom during the wedding ceremony. Mughal emperors carried tiny silver boxes containing cardamom and used it as a mouth freshener.

Chilies/Cayenne pepper (*Lal Mirch*): The seeds are the hottest part of chilies. High in vitamins A and C, they are mellow when fried. For the best chili powder, buy red chilies, de-seed, dry fry, and grind to the required fineness. Dry roasting heightens the flavor of chilies. Good for sore throats but may burn the lining of the stomach, so beware of consuming too much chili-laden food.

Coriander (*Dhania Haree*): Coriander seeds *(dhania)* are grown all over India, especially in Rajasthan and Central India. The seeds have diuretic properties. Has a heady aroma, can be roasted for a few minutes and then fried in a little oil on a hot griddle. Coriander leaves are sprinkled on curries and yogurt dishes to give them a fresh look. It has antibacterial properties and is used for colic, rheumatism, and as a breath sweetener.

Cinnamon (*Dar cheeni*): An essential ingredient of *garam masala*, cinnamon is the inner bark of a tropical evergreen tree and is used in general cooking like pickling vegetables, in beverages, as well as in desserts. Has medicinal properties known in India since the 8th century. Diabetic persons take a teaspoon a day while others believe cinnamon is good for the general health. Used in incense, germicides, soaps, and in *masala chai* (tea).

Cumin seeds (*Jeera*): Strong, spicy, sweet aroma and is used in most curries. Used in rice and dal recipes and kebabs, and roasted cumin is sprinkled on salads or yogurt as a contrasting garnish. Use whole or ground into powder. An appetite stimulant and good for stomach disorders, broken capillaries, and digestion. The drink known as *jeera pani,* or cumin water, has cooling properties and is made of cumin, lime juice, and fresh coriander leaves.

Cloves (*Lavang*): Used in India for centuries. Whole cloves are used in *biryanis*, as well as in hot teas in winter. Refreshing with a powerful flavor and used as a mouth freshener. In North India, men and women keep cloves in tiny silver boxes along with cardamom seeds, and after a rich, spicy meal they place the spices in their mouth. Used to treat flatulence, colic, and indigestion. Clove water is believed to help asthma, and the oil is used in manufacture of soaps, bath salts, and gastric irritability. Often a cotton bud is soaked in clove oil and placed on an aching tooth.

Curry leaves (*Curry patta*): South Indians must use it in practically all dishes. The aromatic flavor is unique. So the chopped or minced or even whole leaves are found in dals, vegetable dishes, and meat curries, as well as fish curries. The leaves are small and deep green. Curry leaves are also used in tempering. Tempering is the final flourish to a cooking session. A little oil is heated in a pan, a small amount of cumin seeds, mustard seeds, black gram dal, and curry leaves are added and cooked until they pop. This mixture is added to a curry or a vegetable fry. Essential fatty acids for the body are contained in the dal and seeds. Certain vegetables like cauliflower and carrots need a medium to release the vitamins in them and this is where the tempering vegetable oils are useful. But when you find curry leaves in a dish, you usually do not eat them as they are slightly bitter and so you set them aside. Curry leaves soaked and boiled in oil and rubbed on the scalp are supposed to prevent the graying of hair. Regarded as a tonic, the paste from curry leaves cures skin eruptions and bites.

Fennel seeds (*Sonf*): Featured in Kashmiri and Kerala cuisine, fennel seeds are very aromatic. They are excellent for vegetables and to sweeten desserts. Used as a mouth freshener and helps in digestion and promotes menstruation. Babies are often given a small drink of fennel water to prevent colic.

Fenugreek (*methi*): A strong powerful spice but mellow after cooking. Small leaves have a delicate flavor; the seeds are eaten to relieve flatulence, diabetes, and diarrhea. A new mother eats nuts and sweets flavored with fenugreek as it is said to improve lactation. Fenugreek seeds are also crushed and given to cattle to increase milk supply. Punjabis love to eat it with potatoes and it is used in *dhansak* (a meat and lentil dish) by Parsi. In South India, fenugreek is an important ingredient in *mulaga podi*, a spice powder eaten with *dosa* and *idli*.

Garlic (*Sonth*): Almost all Indian recipes call for garlic and ginger. Ginger, it is said, tends to raise blood pressure, and garlic is good for keeping it low. When used fresh, garlic and ginger retain all their goodness but can be eaten raw or cooked. Garlic, either crushed, minced, chopped, or blended, is indispensable in Indian cuisine. It has a powerful sharp flavor when sliced or crushed but becomes bitter if it is browned too long. Good for the common cold and obesity. Stimulates blood circulation, lowers blood pressure, purifies the blood, aids digestion, lowers cholesterol, and used in cough medicines. Some people believe that planting garlic under roses produces more perfume.

Ginger (*Adhrak*): One of the oldest known spices, the word *ginger* comes from the Sanskrit *gingahara*, meaning "shaped like a horn." It is used both fresh and dried and is extensively used in Indian cuisine. Ginger tea is becoming very popular. Believed to cure sore throats. Dry ginger powder sprinkled on top of milk before boiling prevents it from curdling.

Mint: Used in chutneys, *dhansak*, and *biryani*. Used in any cold drinks, has a refreshing tang. In curries, a sprig of mint is used as a garnish. Should not be fried with the *masala*, as it turns black. Eases stomach problems and is used to flavor toothpaste, perfumery, and tobacco.

Mustard seeds (*Sarson*): Black mustard seeds, which have little or no smell, are used as a flavoring agent and in the South of India are an essential ingredient when tempering. For some recipes the seeds have to be crushed. Promotes hair growth and believed to keep the mind sharp and alert and to relieve arthritic pain.

Poppy seeds (*Khaskhas*): Before cooking, roast and grind white poppy seeds and use for thickening. Dishes will acquire a nutty flavor. They are used in some Indian breads. Poppy seeds are said to relieve a toothache.

Pepper (*Kali mirchi*): One of the most popular and versatile of spices, black pepper has a sharp, pungent, woody aroma. The name comes from the Sanskrit *pippali* meaning "berry," and India is the world's largest producer and exporter. Ground, or sometimes used whole, it can be found in any regional dish. It has anti-aging properties, is an astringent, is good for blood circulation, stimulates the appetite, and relieves nausea. White and green pepper are milder. Oil of pepper is used for massaging aching muscles, for colds, and even in perfumery.

Rose petals: The petals are sun-dried and then powdered. Powdered rose petals are used in meat dishes as they exude a delicate fragrance. *Kormas* in the north of India favor rose petals as Indian roses have an intense fragrance. Rose water is sprinkled on top of cooked rice dishes like pilafs and *biryanis*. The plants are cultivated especially in the Udaipur region and Kanauj in North India. Known for cooling properties, rose essence is used for making *sherbets* (cooling drinks).

Saffron (*Kesar*): The most expensive spice due to its scarcity, saffron is grown in Jammu and Kashmir. Saffron is the dried stigma of the crocus bulb. Used in worship and wedding ceremonies, it is thought to be an aphrodisiac. Delicate, bright yellow with a red tinge, it has a powerful aroma and slightly bitter taste. Soak in a tablespoon of warm milk for half an hour before using. Gives a golden color to meat, rice, and sweet milk-based dishes along with a fragrant richness. They say that it takes almost two thousand stigmas to produce one gram of saffron. Do not keep it too long and use very little at a time. Believed to be good for urinary disorders, melancholia, and fevers.

Salt: Several kinds of salt are used in Indian cooking. *Kala namak*, or rock salt, is used to perk up snacks (like *chaat*), fruit salads, and desserts. When ground, the gray crystals become a dull brown. In Central India it is favored as a good antidote to dehydration. Other flavored salts come from dry sea beds.

Sesame seeds (*gingelly* seeds): Come winter time, sesame seeds, which have little aroma, are crunched and munched for their warming effect. Their nutty texture is perfect for breads. Can be sprinkled in sweet dishes while cooking, especially *laddoos*, or in chutneys. Used in massage oil, soaps, and cosmetics. In the South, newly married women often wear candied sesame seed necklaces and hair ornaments. Their oil is used as a hot poultice and massaged into the scalp for luxuriant hair.

Turmeric (*Haldi*): Used daily all over India it is perhaps the most traditional of Indian spices. The root of the plant is used as a powder and is an essential ingredient in cooking meats, lentils, or vegetables. The brown root is peeled and out comes the vibrant, rich yellow color which is auspicious and believed to have protective powers. Burns easily, so cook with care. Turmeric can be used as a marinade particularly for fish, or as a preservative. Plain boiled rice takes on a bright tinge when flavored with turmeric. Used as a curative cleansing agent and as a preservative. Its yellow color is supposed to cure jaundice and liver infections. An antiseptic, excellent for a sore throat when added to hot milk. My family and friends can vouch for this cure.

Rice

India is the world's largest producer of rice after China and it is the staple food of half of India. It is believed that rice has been eaten since the fifth millennium BC. Rice contains no fat, is cholesterol free, and is low in sodium. It is the primary source of nutrition in South India. Each part of India grows its own variety of rice. Basmati rice is famous for its long slim grain and its delicate aroma and is grown all over Punjab, Haryana (the neighboring state), the foothills of the Himalayas, and Uttar Pradesh. It is more expensive than ordinary rice, and the older the better. One-year-old basmati rice is perfect for *biryanis*. Then there are the short, fine-grain rice—*jeera* rice, the golden *sela* rice in the north, the thicker and longer *ambe mohur* with a mango fragrance—and *punni*, a long-grain rice from Tamil Nadu.

Rice must always be soaked in cold water while the pot of water comes to a boil. Allow 2 cups of water to 1 cup of rice. Add salt, a stick of cinnamon, and a cardamom pod and then the washed rice to the boiling water. Lower heat. Cooking time varies with varieties of rice. Check to see if the rice is soft. Remove from stove and drain excess water. Fluff up the rice with a fork. Garnish with fried onion, coriander, nuts, and raisins.

For a plainer rice, you can bring a lot of water to a boil, add a pinch of salt and a few drops of oil, then add rice, and when cooked pour out the excess water.

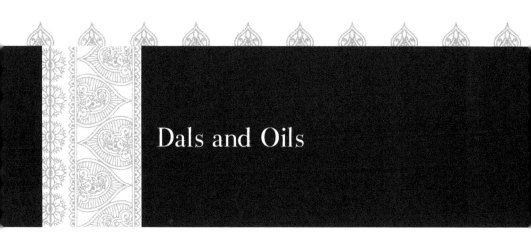

Dals and Oils

Dals

Black *urad dal* eaten with rotis is very popular in North India; *gram dal* or *channa dal* is favored in the eastern regions like Bengal; and *toor dal* is favored in the South (made almost daily). In North and Northwestern India, *moong dal* is preferred and is a signature dish in Uttar Pradesh. It has a beautiful pink color.

Channa dal or **Bengal gram:** Slightly bigger than *tur dal* and stronger in taste. They are cooked and mashed and added to kebabs, vegetable, and meat curries.

Masoor dal: Whole and split lentils, they cook fast for a quick, nutritious meal. When whole they are dark brown. Split lentils are orange in color. If whole, soak overnight.

Moong dal or **green gram:** A versatile dal, used in snacks or sprouted. When whole, these lentils are small, olive green, and have a strong flavor. When split, they are easy to cook. Cooked moong dal is typically mashed and given to babies as it is very nutritious.

Tur or **arhar dal:** A yellow dal that can be pureed after soaking. Do not add salt until the end of the cooking or lentils will become hard. Easy to digest and has a nutty flavor.

Urad dal or **black gram:** Used whole in North India and split in the South. Whole black lentils are small and when split are creamy white inside. Their aroma is also different between whole and split *urad dal*.

Ghee

The purest form of butter fat. It is clarified butter made from the milk of cows and buffaloes. Used for sautéing, smearing on top of rotis, and in desserts. Also used for tempering lentils.

Oils

Coconut oil is poured on dishes for extra flavor or used in cooking meat and vegetable dishes, especially in Kerala and Tamil Nadu.

Groundnut oil is colorless, odorless, and full of proteins.

Mustard oil, which is rather thick and has a strong flavor, is favored in Bengal, eastern India, and the Punjab.

Sesame oil is light and colorless and can be used to add flavor to dishes.

Vegetable oils, such as canola or corn, have a light flavor and can be used for sauteing and frying in most of the dishes in this book.

Regional Recipes

Note: *Since Hindi is the national language in India, the names of recipes are written in Hindi with translations in English to help readers learn the original names. Local regional names which are commonly associated with the cuisine of non-Hindi speaking regions are also included.*

MASALAS (Spices)

Hara Masala
Garam Masala
Panch Phoren
Chaat Masala
Kashmiri Masala
Tandoori Masala
South Indian Sambar
   Powder
South Indian Karapudi
   Spice Blend

KASHMIR

Kashmiri Gustaba
Kashmiri Gaadh
Hareesa

NORTH INDIA

Rotis
Makki ki Roti
Puris
Matar Paneer
Sarson ka Saag
Aloo Gobi
Gajjar Halwa
Mughal Lamb Biryani
Tandoori Shrimp Masala
Rogan Gosh
Shahi Koftas
Chicken Tikka Masala
Tandoori Murg
Yam Kabab Pilaf
Chicken Pistachio Korma

UTTAR PRADESH

Navaratan Curry
Masoor Dal

ORISSA and BIHAR

Rasbara
Jahni Posta
Chatu

MADHYA PRADESH

Chatpata Baingan

RAJASTHAN

Watermelon Curry
Badam Sherbet

BENGAL

Rasagolla
Singharas
Machili aur Kela Patha

GUJARAT

Dahi Kahdi
Ghosh aur Zard Aloo
Dhansak
Sevai

MAHARASHTRA

Dahi Aloo
Shrikand
Parsi Patra ni Machi
Sind Siyala Gosh
Sai Bhaji
Besan Curry
Suj Jo Seero

GOA

Pork Vindaloo
Kenkda Curry
Goan Beef Curry

TAMIL NADU

Sabzi Chaval
Idlis
Murukus
Sada Dosa
Masala Dosa
Coconut Chutney
Avial
Manga Paruppu
Baingan Sambar
Vermicelli Uppuma
Adhrak Nimbu Rasam
Payasam

CHETTINAD

Nariyal Chili Chicken
Anda Kurma
Manga Oorga
Nimbu Pickle
Badam Kesari Halwa

ANDHRA PRADESH

Nariyal
Garam Garam Aloo
Tomato Yogurt Chutney
Gongura Mamsaam

HYDERABAD

Shammi Kebabs
Tamatar
Hyderabadi Chicken
   Biryani
Mirch Ka Salan
Baingan Bartha
Paya
Double Ka Meeta

KERALA

Meen Varatharcha
Kofta
Kala Mirchi Murg
Kathar Curry

KARNATAKA

Coorg Pandi
Bell Pepper and Potato
   Sukke
Mysore Pak
Bise Bele Baath
Pork Bafath
Prawn Curry

STREET FARE

Aloo Ki Tikki
Samosas
Sev Puri
Onion Pakoras
Soan Papdi

QUICK TAKES

Cucumber Raita
Mint Chutney
Kachumber
Appalam
Carrot Sherbet
Kela Kheer
Honey Dew
Masala Chai
Lassi

Masalas

The recipes for a *masala* (mixture of spices) differ from region to region, household to household. A family's *masala* recipe can be as zealously guarded as a political secret, and is often handed down from generation to generation. Although readymade spices can be found in Indian grocery stores, the flavors are best when prepared fresh at home.

Hara Masala

Green Spice Blend

Aromatic and tangy with a fresh light flavor, the green spice masala is a perfect base for chicken and steamed fish or a simple dal.

MAKES 2 CUPS

2 bunches cilantro, chopped

5 tablespoons mint leaves

10 whole cloves

2-inch piece fresh ginger, peeled

2 green chilies

A few curry leaves

Sprig of basil

1 medium onion, sliced

2-inch piece cinnamon stick

1 tablespoon poppy seeds

Combine the ingredients in a blender or food processor. Grind, adding a few tablespoons of water to make a smooth paste. Store in an airtight glass jar in a cool dry place for up to 2 weeks.

Garam Masala

Hot Spice Blend

The word *garam* in Hindi means "hot." This hot spice blend can be a mixture of whole or ground spices and is an essential ingredient in most recipes across North India. The *masala* contributes to taste, enhancing the flavor when added in the early stages of cooking, and intensifying the aroma when sprinkled at the end. It is used in meat dishes, chutneys, and when serving fruit like bananas or guavas. It is rarely used in fish or vegetable dishes as the aroma is too strong. The recipe below is a simple easy-to-make one, but *garam masala* can also be purchased ready-made at an Indian grocery store.

8 cardamom pods, peeled

2 bay leaves

1 teaspoon black peppercorns

2 teaspoons cumin seeds

2 teaspoons coriander seeds

2-inch piece cinnamon stick

1 teaspoon cloves

Remove seeds from cardamom pods and break the bay leaves into pieces. Grind in a spice or coffee grinder with remaining spices until a fine powder. Store in an airtight container.

Panch Phoren
Five Spice Blend

Panch means "five" in Hindi. This five spice blend, an integral part of Bengal cuisine, gives an aromatic flavor to vegetables and lentils. You can use it while cooking or in the final seasoning. Feel free to vary ingredients according to taste.

1 teaspoon cumin seeds
1 teaspoon fennel seeds
1 teaspoon fenugreek seeds

1 teaspoon mustard seeds
1 teaspoon *kalonji* (*nigella* or onion seeds)

Grind spices to a powder and store in a small airtight container. To use: Add to hot oil before adding lentils or vegetables. Or sauté in ghee and put on top of a cooked food for flavor.

Chaat Masala

Found in street foods such as *bhelpuri* (a mix of sweet, sour, hot, crunchy fried dough), this *masala* is a wonderful sweet, salty, tangy seasoning to tickle the palate. Can be used on fresh fruit and vegetables and on savory snacks.

4 tablespoons coriander seeds
2 tablespoons cumin seeds
1 teaspoon *ajwain*
3 tablespoons black salt

1 tablespoon *amchur* (dried mango) powder
2 dried chilies
1 teaspoon black peppercorns

On low heat in a small skillet, fry coriander seeds without any oil for 1 minute. Remove from skillet. Roast cumin seeds in the same small skillet over medium heat until lightly browned. Remove. Roast *ajwain* in the same way. Grind roasted spices to a fine powder with the other ingredients. Store in airtight container.

Kashmiri Masala

Fragrant and warmly spiced this is perfect for the cold regions of Kashmir but the subtle blend of flavors works in any dish.

10 green cardamoms
2-inch piece cinnamon stick
oil
1 tablespoon cloves
1 tablespoon black peppercorns

1 tablespoon black cumin seeds
2 teaspoons caraway seeds
2 bay leaves
1 teaspoon ground nutmeg

Split cardamom pods and break cinnamon stick into pieces. Heat some oil in a deep heavy-bottomed pan or wok, and deep-fry all spices except the nutmeg, stirring continuously. Remove from pan and allow to cool. After they have cooled, finely grind all the spices together. Add nutmeg. Store in an airtight container.

Tandoori Masala

This masala can be used in marinades or added to hot oil before you put in the main ingredients. When baking meats like chicken, marinate the chicken in yogurt mixed with this masala before baking.

2 teaspoons cumin seeds
2 teaspoons coriander seeds
½-inch piece cinnamon stick
1 teaspoon cloves
1 teaspoon ground black pepper

1 teaspoon ground ginger
1 teaspoon ground turmeric
1 teaspoon garlic powder
1 teaspoon salt
¼ teaspoon red food coloring

Dry roast the whole spices (cumin, coriander, cinnamon, and cloves). Cool and grind with the ground spices, salt, and food coloring in a spice or coffee grinder. Store in an airtight container.

South Indian Sambar Powder

The earthy, deep brown *sambar* powder has a permanent place of pride in any South Indian kitchen. The powder is used in lentil curries and can also be used as a thickening agent. A teaspoon of this powder will add zing to any vegetable dish.

MAKES 3 CUPS

8 dried red chilies
5 tablespoons coriander seeds
1½ tablespoons cumin seeds
2 teaspoons black peppercorns
2 teaspoons fenugreek seeds
2 teaspoons *urad dal* (white split gram)

2 teaspoons *chana dal* (yellow split peas)
2 cups *moong dal* (yellow *moong* beans)
2 teaspoons ground turmeric

Remove seeds and stalks from chilies.

Heat a heavy-bottomed pan and fry (without oil) chilies, coriander seeds, cumin seeds, black peppercorns, and fenugreek seeds over medium heat until there is a rich aroma, about 2 minutes. Remove from pan.

Repeat the process with the dals and fry over medium heat, stirring constantly.

Grind dals and spices and mix together. Mix in turmeric. Store in airtight containers.

South Indian Karapudi Spice Blend

North Indians call this spice blend gunpowder! It is a strong mix but drizzle with some olive oil or ghee to temper it down. Roasted curry leaves add flavor.

1 teaspoon oil or ghee
½ cup *urad dal*
½ cup *chana dal*
6 dried red chilies
6 black peppercorns
1 teaspoon ground cumin

1 teaspoon coriander seeds
1 teaspoon mustard seeds
1 teaspoon cumin seeds
½ teaspoon salt
½ teaspoon fenugreek seeds
1 teaspoon tamarind

Heat oil or ghee in an iron skillet over medium heat. Add the remaining ingredients and roast for a few minutes, stirring so that the spice mixture does not burn. Cool mixture to room temperature, grind, and store in airtight container. Stays fresh for 3 months.

Kashmir

Eating in Kashmir is a gustatory experience. Imagine being invited to a *waazwaan* where you are served a 36-course meal, fragrant with spices, meats, and fish. The *waazwaan* is a formal feast hosted on a religious occasion, festival, or for a wedding ceremony. It is said that the original *wazas* (cooks) came to India in the fifteenth century along with the ruler Timur from Central Asia. Guests sit in groups of four while the *waza*, the top chef, oversees the dishes brought out. Meanwhile the guests have washed their hands in warm water from a jug and basin passed around. Large platters laden with choice delicacies accompanied by *kormas*, fish, chicken cooked in saffron-scented yogurt, sticky dense rice, crunchy rib chops, *rogan gosh*, and spicy ground meat are presented in a never-ending procession of dishes. I did not expect a reproduction of these fantastical dishes when I planned my visit to the valley of Kashmir, but I was fascinated and intrigued by a land much extolled by poets, who wrote intoxicatingly of Kashmir's rivers, forests, flowers, and lofty mountain ranges. One Mughal emperor is said to have cried out to the heavens in ecstasy, "If there is a heaven on earth, it is here, it is here …"

After the Partition of India in 1947 most Muslims left India to found Pakistan. Kashmir (the northernmost extremity of India, bordered by Afghanistan, Pakistan, and China) was in a state of uneasy truce with vested political interests. Even though Kashmir was torn by strife and violence, it still welcomed visitors.

I found myself on a vacation, taking the long, arduous, bone-rattling bus journey from Jammu, swaying with every hairpin bend, passing sunlit glades, valleys, rushing streams, pines, poplars, chinars, lush meadows, and deodar forests. Suddenly before me was the deep pink lotus-filled Dal Lake. The revered lotus, the flower of the gods, is considered sacred by both Hindus and Buddhists. Writers have used the tranquil lotus flower as a metaphor for purity and independence since the exquisite bloom is quite unaffected by the mud surrounding the roots. Notwithstanding the profundity of my reflections, I found myself an hour later crunching lustily on delicious crisp lotus fritters coated in rice batter which had been made from lotus roots. In subsequent meals, the lotus roots often appeared in meat and fish dishes, giving the dish extra texture. Sometimes, the leaves of the lotus were used as plates since they are waterproof and retain heat.

We stayed on a sumptuous houseboat, a *shikhara*, fortuitously named *Paradise*, embellished with soft Kashmir carpets and silk curtains. The *shikhara* was linked to the kitchen boat where the cooks, a husband and wife, supplied us with fragrant basmati rice, succulent lamb curries, delicate fish broths, fruits, and vegetables. Meanwhile vendors in boats circled us, selling fresh apricots, figs, almonds, apples, dried fruits, intricate crafted papier-mâché objects, silver jewelry, and carvings made of walnut wood. Often we strolled through Mughal gardens with enchanting names such as Nishat, Shalimar, and Chashmashahi. I bought a fine embroidered wool shawl in peacock colors, while the shopkeeper told me that the local weaving art had existed since AD 1470, and the weaving was so complex that only a quarter of an inch is completed every day. The yarn itself was stiffened by a paste from the vegetable yam making it easier to weave.

Meanwhile I was tasting inspired Kashmiri foods, strangers to my palate but welcomed heartily. Many Kashmiri dishes, I discovered, are built around rice, chicken, wild fowl, wild geese, and sheep that have pastured on verdant mountain ranges. Meats are cooked in curds or milk and marinated in spice blends. *Rogan gosh* is made from the mutton of a mountain-fed goat. The goat meat, which has a thin layer of fat, is stewed in a thick gravy made of various spices, including cumin, poppy seeds, chilies, yogurt, cardamom, tomatoes, garlic, ginger, and thick cream or milk. Sometimes the meat is so flavorful that neither onions nor garlic are used. The meat curry surprised me with its startling fiery red tinge due to the addition of the powdered cockscomb flowers (*lal murga).* Another favorite, the Kashmiri *tabbak maaz,* is made from tender ribs of lamb. The aromatic flavor is bound to make you swoon.

A meat dish that always tastes exactly right is meatballs. When making meatballs, a Kashmiri cook pounds the meat so vigorously that not even the membrane remains. The meatballs are then saturated with a creamy, rich sauce of cardamom, thick milk, and broth, and cooked. They are then pressed around iron spikes which are laid over large plates to divide them into four quarters so that each quarter belongs to one guest. The meat is so tender and full of goodness, it deserves a poem. Instead I merely asked for another helping.

The *biryani* is a festive elaborate dish that can be served as a complete meal. It is made from basmati—a special, aromatic rice—and flavored with diverse spices, meat, fish, prawns, or vegetables. Nuts and edible silver foil embellish. They say that the test of a good *biryani* is to throw a fistful on the floor and see if each grain falls separately. You will then know that the finest basmati rice has been used. There is a legacy of *biryani* recipes as it came to

India accompanying invaders and conquerors. Some say it came with the Persians, others with the Mughals. Today each state has its own individual signature *biryani* flavored with local ingredients.

Another appetizing dish is *alu bokhara korma*, lamb curry cooked with dried plums and nuts, like almonds, together with tamarind water, pistachios, and spices. Walnuts are a specialty of the region and their oil is used as a salad dressing and cooking medium. Ground roughly to retain their nuttiness, walnuts are used in desserts and chutneys or as a garnish for Kashmiri rice dishes. Fresh fish, especially trout, is smeared with salt, butter, and herbs from the banks of the river and smoked in the embers of a low fire to produce a simple, delicious dish. Popular vegetarian cuisine includes morel mushrooms called *gahchi*. The shallot-like garlic called *praan* is also used to thicken sauces. Because of the never-ending golden mustard fields, mustard oil is often used in cooking.

A thick green leafy vegetable called *hak* grows almost everywhere in profusion and is used in the preparation of *saag*—a dish of nutritious greens that can be eaten with plain cooked rice. The dark green fibrous leaves of the *kale* are full of calcium and potassium and believed to change flavor seven times. It can be steamed or added to fish, chicken, and meat. Coriander is a predominant flavor in some dishes, while thick lentil soups are complemented with fenugreek seed and pomegranate juice. Flat bread made of kneaded white flour dough called *kulcha* is the perfect accompaniment to the sauces. *Sheermal*, a sweet bread doused in a saffron milky liquid, is characteristic of the Kashmir region.

On a special day in winter, the good spirits are served their yearly dinner. A meal of their favorite foods, like lamb, *mung dal* (lentils), and rice, is prepared and placed outdoors for the wandering spirits to partake.

The best saffron, one of the costliest spices in the world, comes from Kashmir. It was cultivated in Kashmir when Persian merchants introduced this flower. It is said that seventy thousand *crocus sativus* flowers have to be harvested to extract 200,000 stigmas for one pound of saffron. Used as an aphrodisiac, it is often included in the gifts for a bride. Many dishes are enhanced with saffron. It is also used as an organic coloring for food. Of a deep reddish orange color with a unique fragrance, even two strands of saffron can enhance a dish.

Fruits form a major part of the regular diet as they grow in abundance in the Kashmir valleys. Mulberries, cranberries, peaches, apricots, apples, strawberries, plums, cherries, loquats, and nectarines are some of the luscious fruits eaten fresh with the flesh rippling beneath your fingers or used in preserves. In summer, fruits and vegetables are plucked and dried in the upper rooms of a home and preserved for winter. Kashmir chilies, the large, not so pungent, wrinkled, vibrant red kind, are also gathered during the hot days. I find these chilies in the stores these days and use them to give a vibrant red color to curries. In the long Kashmir winters, sun-dried fruits, nuts, turnips, and dried fish are relished.

Returning to the *shikhara* late one evening shivering with the cold, wrapped in exquisitely embroidered Kashmir shawls light as a leaf, we passed men and women hugging *kangris* (clay lamps filled with glowing charcoals) inside their thick cloaks to keep warm. Passing a restaurant I heard a melody from an old Hindi film *Andaz.* I remembered that Kashmir was the favorite shooting location of many a Hindi film in the 1950s, 1960s, and 1970s and the titles like *Kashmir Ki Kali, Mere Sanam, Junglee,* and *Silsila* filled me with memories of beautifully crafted films set against the backdrop of snowy mountains and meadows of flowers and mist.

When we entered our houseboat, a feast of *biryani*, fruit, and nuts made by the cook awaited us. Then for dessert, fresh peaches and a heavenly *phirni* made from clotted cream, thick milk, almonds, raisins, and sugar. We gazed on the mountains deepening in the twilight from rich orange and dazzling pinks to mysterious dark hues of purple and grey as the night blanketed the cold waters of the lake and sipped a soothing spice-scented green tea (*cawa*).

Kashmiri Gustaba

Lamb Koftas

Koftas are one of India's favorite dishes, and the Mughals are credited with introducing minced meat or meatballs in their meals. Goat and beef can be used for the making of *koftas*. This is a rich and creamy meat dish, but must be treated gently as the meat may break. *Koftas* can be made a day in advance, kept in the refrigerator, and reheated before serving. You can eat them as part of a meal or as a snack.

SERVES 4

½ pound lamb
2 teaspoons ground black pepper
2 teaspoons fennel seeds
1 teaspoon ground ginger
1 small bunch cilantro, minced
1 teaspoon Kashmiri masala (page 71) or garam masala (page 69)
½ cup yogurt

2 tablespoons ghee
1 teaspoon sugar
4 cardamom pods
1 cup *khoya* or heavy cream
Salt
1 cup milk

To make the *kofta*: Chop the meat and finely grind with the black pepper, fennel seeds, ginger, cilantro, and masala. Add a little of the yogurt and ghee until the meat is a smooth paste. Form into balls that are 2 inches in diameter, and set aside.

Heat remaining ghee in pan and add sugar, cardamom pods, *khoya*, the rest of the yogurt, and salt to taste. Pour in milk and stir. Add the *koftas* and simmer until *koftas* are tender and liquid evaporates.

Kashmiri Gaadh
Kashmiri Fish

Kashmiri fish is believed to taste better the day after cooking. A fish dish is a must on religious occasions like *Shivaratri*, the festival that marks the day when the Goddess Parvati prayed the whole night to her husband Lord Shiva and asked him to save the world from destruction. He granted her wish. On that particular night in the year, Hindus pray the whole night and fast and ask for boons. Kashmiri fish is also cooked on special occasions like *Shraan Sundar*, the ceremonial bath of a newborn baby that is usually done on the eleventh day after the birth. Check the fish frequently so that it does not become shredded while cooking. Very few spices are used, thus retaining the full flavor of the fish.

SERVES 4

1 pound fish (mahi-mahi, halibut
　or catfish)
Cooking oil
1½ teaspoons red chili powder
Pinch of asafetida

1 teaspoon ground turmeric
½ teaspoon ground ginger
½ teaspoon ground fennel seeds
2 cloves
Salt to taste

Wash and clean the fish, removing all scales. Cut into pieces. Heat some oil in a pan and deep fry 3 pieces of fish at a time until golden brown. Set aside on paper towels.

Heat 3 tablespoons of oil and add chili powder, asafetida, turmeric, and a little water. Sauté on low heat for about 1 minute. Add 2 cups of water, ground ginger, ground fennel, and cloves.

Add fried fish to chili mixture. Cover pan and simmer for 15 minutes, adding more water if needed. Do not stir as fish can break.

Hareesa

Lamb and Wheat Stew

Hareesa is cooked the night before as it takes many hours to prepare. It is a combination of lamb and kernels of wheat cooked for many hours. Kashmiris take pride in excelling in the preparation of a dish which is a legacy of the Mongols, who it is said cooked the meat in their helmets when traveling.

SERVES 6 TO 8

1½ cups cracked wheat
3 pounds boneless lamb or minced lamb
1 teaspoon garlic paste
6-inch piece fresh ginger, peeled and ground to a paste
2-inch piece cinnamon stick
1 tablespoon cumin seeds
1½ teaspoons minced red chilies

1 teaspoon black peppercorns
Salt to taste
2 cups rice
1 tablespoon garam masala (page 69)
¼ cup ghee
2 tablespoons dried fenugreek
2 small onions, chopped

Soak wheat in 2 cups of water for at least 6 hours and then drain.

In a large vessel, boil lamb, garlic paste, ginger paste, cinnamon stick, cumin seeds, chilies, peppercorns, and salt in 8 cups of water over medium heat for 2 hours, until meat is tender.

In another vessel, boil rice and wheat with 4 cups of water until it resembles a thick porridge.

Stir the meat into the rice mixture and cook for 1 hour over low heat while mashing the mixture with a large wooden ladle, adding additional water for a smooth consistency.

Sprinkle garam masala on top, cover with a lid for 4 minutes. Fry the fenugreek and onions in ghee for a minute and use them to embellish the *hareesa*.

North India

Punjab

Royal families in Punjab (the north Indian state that lies south of Kashmir) are remembered for lavish banquets. The late Maharajah of Patiala was famed for his feasts that summoned three thousand guests who reclined amidst gurgling fountains on brocaded divans and velvet pillows encrusted with precious stones, partaking of forty or more exotic dishes. They ate with their fingers the fine breads, the succulent meats, the fresh fruits, and rich traditional foods smothered in ghee.

Legend has it that the Maharaja of Kapurthala built a replica of Versailles, made his attendants speak French, and hired a top chef from Paris who specialized in French cuisine. But the Maharaja's three wives who loved Indian food conspired with the chef to conceal a spiced curry inside a creamed chicken. From true to make-believe there is always a story about food.

Irrigated by five rivers, the Jhelum, Chenab, Sutlej, Beas, and Ravi, the state of Punjab, with a dominant Sikh community, has adopted new innovative methods of farming and irrigation. Milk products form a part of every nutritious meal, accompanied by lentils, breads, and fresh vegetables. A Punjabi farmer who goes out to work in the noonday heat takes a pile of rotis (wheat breads), raw onion (good for preventing heat stroke), cool cucumbers, and ripe tomatoes, accompanied by a tumbler of sweetened or salted buttermilk (whipped yogurt). Enter a Punjabi home, and you will be offered a glass of foaming, fresh, frothy buttermilk even if you are a stranger. You will then be invited to eat rotis smeared with a dollop of butter topped with a raw onion. A simple satisfying meal.

The onion is an important part of the meal. In Punjabi homes I often saw families place a round onion in front of them and give one mighty thwack with the fist; as the juices ran out, they would mop it up with the roti and munch on the succulent onion, good for the heart and digestion.

Punjab, the breadbasket of India, produces 60 percent of India's wheat. It is the main winter crop, sown in October and harvested in March or April. In North India, whether it is summer or winter, rotis are the staple food. Different kinds of rotis or breads add variety to a meal. The making of the *roti* is simple. A little water is added to the wheat flour, the dough is kneaded, a small ball is broken off, patted into a round shape, rolled out, and roasted on an open wood fire. When the iron skillet (*tawa*) was discovered, the roti became firmer and improved in taste and texture. A dab of vegetable oil, butter, or ghee (considered sacred) is often smeared on the hot roti to enhance flavor. Rotis are made soft or thick, depending on the way you flatten the dough. If you knead the dough with milk and water, it becomes soft.

The *paratha,* a thicker and richer roti, needs more oil, and can be stuffed with mashed potatoes, spinach, peas, shredded cabbage, or ground meat and spices. Wheat flour is so flexible the rotis adapt to almost any kind of filling. Radishes, potatoes, peas, dal, tomatoes, cauliflower, sugar cashews, chickpeas, and even layers of skimmed milk are used as textured fillings. For a bit of drama, request the handkerchief roti. The *roomali* (handkerchief) roti is a combination of refined flour and wheat flour. Once the dough is kneaded well, the rolled out roti is tossed into the air and caught deftly as it comes down, resembling a large handkerchief. Then it is placed on the scalding *tawa. Kulchas,* another rich type of roti made from maida flour, are more flexible in texture and contain a lot of milk and butter, giving them a rich, smooth flavor. *Makki* (cornmeal), *bajra* (millet), and *jawar* (barley) are very nutritious grains used to make rotis, which can be roasted over an open flame or on a *tawa.* Satwant Narang, the 85-year-old matriarch in my husband's family, was famed for her rapid turn of the wrist and hands that can transform a lumpy dough into pure silk.

The *puri,* another form of roti, is deep-fried. The *bhatura* is a balloon-like puri—delicately crisp and crunchy, with the dough being fermented with yogurt and then rolled out and fried. Another interesting flavored *puri* is the *kachori* stuffed with vegetables. *Naan* is made of maida or white flour. The damp dough is patted with the hands into an elongated shape resembling a teardrop and slapped on the sides of the glowing *tandoor* oven. The dough puffs up and the moment brown patches appear the cook quickly lifts the bread out of the oven with an iron spike. After the *naan* is made, it can be coated with a tomato and garlic paste or pounded dates mixed with jaggery and embedded with almonds or bits of *paneer* (cheese). The *khurmee naan* is coated with a mixture of dates and jaggery, while the *roghani naan,* which means "red *naan,*" is given a quick brushing with saffron water or saffron mixed with ghee. Dexterity, nimble hands, and imagination are the defining features of rotis, which vary from region to region. The Bombay roti (*Andey ki roti*) is filled with minced meat, eggs, coriander, mint leaves, and green chilies.

The *tandoor* oven is the pride and joy of Punjabis and found in many a courtyard in the Punjab. *Tandoori* cooking may have been introduced by Turkish invaders. The word *tandoor* comes from the Arabic word *tannoor* which means "the oven or a pit for baking." *Tandoor* could also be a derivation of *noor* which means "radiant light or heat." The *tandoor* is a massive five-foot-tall oven with an open top, fitted with a lid. A wood or charcoal fire stokes it. Though lit much in advance, the actual cooking is rapid. There are iron-lined and clay-lined *tandoors*. The iron one gives off more heat and is used for meats, while the clay one is excellent for baking bread. Meats are marinated with spices, ginger, garlic paste, and curd before being cooked in iron-lined *tandoors*. Thick chicken drumsticks called *tangri, chicken tikka* (chicken roasted on skewers), and *boti*, bits of boneless lamb, are relished by meat eaters. Fat from the meat drips onto the coals and reacts with the carbon. The carcinogens in the carbon are not healthy for the body so to offset this, meats are marinated with garlic, curds, turmeric, and crushed onion. If you go to a restaurant or a home and you are served *tandoori chicken*, you will always find a wedge of lime and raw sliced onions on your plate. By munching on the lime and onions, the body is cooled down after the consumption of hot spices.

Rotis are often accompanied by lentil dishes. Punjabis are said to cook with sixty varieties of dals or lentils. Most Punjabi dishes require a ground paste of ginger, garlic, and onions, with chilies, tomatoes, cumin, garam masala, dried fenugreek leaves, and onion seed called *kalonji* forming the base of any curry. *Aloo mattar* is a simple signature curry of potatoes and green peas, while *aloo gobi* is curried cauliflower and potato—a fixture in every Punjabi household and restaurant. My favorite Punjabi dish is *sarson ka saag*, a delectable spiced blend of tender mustard greens and spinach complementing a cornmeal roti. Subtle, delicate, and full of goodness.

And to round off the meal, try *khoya*, a thick cream. The milk is reduced to a thick paste, which may take a few hours, and mixed with powdered almonds, pistachios, sesame seeds, dried melon seeds, coconut, fruits, and *paneer*, the Indian cheese. Quintessentially Punjabi.

Roti/Chappati

A soft roti expects a gentle patient kneading. Satwant Narang, the matriarch of the Narang family (my in-laws), had the divine gift of being able to roll out rotis for hours sitting on a stool near the stove. Light and nourishing, the rotis can be eaten any time of day and whenever I make an appearance, she quickly heats up the *tawa*, and sends me home with a half dozen perfect rotis, the everyday bread of the Indian home.

MAKES 8 ROTIS

2 cups all-purpose flour
1 teaspoon salt

1 cup water

Combine all the ingredients and knead gently into a soft dough. Dust your hands with flour so that the dough does not stick to them. You can also use a little oil or ghee to smear your hands when kneading. Once the dough is made, wrap it in a thin cloth and cover for at least 20 minutes.

Divide dough into 8 portions and dust with flour. Make each portion into a small ball and flatten with tips of fingers. Roll out each ball into a circle 6 inches in diameter and use a little flour to dust. Place on a platter and cover lightly with a cloth.

Heat a *tawa* or other heavy flat cast-iron skillet over medium heat for 4 minutes. Lower heat and place a roti in the middle. When the bottom becomes a little brown, turn the roti over. Continue to cook for 30 seconds. Turn again and use a small piece of folded cloth to press the edges of the roti down as they will start puffing up. Remove from pan.

Keep rotis wrapped in a thick napkin while making the rest, and serve with vegetables or a meat gravy.

Leftover Rotis

Leftover rotis can be used in a delicious dish: Cut rotis into small pieces. Chop some green chilies and mince some cilantro. Heat oil in pan. Add a small amount of asafetida, turmeric, curry leaves, the green chilies, and mustard seeds. When the seeds sputter, add some garlic powder, ground ginger, salt, and the leftover rotis. Mix well. Sprinkle a little water over the rotis and cook for a few minutes. Add a little lemon juice, the minced cilantro, and peanuts or coconut for garnish.

Makki ki Roti

Maize Bread

Known for entertaining lavishly an extended family of 120 members in Southern California, my brother-in-law Harbir and Sushil Narang often serve this Punjabi classic roti filled with earthy goodness and nutrition.

MAKES 8 TO 10

2 cups maize flour	**½ teaspoon salt**
1 cup whole wheat flour	**Warm water**
½ bunch cilantro, chopped	**Oil**

Sift the two kinds of flour and salt into a bowl. Add cilantro. Slowly add enough warm water to make a smooth dough. Knead the dough with a clenched fist to make it soft. Cover the dough with a damp cloth and set aside for 30 minutes.

Divide dough into 8 to 10 equal parts and flatten with hand. Roll out each into a small thick circle of dough, sprinkling with a little flour to keep from sticking.

Heat a griddle or *tawa* made of heavy cast iron, place one roti in it, pour 2 teaspoons of oil around it, and cook until bottom is just starting to turn golden brown. Flip over and cook the other side. Repeat with remaining dough circles.

Makki Ki Roti can be served with butter and a green chili, or with *saag* (spinach) and *lassi* (buttermilk).

Puris

.... Deep-fried Bread ....

A rich and nutritious *puri* is the *Nargisi puri* in which mashed potatoes, mashed boiled eggs, chili, mint, and cilantro are chopped fine and kneaded into the dough. But if you want a simple, traditional *puri* that can be accompanied by a sweet *halwa* or mashed potatoes this is the recipe for you.

MAKES 20 *PURIS*

3 cups whole wheat flour
½ teaspoon salt
2 teaspoons ghee

1 cup warm water
Oil

Put the flour in a bowl and mix in salt and ghee. Slowly pour in warm water to make a moist dough. Knead gently until it forms a stiff dough. Divide into 20 small balls. Dust balls with flour and roll out into 4 or 5-inch circles. Put the circles of dough on a plate or large board.

Heat oil in a *kadai* or wok. Fry one *puri* at a time pressing down with a slotted spoon. This helps the *puri* to rise up as a puffed ball. Turn over after a minute and repeat the pressing. Remove when the *puris* are soft and a light brown. Be careful, if the oil becomes too hot the *puri* will become hard. Repeat with remaining dough.

Matar Paneer
Peas and Paneer

The Maharajas in Punjab would often host feasts to honor three thousand people. Seated on richly brocaded pillows, guests would dine from silver platters filled with twenty or thirty individual *katoris* (bowls) of delicious foods. This would have been one of the unusual side dishes served with rice or rotis.

SERVES 4

½ pound *paneer**
2 tablespoons ghee or oil
½ cup chopped onion
Pinch of salt
1 cup peas
½ teaspoon sugar

2-inch piece fresh ginger, grated
3 green chilies, minced
Small bunch of cilantro leaves, chopped
½ teaspoon garam masala (page 69)

Cut the *paneer* into small cubes. Heat ghee in a pan and carefully fry the cubes until they are golden brown. Remove and set aside.

Fry the onions in the same ghee until soft and translucent. Remove and set aside.

Add a pinch of salt and 5 tablespoons of water to the pan. Add the peas and sugar and cook for 2 minutes. Add the *paneer*, onions, ginger, and chilies. Cook for 2 minutes.

Add cilantro and garam masala and salt to taste.

*Note: *Paneer* is Indian cheese and is usually homemade. Mix lemon juice with milk and place in a muslin bag. Allow it to drain overnight. The whey separates from the curd, and what remains is solidified. Press into small square blocks. You can often find *paneer* in Indian grocery stores. In Punjab, *paneer* is a staple cheese usually accompanied by rotis.

Sarson ka Saag
Sautéed Mustard Greens

Irrigated by five rivers, the Punjab region offers wholesome, satisfying food. *Sarson ka Saag* is a favorite as the mustard leaves from the fields are nutritious and delicious when cooked with a dab of butter on top. The *saag* is usually accompanied by rotis and fresh buttermilk churned in clay pots—a simple unique experience. Look for bright colored leaves, with smooth and supple tips.

SERVES 6

2 pounds mustard green leaves, cleaned and chopped
1 cup spinach leaves, cleaned and chopped
3 medium onions, thinly sliced
3 garlic cloves, minced
½ teaspoon minced fresh ginger
6 green chilies, thinly sliced
1 teaspoon chili powder
Salt
¼ cup maize flour

TEMPERING
2 teaspoons ghee
1 teaspoon chopped onion
¼ teaspoon chopped garlic

In a heavy-bottomed pan, place cut mustard greens and spinach with onions, garlic, ginger, green chilies, chili powder and some salt. Add some water and cook over low heat for half an hour. Remove from heat, drain, and grind to a smooth paste. Add maize flour and mix well.

To temper, heat some ghee and sauté onions and garlic. Add ground mixture and simmer for 15 minutes over low flame.

Garnish with sliced green chilies and butter. Serve hot with *Makki ki Roti* (page 84).

Aloo Gobi

Potato and Cauliflower Fry

This vegetable dish has a crunchy texture, is simplicity itself, and quick to cook with an interesting combination. Eat with rice, breads, or a cup of yogurt sprinkled with mint leaves. This hearty comfort food is excellent with rotis or *parathas*.

SERVES 4

1 tablespoon vegetable oil
1 teaspoon black mustard seeds
1 teaspoon *urad dal*
1 teaspoon *chana dal*
¼ teaspoon cumin seeds
¼ teaspoon ground ginger
1 teaspoon ground turmeric

1 teaspoon chili powder
2 medium potatoes, peeled and diced
1 medium head cauliflower, cut into florets
Salt to taste

Heat oil over medium heat. When oil is hot, add mustard seeds, *urad dal, chana dal,* cumin seeds, and ground ginger. Stir and fry until mustard seeds begin to pop. Add turmeric and chili powder.

Add the potatoes and cauliflower to the pan and stir well to coat with the spices. Cook until potatoes are cooked through, stirring to prevent burning and sprinkling with a little water if it becomes too dry. Add salt to taste.

Gajjar Halwa
Sweet Carrot Confection

This homemade specialty of many North Indian households is easily made with fresh carrots. You can add lightly whipped heavy cream at the end to make it richer.

SERVES 8

2 pounds carrots
4 cups milk
6 tablespoons sugar
½ cup ghee

10 crushed cardamom seeds
Few raisins, almonds, and dried fruits

Wash, dry, and peel carrots. Grate finely.

Bring milk to boil. Add carrots. Simmer, stirring, until liquid has evaporated. Add sugar and ghee and cook until the mixture is dry.

Cool mixture. Add cardamom and dry fruit and warm before serving.

The Splendor of the Mughals

"Regal sumptuousness" are the words that come to mind when describing feasts during the Mughal period. Presented on gold and silver platters, dishes had exotic names like *Shah Jahani Biryani*, named after the Mughal emperor Shah Jahan. A *biryani* could be cooked as an entire one-dish meal with lamb, fish, chicken, or vegetables, accompanied by *raitha*, the cooling mix of cucumber and yogurt. One distinguishing feature of the *biryani* is that the rice and meat are arranged in layers for the final cooking phase. It is said that the Mughals brought recipes for twenty-six variations of the *biryani*. The *biryani* entered the Guinness Book of Records in 2008 after sixty chefs from Delhi, the capital of India, cooked 13,000 kg (26,000 pounds) of vegetarian *biryani*. A gastronomical fantasy come true. Since the stirring could not be done manually, a special mechanized rotor was installed and laser-operated thermometers gauged the temperature of the cooking.

A *pilaf* is a variation of the *biryani* in which meat and rice are cooked together. One particular pilaf has an interesting embellishment. The *samosa* pilaf is seasoned with spices and ghee, and embellished with choice meat as well as small, dainty shaped minced meat-filled *samosas*. *Samosas* are rolled out thin *puris* made of flour, the white of an egg, and ghee; they are folded over and stuffed with minced meat, ginger, onion, and garam masala and then deep fried.

Cinnamon, cardamom, clove, pepper, ginger, and fennel seeds were common if not required ingredients in any form of cooking. A variety of game birds, fish, lamb, and beef marinated in yogurt were enjoyed by the Mughals. One popular cooking method was called *dum phukt*, in which the meat was tightly sealed in a vessel and cooked very slowly over a low fire, resulting in incredibly tender meat. And of course, since every meal ended with a repast of exotic fruits, Mughal gardens typically overflowed with grapes, plums, pomegranates, apricots, pears, peaches, and mango trees. A taste of luxury for all seasons.

Mughal Lamb Biryani

Sangeetha Ahmad, my daughter who lives in Zurich with her family, has an insatiable appetite for parties. There are always guests and special festive events that inspire her to cook up a storm whether it is Indian, Pakistani, Italian, or American dishes. For me there is always an exquisite refinement in a *biryani* and she excels in bringing out the flavor, fragrance, and aura of the Mughal dynasty. *Biryani* can be made with *keema* (ground meat), or cubes of lamb, chicken, fish, prawns, or vegetables. It should be accompanied by *raita*, a cooling mix of yogurt and cucumber (page 208) .

SERVES 6

10 tablespoons oil
4 large onions, minced
2 pounds lamb shoulder, cut into
    small pieces
2 teaspoons ginger paste
2 teaspoons garlic paste
2 teaspoons coriander powder
1 teaspoon chili powder
1 teaspoon turmeric powder

1 teaspoon garam masala
1½ cups plain yogurt
½ teaspoon lemon juice
2 teaspoons salt
3 cups basmati rice
1 bunch mint leaves
1 bunch cilantro leaves
8 green chilies, sliced
½ cup warm milk

Heat oil and fry onions until golden brown. Set onions aside.

Add lamb pieces, ginger paste, and garlic paste to pan and fry. Add coriander powder, chili powder, turmeric powder, and garam masala and fry with a little bit of water till the oil separates.

Add yogurt and cook on low flame for 5 minutes. Add 4 cups water and cook on low flame till meat is tender. Add browned onions, lemon juice, and salt.

Meanwhile, soak rice in cold water for 30 minutes. Place rice in deep saucepan and add 4 cups water and cook till half done. Drain. Remove half the rice and set aside.

Put the lamb mixture on top of the rice in the saucepan and layer with mint, cilantro, and green chilies. Cover the lamb with the remaining rice and pour warm milk over the rice. Cover and cook over low heat for 25 minutes without stirring until rice is tender. Serve hot.

Tandoori Shrimp Masala

Tandoori shrimp is a delicacy served with small onions and green chilies. In restaurants and in villages it is cooked in a large clay oven, although a metal *tandoor* is now available and can be used on a gas burner. I find that the *tandoori* recipe works very well with shrimp. You can roast the spices on moderate heat for 1 minute until the kitchen becomes aromatic.

SERVES 4

½ cup plain yogurt
½ cup cream
1½ teaspoons ginger paste
1 teaspoon garlic paste
¾ teaspoon chopped green chili
¾ teaspoon garam masala (page 69)
1 teaspoon red chili powder
½ teaspoon ground turmeric

1 tablespoon gram flour (*besan*)
½ teaspoon *ajwain*
Salt to taste
2 tablespoons lemon juice, plus additional for garnish
2 tablespoons vinegar
10 large shrimp, cleaned and deveined
Melted butter

Combine all ingredients except the shrimp in a large bowl. Add the shrimp and stir to coat. Marinate for a few hours or overnight.

Cook the shrimp in a regular oven or on skewers on the barbecue. If you use the oven, preheat to 500 degrees F. Put shrimp in a foil-lined pan in a single layer. Roast for 10 minutes. Remove and allow to cool slightly. Brush some melted butter on shrimp and place in oven for another 10 minutes. Squeeze lemon juice on shrimp before serving.

Note: Any meat can be marinated in this yogurt-masala marinade. Potatoes, peppers, and fish can also be basted with the yogurt-masala mixture.

Rogan Gosh

Curried Lamb in Thick Sauce

A spicy curry with a strong Mughal influence. Select lean tender lamb. One of the best ways to tenderize meat is to marinate it in unripe ground *papaya*. The secret of the essence of this curry is the use of fennel and Kashmir red chilies, which give the curry a rich, vibrant color and excellent flavor.

SERVES 6

2 pounds lamb or lamb chops
12 ounces lamb bones
6 garlic cloves, chopped
4 teaspoons black peppercorns
1 cup plain yogurt
1 cup chopped shallots
¼ cup oil or ghee
3 cloves
2 black cardamom pods
6 green cardamom pods

2 small pieces cinnamon stick
2 teaspoons ground coriander
2 teaspoons ground fennel seeds
2 teaspoons ground ginger
½ teaspoon ground turmeric
1 tablespoon chopped chili pepper, ground with a little water to make a paste
Salt to taste

In a large pot, bring lamb and bones with chopped garlic and 7 cups of water to a boil and simmer for 25 minutes. Remove from the heat. Strain and reserve cooking water.

Make a paste by grinding peppercorns with a little water. Whisk yogurt.

Fry shallots in ghee or oil until brown. Add cloves, cardamom pods, and cinnamon sticks. Fry for a minute. Then add ground coriander, fennel, ginger, and turmeric, chili paste, peppercorn paste, and 3 tablespoons of water. Stir and cook for 3 minutes.

Add meat, and sauté for 6 minutes. Lower heat and add yogurt. Stir and sauté. Add some salt and 5 cups of the reserved cooking water. Cook until meat is tender. Remove cardamom pods and cinnamon sticks before serving.

Shahi Koftas
Flavored Meatballs

Our unforgettable aunt Dora Venkatesulu was a delightful storyteller and cooked joyful dishes ranging from the simple to the extravagant. She always arrived with myriad dishes in a tiffin carrier on Sunday afternoons, to regale us with hilarious stories and a classic dish like this one. It is delicate, but very flavorful. If you need to spice it up, add a green chili chopped into fine pieces.

SERVES 4

KOFTAS:
Oil
1 pound ground lamb
2 onions, minced
1 tablespoon garlic paste
1 tablespoon ginger paste
1 teaspoon green chili paste
Salt
1 teaspoon *urad dal*, ground
1 teaspoon garam masala (page 69)

COATING FOR KOFTAS:
1 cup *urad dal*
1 teaspoon green chili paste
Salt

GRAVY:
1 small bunch mustard leaves
8 tablespoons oil
2 small onions, chopped
½ teaspoon garlic paste
3 large tomatoes, grated
2 teaspoons green chili paste
Salt to taste
1 teaspoon garam masala

Make *koftas*: Heat oil in a medium skillet. Cook ground lamb with onions, garlic paste, ginger paste, green chili paste, and some salt until dry. Remove from heat and add *urad dal* and garam masala to meat. Stir. When cool enough to handle, divide into small balls about 1 inch in diameter and set aside.

Soak *urad dal* for coating for 2 hours in enough water to cover. Drain and make coating by grinding the soaked *urad dal* with chili paste and some salt, adding a little water as needed to make a paste.

Heat enough oil in a pan for deep frying. Dip *koftas* in coating mixture. Deep fry until golden brown. Set aside.

Make gravy: Cook mustard leaves and mash. Fry chopped onions in oil and add garlic paste, tomatoes, green chili paste, and some salt. Fry well. Add mustard leaves and simmer.

Put *koftas* in gravy and simmer for 5 minutes. Sprinkle with the 1 teaspoon garam masala.

Chicken Tikka Masala

Chicken tikkas—pieces of chicken—can be eaten as an appetizer, a snack, or part of a meal. Serve the *tikka* with a salad if you plan to use it as a welcome treat for guests. *Tikka* paste can also be bought at a store.

SERVES 4

TIKKA PASTE:
½ teaspoon cumin seeds
½ teaspoon coriander seeds
2 cloves
½ teaspoon paprika
½ teaspoon garam masala (page 69)
½ teaspoon ground turmeric
½ teaspoon ground ginger
½ teaspoon chopped fresh mint
1 teaspoon chili powder
1 tablespoon lemon juice
2 tablespoons water
2 tablespoons vinegar
6 tablespoons oil

CHICKEN:
1½ pounds skinned chicken breasts
5 tablespoons *tikka* paste
½ cup plain yogurt
1 tablespoon oil
1 onion, chopped
1 teaspoon minced garlic
1 green chili, chopped
1-inch piece fresh ginger, grated
1 tablespoon tomato puree
1 cup water
1 tablespoon butter, melted
1 tablespoon lemon juice
Fresh cilantro

Make the paste: Grind cumin seeds, coriander seeds, and cloves. Mix with paprika, garam masala, ground turmeric, ground ginger, mint, and chili powder. Stir in lemon juice, water, and vinegar to form a paste. Heat oil. Cook paste gently for about 7 minutes. Set aside.

Cut chicken into cubes. Put 3 tablespoons of *tikka* paste and 4 tablespoons of yogurt in bowl and blend. Marinate chicken in the mixture for 20 minutes.

Make sauce: Heat oil in heavy-based pan and fry onion, garlic, chili, and ginger for 5 minutes. Add tomato puree and water. Bring to a boil then simmer for 15 minutes.

Thread chicken pieces onto wood kebab skewers. Preheat broiler. Brush chicken pieces with melted butter. Broil on medium heat for 15 minutes, turning skewers halfway through.

Carefully pour sauce in a blender and puree until smooth, or alternatively use a hand-held immersion blender. Add remaining yogurt, 2 tablespoons *tikka* paste, and lemon juice to sauce and stir until heated through.

Remove chicken from skewers, place in the *tikka* sauce, and simmer for another 5 minutes. Garnish with cilantro.

Tandoori Murg

Tandoori Chicken

If you do not have an open clay oven, or *tandoor*, a conventional oven will work. The wonderful red color can be achieved by using red chili powder or a blend of cayenne pepper and paprika. Or you can buy the red food coloring in an Indian grocery store.

SERVES 2

4 chicken quarters
¾ cup plain yogurt
1 teaspoon garam masala (page 69)
1 teaspoon ginger paste
1 teaspoon garlic paste
1½ teaspoons red chili powder
½ teaspoon ground turmeric

1 teaspoon ground coriander
1 tablespoon lemon juice
Salt to taste
Few drops of red food coloring (optional)
1 tablespoon oil
Lime wedges

Wash and pat dry chicken. Make a couple of slits in the flesh. Set aside.

Mix yogurt, garam masala, ginger paste, garlic paste, chili powder, ground turmeric, ground coriander, lemon juice, salt, red food coloring, and oil.

Coat chicken with yogurt mixture and marinate in the refrigerator for 5 hours.

Preheat oven to 475 degrees F and place chicken in oven-proof dish. Bake for 25 minutes or until chicken is evenly browned and cooked well. Remove from oven and garnish with lime wedges.

Yam Kabab Pilaf

········· ### Fragrant Rice and Yams ·······································

A pilaf, or *pulao*, is not very different from a *biryani*. It is rice cooked with meat, ghee, and spices. This is a delicious vegetarian pilaf made with yams, but cauliflower or even cooked corn also make a delicious pilaf.

SERVES 5

YAM BALLS:
1 pound yams
½ teaspoon cumin seeds
1 teaspoon chopped green chili
1 teaspoon chopped red chili
1 tablespoon crushed cilantro
  leaves
3 tablespoons grated coconut
1 teaspoon poppy seeds
3 tablespoons *besan* (chickpea
  flour) or gram flour
½ teaspoon ground turmeric
1 teaspoon fresh crushed ginger
1 teaspoon garlic powder
1 teaspoon garam masala (page 69)
salt to taste
2 tablespoons grated Parmesan
  cheese
Oil for frying

RICE:
2 cups rice, washed thoroughly and
  drained
Salt to taste
Ghee
2 onions, chopped
Oil
3 green chilies, chopped
½ teaspoon ground cardamom
2 cloves
1 teaspoon ground coriander
1 teaspoon grated fresh ginger
1 teaspoon grated garlic
2 cups pureed fresh tomatoes
½ cup milk
Cashew nuts, sliced and fried

Make yam balls: Wash yams and boil until soft. Remove skins and mash. Grind cumin seeds, green chili, red chili, cilantro, coconut, and poppy seeds. Add the paste to the yams with *besan*, ground turmeric, ginger, garlic powder, and garam masala. Add salt to taste. Shape mixture into one-inch balls, stuffing each with a little cheese as you make them. Fry in hot oil, drain, and set aside.

Make rice: Parboil rice in salted water and drain. Heat some ghee in a medium skillet and fry chopped onions. Crush half of onions and add to rice. Set aside remaining onions. Heat a little oil in another skillet and fry green chilies, ground cardamom, cloves, ground coriander, ginger, and garlic. Stir mixture into rice.

Place tomato puree and milk in a pot and bring to a boil. Add rice mixture. Place yam balls in rice, cover and steam for 10 minutes. Garnish with remaining fried onions and cashew nuts.

Chicken Pistachio Korma
Nutty Chicken Stew

North India, especially the region around New Delhi, is famous for marinated meats, which may include kidney, liver, and even udders, ground to a paste with yogurt and then patted around a glowing skewer and roasted outdoors. A lashing of ghee makes the meats rich and succulent. This recipe is perfect for breast of chicken.

SERVES 4 TO 6

2/3 cup shelled pistachio nuts

4 whole green chilies, plus 6 green chilies, seeded and chopped

5 tablespoons heavy cream

4 tablespoons plain yogurt

oil

3 medium onions, chopped

1-inch piece fresh ginger, peeled and chopped

6 garlic cloves, chopped

3/4 teaspoon garam masala (page 69)

1 teaspoon ground turmeric

1/2 teaspoon ground cinnamon

2 bay leaves

1/2 teaspoon ground white pepper

1 teaspoon fennel seeds

2 pounds boneless, skinless chicken breasts, cut into cubes

1 large tomato, chopped

1 teaspoon ground green cardamom

2 tablespoons chopped cilantro leaves

Boil pistachios for a few minutes in 1 cup water. Drain and cool. Remove skin of pistachios with fingers and grind with the 4 whole green chilies into a paste. Whisk with cream and yogurt and set aside.

Fry onions in small amount of oil until translucent. Add ginger, garlic, garam masala, turmeric, cinnamon, bay leaves, white pepper, and fennel seeds. Fry for 3 minutes.

Add chicken pieces and sauté for 5 minutes. Add the yogurt mixture, seeded and chopped green chilies, tomato, and salt to taste. Add enough water to make a thick gravy and cook for 20 minutes until chicken is done. Sprinkle with ground cardamom and cilantro leaves before serving.

Uttar Pradesh

Himachal Pradesh and Haryana are independent states that have separated from Punjab but still maintain almost the same cooking traditions. The northwestern part of Uttar Pradesh, attracts trekkers and hikers who revel in simple rustic vegetarian fare as well as non-vegetarian dishes.

The sacred site of Varanasi, also known as Benares, in Uttar Pradesh is the holiest city revered by Hindus. Jostling with temples, Benares stands on the banks of the River Ganges and has been a center of learning for over two thousand years. More than a hundred bathing *ghats* (shallow tiered steps) lead to the sacred river where Hindu worshipers perform funeral rites and a ritual purification by submerging ashes in the sacred waters.

Hindus believe that by visiting Benares they are purified, or by dying there that they ensure freedom—a release from rebirths. Millions seeking penance and salvation throng this ancient city. The dead are cremated here amidst smoke and flower garlands and the chanting of Sanskrit *slokas* (hymns) as the ashes float away on the holy river. Ganges is believed to be the Goddess who resides in the matted locks of the deity Shiva's head. It is said that a king beseeched the Goddess to come down and purify the earth and thus was a river born.

The city of Benares resounds day and night with the clamor of bells, prayers, and street vendors. Surrounded by the thick smell of incense, wood fires, flowers, and cremation rites, you walk through a city that invites millions of people to pay homage to the holy waters and the deities. This is also the place where hundreds of widows have been confined with shaven heads over the years to pray, beg, and eat a bowl of cold rice and vegetables. One of the sad, horrifying contradictions of India is that many widows are still ignored and humiliated. Although it must be said that a few deliberately make the choice of this ascetic lifestyle and renounce the world.

In the secular part of the pilgrimage city, vegetarian food is made for the most part without onions and garlic. Popular vegetables include pumpkin, potatoes, okra, eggplant, and spinach. *Aloo Benarasi* is made with fried small, whole potatoes in a spicy yogurt dish garnished with cilantro and tamarind. Hot *kachoris* are ideal for a quick snack. A *kachori* is a round flattened ball of dough stuffed with lentils, like *moong* or *urad dal*, gram flour, potatoes, chili powder, and spices; it is served with tamarind, mint, or cilantro chutney. Lots of pushcarts tempt with delicious potatoes in a thick gravy, fried batter swimming in syrup, and sizzling rotis and dried fruits. Fried *papads*, or *pappadams*, are wafers made from dals and are a favorite at any meal. A typical meal of rotis, lentils, and vegetables served on a *pattal* (a plate made of dried leaves pinned together with tiny sticks) is topped with *jelabis*, a very sweet dish made from *urad dal* and deep-fried in flavored sugar syrup.

Another delectable sweet is the *peda* made with thick cream, pistachios, saffron, and cardamom. If you fancy a sweet dish, go to the numerous outdoor sweet shops and you will find cooks sitting in front of large shallow pans boiling milk, known for its rich cream. Sometimes the sweet maker will skim off the heavy cream and press it into small squares. He then places it in another vessel in which milk tinged with saffron and ground pistachio nuts gently simmers. This sumptuous delight is called *rabri*. And in this holiest of cities in India, you will attain a state of bliss merely by sucking on a mound of ice shaped into a ball, drowned with the sweetest of *sherbets* (drinks) made of melon, almonds, anise, cardamom, cashews, and saffron, with a stick poked into it for you to hold and savor—the *thandai*. A nod and a wink may even get you the intoxicating *bhang* (made from the hemp plant) lacing your *thandai*.

In Stately Lucknow

Located five hundred miles from Delhi, the state capital of Uttar Pradesh, Lucknow derived its name from Lakshman, the younger brother of Rama. According to the *Ramayana,* Rama the elder brother gifted this territory to Lakshman in gratitude, since Lakshman had chosen to spend fourteen years of exile along with his brother. The region later ruled by Nawabs is associated with gracious hospitality and elaborate etiquette, reviving the memory of past grandeur and Mughal culture. Persian, Turkish, and Arabian influences and courtly traditions reflect the royal history of the past. If there were twenty dishes being prepared then twenty individual fires were lit as each item was prepared separately and aesthetically, recalling a culinary heritage of hundreds of years.

Cooking in Lucknow became an aesthetic art. Chefs were encouraged to compete with each other. The secrets of various *masalas* were handed down through the generations. The story is that many a time guests were tricked into thinking that preserved fruit was meat; and a chef once shaped small birds out of meat so that when the dish was served, guests were astonished to find almost lifelike birds in the mound of pilaf. Cooks were honored and treated with great respect. They were paid enormous salaries and dominated the kitchens. Individual names were given to cooks who specialized in a certain process of cooking. There were several kinds of cooks (*bawarchis*). Gourmet cooks were called *raqabdars* and cooked in small quantities, garnishing and presenting single dishes with individual flair and elegance. *Bawarchis* cooked food in bulk. The *masalchi* would grind the spices; and the *mehri* would carry the food trays. *Nanfus* made the breads—*rotis, naans,* and *sheermals*.

Kakori kebab, named after a town nearby, is a legendary Lucknow meat dish with a smoky flavor. The lamb is minced, folded over, spiced with ginger, onion, garam masala, and then deep fried. *Galavaat kabab,* another Lucknow specialty, is tenderized meat patties that one does not chew. The succulent meat is savored on the tongue and slips gently into your gullet. The indulgent story goes that it was dreamed up for a *nawab* who had lost all his teeth. The secret to the softest melt-in-the-mouth gravy comes from items like onions, fried well, ground fine, and then strained.

Moti pilaf is a creation of deep-fried balls of cheese, ground cashew nuts, corn flour, and silver foil used to garnish a rice pilaf. *Shami kabab,* mincemeat boiled and ground with chickpeas and spices with raw papaya added, is another favorite. Profuse quantities of nuts and spices were used extravagantly to give the food a rich taste. And who has not heard of *Shahi dal* where the dal was cooked with such delicacy that each grain was separate?

The province of Avadh in Lucknow is noted for its use of large quantities of ghee, nuts, raisins, saffron, and edible gold and silver foil in cooking. Pilafs here were given exotic names like jasmine, radiant light, perfume, pearl, ruby, and garden. Cottage cheese, ground lentils, and evaporated milk made inimitable desserts. The *sheermal* dough for rotis in Avadh is made without any water; only milk and ghee are used, resulting in an exquisite softness of texture and a rich taste that lingers in the memory.

Another Lucknow favorite is *Malai paan,* made from layers of cream, nuts, and spices, and fashioned to look like a betel leaf; and *Lasoon ki Kheer* melded with garlic, evaporated milk, cashews, and sauces is another signature Lucknow sweet confection. The feast of culinary delights was placed before you on a multi-colored, dazzling, mirror-sequined cloth called the *dastarkhwan* which invited guests to sit together and share a culinary tradition.

The *nawabs* of Lucknow were known to chew cardamom throughout the day to sweeten the breath. Cardamoms were dipped in rose water with a tinge of tobacco and covered in gold or silver foil to induce an exotic flavor. Many *nawabs* of Lucknow partook of tobacco melded with exotic potions. Beauteous courtesans—after singing, dancing, reciting poetry, and playing music—ended the evenings offering a seductive dish of cardamoms or a *paan* (betel leaf garnished with sweet herbs and spices) to guests.

Navaratan Curry

Nine Gem Curry

Nine Gem Curry, as it is called, is a mix of nine fresh vegetables that cook quickly and require less oil. It can be served in a variety of creative ways including with rotis, rice, *dosas*, or *idlis* (South Indian rice preparations).

SERVES 4

2 tablespoons oil
2 onions, chopped
1-inch piece fresh ginger, ground to a paste
4 garlic cloves, ground to a paste
1 teaspoon cumin seeds
1 cup diced potatoes
1 cup diced carrots
½ cup diced radish
½ cup sliced green beans
2 cups cauliflower florets

1 cup chopped eggplant
1 cup peas
1 pound tomatoes, peeled and quartered
1 teaspoon garam masala (page 69)
1 cup plain yogurt
1 cup water
3 tablespoons grated coconut
Salt to taste
1 tablespoon chopped cilantro

Heat oil in pan; fry onions, ginger, garlic, and cumin seeds until brown. Add vegetables (potatoes thru tomatoes) and cook gently for a few minutes. Add garam masala. Mix in yogurt and water to form a thick curry.

Add coconut and some salt to taste. Keep on high heat for 3 minutes stirring constantly. Cover and cook on low flame for another 20 minutes. Garnish with cilantro.

Masoor Dal

Orange Lentil Curry

This dish is also called *arhar dal* and can be cooked with vegetables like squash, zucchini, eggplant, or onions. Dals may be oiled or not, whole or split, with the skin off or on. Always wash dal thoroughly before cooking.

SERVES 4

1 cup *masoor dal*	3 green chilies, chopped
Salt	1 teaspoon ground coriander
Small pumpkin, chopped	½ teaspoon ground cumin
1 medium onion, chopped	1 teaspoon ground black pepper
4 small tomatoes, chopped	½ teaspoon tamarind paste
6 garlic cloves, chopped	2 teaspoons lime juice
½-inch piece ginger, peeled and chopped	1 tablespoon oil

Wash dal well and soak for 30 minutes. Bring 7 cups of water to a boil in a pot. Add dal and 1 teaspoon salt, and cook for 10 minutes.

Add pumpkin, onion, tomatoes, 5 of the chopped garlic cloves, ginger, chilies, coriander, cumin, and pepper, and cook over moderate heat for 30 minutes.

Add tamarind paste and lime juice. Boil for 2 minutes. Remove and mash vegetable mixture gently.

Before serving, temper by heating oil and frying remaining chopped garlic clove for a minute. Add to dal.

Orissa and Bihar

In the eastern part of India lies the state of Orissa, luring travelers from around the world with its ancient temple towns, many over a thousand years old. Three temple towns—Puri, Bhubaneswar, and Konarak—are situated near each other. Thousands of pilgrims gather every year at Puri's Jagannath Temple for a religious festival, when giant floats carrying the revered image of Lord Jagannath are pulled through the streets by worshipers, followed by feasting.

Predating the Renaissance and dedicated to Hindu deities, the Khajuraho temples of Orissa possess a unique beauty of proportion. All are placed within an eight kilometer triangle. The sandstone temples are supported by carved pillars, with hundreds of sculptures of celestial nymphs, cavorting erotic couples, warriors, gods and goddesses, and dancing women that inspire, awe, and even shock those who gaze upon this cornucopia of timeless, joyful, magnificent art and creativity.

After an intense day of worship and devotion, you can enjoy vegetarian fare, as well as both saltwater and freshwater fish and seafood such as crab, prawns, shrimp, and stingray. Fish is a favorite and prawns are cooked with mustard paste and dried mangoes and served with rice. Tamarind is used for a touch of sourness, and a mix of cumin, mustard, fennel, fenugreek, and *kalongi* (nigella) enhances dishes that need tempering. *Ghanto tharkari* is a spicy blend of roasted cumin, red chilies, cooked peas, potatoes, eggplant, cauliflower, yam, and whole gram garnished with coconut. You can indulge in *rasagollas* and *kheer* (milk pudding), which it is said was enjoyed in Orissa for centuries before it became the pride and joy of Bengali sweet fare. Deliciously thick and rich the *pitha* made from semolina or rice flour is a dumpling sweetened with jaggery, coconut fillings, and raisins and steamed in leaves.

The state of Orissa is home to sixty-two tribal groups with the Kondh tribe being the largest. A subgroup named Dongria Ondhs live on the lush green hills in thickly wooded valleys in houses of bamboo and broom sticks plastered with mud and cow dung built so low you have to crawl into them. They are agriculturists, and a Dongria village is established after a ritualistic ceremony. A lump of rice is sanctified and left at a particular site. If the rice is untouched the next morning the location is considered propitious.

Bihar, midway between West Bengal in the east and Uttar Pradesh in the west, is called the Land of the Buddha as Buddhism and Jainism originated there. Bihar itself is derived from *vihara*, a Buddhist monastery. A monastic university, Nalanda, flourished there from the fifth century. It is said that 2,000 teachers and 10,000 students from Japan, Java, Korea, and South Asian countries studied here surrounded by 9 million volumes between the fifth and twelfth centuries. Many monasteries still remain as well as imposing temples, bas reliefs, and sculptures.

The impact of Jainism has made the people of Bihar largely vegetarian, and yet the Mughal influence has enhanced non-vegetarian cuisine. Biharis are fond of meat and lamb steeped in a garam masala curry. But daily fare is mostly vegetarian food—rustic and simple but filling and nutritious with a mash of potato, bitter gourd, eggplant, and pumpkin cooked with mustard oil, green chilies, garlic, and cilantro leaves. This dish is called *chokha*. Roasted chickpea flour (*sattu*) is mixed with tangy onions and hot chilies to make a quick and tasty meal when working in the fields. Farmers make this a satisfying meal and carry it in their handloomed towels (*gamcha*) on their way to work. Vegetables are often mashed together to make a chutney (sauce). Potatoes, eggplants, pumpkins, and gourds are all mashed and fried with mustard oil, onions, coriander, green chilies, and sliced onions. A nutritious meal can be made from merely eating boiled rice covered with water and kept overnight, then eaten the next morning with the leftovers of a fish or vegetable curry. Sweets are made from sugar or jaggery while the *til laddo* is made with sesame seeds.

Rasbara

.... Sweet Lentils ....

An easy and quick sweet dish with lentils to provide a satisfying base, this is ideal for snacks. You do not need a festive occasion to make this sweet. You can even buy this in a sweet shop as it is a favorite for anyone who wishes to indulge in an instant gratification moment.

MAKES 15 PORTIONS

1 cup *moong dal* (green gram)
1 teaspoon baking soda
2 tablespoons buttermilk

4½ cups sugar
3 teaspoons ghee or vegetable oil

Soak *moong dal* for 2 hours. Drain and grind into a fine paste until it is a batter. Add baking soda and buttermilk. Set aside for a couple of hours.

In a saucepan, add sugar to 4 cups of water and boil until sugar is dissolved and it is a syrupy consistency.

Heat oil in pan. Pour 1 tablespoon of batter in the center to form a pancake. Fry until golden brown. Repeat with remaining batter.

Soak the *rasbara* in syrup for an hour before serving.

Jahni Posta

Zucchini and Poppy Seed Curry

Poppy seeds are used as a thickening agent, lending a nutty taste to this dish.

SERVES 4

3 medium zucchini
3 tablespoons poppy seeds
Oil
1 teaspoon cumin seeds

4 green chilies, chopped
Pinch of turmeric
Salt to taste

Slice zucchini into pieces. Crush poppy seeds adding enough water to make a paste.

Heat oil and fry cumin seeds until they pop. Add green chilies and poppy seed paste. Fry for a few minutes. Add turmeric and fry for 5 minutes. Add zucchini with a little water and salt. Sauté until the zucchini is fully cooked.

Chatu

······· Mushroom Curry ··

Simple and delicious, this dish is eaten with rice or rotis.

SERVES 4

2 cups mushrooms	1 teaspoon red chili powder
½ teaspoon ground turmeric	1 teaspoon garam masala (page 69)
5 tablespoons oil	
1 onion, chopped	Salt to taste
½ teaspoon ginger paste	1 cup milk
1 teaspoon garlic paste	¼ cup fine white flour (*maida*)
1 cup tomato paste	1 teaspoon chopped cilantro leaves

Clean mushrooms and dice. Put mushrooms in enough water to cover, add turmeric and soak for 30 minutes. Squeeze out water. In deep pan heat 2 tablespoons of oil and fry mushrooms. Set aside.

Put 2 more tablespoons of oil in empty pan. Fry onions, ginger paste, and garlic paste.

Add tomato paste and cook for 5 minutes. Add chili powder, garam masala, and salt. Cook for 3 minutes.

Mix the milk and flour. Pour into pan and cook for 3 minutes. Add mushrooms. Cook on low heat for 5 minutes. Garnish with cilantro leaves.

Madhya Pradesh

Going south, sprawling Madhya Pradesh (the largest state in Central India) prides itself on three sites that have been declared World Heritage sites by UNESCO—the temple sculptures of Khajuraho, the Buddhist monuments of Sanchi, and the rock shelters of Bhimbetka. The original inhabitants of Madhya Pradesh were tribal. Today migrants from other states have arrived bringing with them their own individual cuisines. A separate state, Chattisgarh, was carved out of Madhya Pradesh where tribals live now. Their food is simple—gourd and pumpkin flowers, mushrooms, tubers, and vegetables. The staple food is maize gruel and a cornbread called *pannia*. Forest dwellers make small balls of dried lentils or cornbread cooked in various edible leaves. One leaf that is used in many recipes for many ailments is the *neem*. I remember my own grandmother in southern India mixing *neem* leaves in cooked rice, making it into a ball and telling me it was good for my liver. In Chattisgarh, *neem* leaves are plucked when tender and fried in ghee. *Neem* has so many beneficial effects that there are at least forty patents that have been issued in the U.S, as the bark, seed, and oil are all valuable products used to treat many diseases.

The food in the rest of Madhya Pradesh is also uncomplicated and known as Malwa cuisine. It is grain and dal-based, with vegetables like cauliflower, chickpeas, sweet breads, steamed wheat cakes, rice, sugarcane, cardamom seeds, chilies, milk, and ghee on the everyday menu. The spontaneous hospitality of people is legendary. You will always be offered a glass of hot milk or a cold *lassi* (buttermilk) when you enter a home.

The capital city of Bhopal, with a long tradition of Muslim rule, retains a taste for fragrant meat dishes, spiced with garam masala, nutmeg, ginger, fresh herbs, and *kewra*, an essence taken from the screwpine flower. Spicy mutton dishes like *ishtu* are popular, as well as fragile *rumali rotis* and *kababs*. The Bhopali *paan* literally rounds out the meal with a flourish as the making of the paan is indeed a fine art.

Two-hours outside of Bhopal you can see some of the oldest Buddhist stupas (shrines) in Sanchi. The dome-shaped stupas date back more than 2,200 years and have a magnificent carved gate rising to thirty-four feet with episodes of the Buddha and his previous incarnations depicted on its square columns. In Bhimbetka, near Bhopal, the rock caves contain the largest collection of prehistoric art in India dating back to the Old Stone Age and are possibly 35,000 years old. If you have the wanderlust, wish to rediscover history, and have a yen for authentic, interesting, simple fare head to Madhya Pradesh.

An entertaining story about this area is popular even today. During the British rule in 1911, King George V decided to visit India to greet his loyal subjects and shoot tiger and leopard. In anticipation of his royal visit, a Maharaja who owned a game preserve in Shivpuri called Madhya Pradesh, which is now the Madhav National Park, ordered furniture, curtains, floor tiles, chandeliers, and even ceramic toilets from England to host the king. While all this was being brought by steamship, the local architects built a Tudor castle of stone with turrets in the heart of the jungle. King George was supposed to spend just one day in this jungle, but he never even made an appearance. Travelers today will be amused to find that the George Castle still stands in a wooded jungle in Madhya Pradesh.

Chatpata Baingan
Eggplant Fry

This dish is wholesome and nutritious and has an earthy flavor. It has local touches but also resembles the cuisine of neighboring regions.

SERVES 4

8 baby eggplants
1 teaspoon ground turmeric
Salt to taste
1 cup plain yogurt
Oil for frying
1 teaspoon fenugreek seeds
1 onion, chopped
1 tablespoon ginger paste
4 green chilies, ground

1 tablespoon mustard paste (made with dry mustard mixed with a little water)
1 tablespoon garlic paste
1 tablespoon crushed coriander seeds
Salt
Sprig of cilantro

Cut eggplants lengthwise into four sections but do not cut through stems. Rub with turmeric powder, salt, and 1 tablespoon yogurt. Marinate for 10 minutes.

Heat some oil and fry eggplants until golden brown. Remove eggplants from pan and drain on paper towels.

Meanwhile add fenugreek seeds to the same pan. When seeds pop, add onion, followed by ginger paste and green chilies, then mustard and garlic pastes and cook for 2 minutes. Add coriander, rest of yogurt, and a little water.

When the gravy becomes thick, add fried eggplants and simmer for 5 minutes. Garnish with cilantro leaves.

Rajasthan

The cities of Rajasthan, a collection of princely kingdoms, are called "Technicolor Cities." Each city has its own characteristic color. Udaipur is a white city with a palace painted white built on the sapphire blue Pichola Lake. Jaipur, the capital city, is startlingly pink. Jodhpur has whole parts of the city painted blue, and Jaisalmer is shrouded in soft yellow. Spectacular sandstone palaces, ornately carved Jain temples, arches, towers, cupolas, courtyards ringed with balconies, and houses embellished with a lacy filigree of pierced stonework are everywhere in this stark, arid landscape. Historic forts with rounded bastions and massive cannon balls capable of making a large enough hole to let eight horsemen ride through the gates literally sing with ballads of heroic feats.

Rajasthan, meaning "land of the kings," was the home of the Rajputs, a warrior race who controlled northwestern India for over a thousand years. Their courage and valor has inspired ballads sung even today by wandering minstrels who still remember the exploits of Rajputs, both men and women who chose death over defeat in bloody wars with invaders. Rajasthanis wear brightly colored fabric to protect them from the harsh sun and have learned to survive in the hostile desert landscape using inventive methods of water conservation and making the best of the available cereals, pulses, and spices. Meats are cooked with milk and curds, buttermilk, and ghee giving a different kind of nuance to the meat. This kind of food can keep for days. *Murgh ko khaato* is chicken steeped in curds while dry lamb cooked for a long time in spices like asafetida, ginger, and ajwain is a classic desert dish called *kacher maas*.

The she-camel is the cow of the stark arid landscape. Camel milk is rich in vitamin C and nutritious although it has a salty taste. At the frequent camel fairs, there is always an exciting milking competition where the female camels are led to a viewing area and a calf begins to suckle. The moment the milk appears, the contestants start milking the camels until the whistle blows, and the judging begins to see which container holds the most milk. Very exciting.

The majority of people in this state are vegetarians. The Thar desert has inspired people to use rustic famine foods like *kair sangri kumita*, a small berry of a thorny tree that interestingly does not have a single leaf. *Kangri* and *kumita* are two types of desert berries that can survive even when every other plant has shriveled in the desert heat. Minimum water is used in cooking due to scarcity; instead clarified butter, milk, cereals, pulses, and curds are used liberally. Barley, millet, maize, corn, and spiced chickpea flour are used to make rotis. A dish that can be preserved for days is the classic *dal batti churma* in which five different dals are cooked and pounded together with sugar and nuts and made into flour balls. When warriors went to battle this dish accompanied them tied to their saddles as they were many days from home. It could be eaten without heating and remain unspoiled for days.

Slow-cooked lentils were eaten with *batti*, a baked wheat roll. Another desert dish is powdered barley mixed with curds, and wheat rolls encrusted with raw sugar, nuts, and ghee. The scarcity of vegetables, and more importantly water, has definitely had an effect on cooking in this state. Instead of tomatoes, which do not grow in the desert, the sour taste is provided by mango powder (*amchoor*). I use it in practically every dish I make. It gives the added bite. Some Rajputs who hail from the warrior clan in Rajasthan are meateaters, so grilled meat and game dishes are popular.

Pickled fruits, cereals, vegetables, gram flour, and chili peppers are part of the strict vegetarian diet of the business Marwari community who live in Rajasthan. Rice, barley, and wheat are used daily; and *tilauri*, balls of *urad* or *moong dal* along with sesame seeds is dried in the sun and deep-fried. A thick roti with garlic, red chili sauce, and raw onions is a true rustic dish. Another popular dish are *gatti* and *papdi*, balls of wheat flour with *besan* and *moong dal* as the base batter. They are roasted, cracked open, and eaten with ghee.

The unique, statuesque, vegetarian Bishnois community have been living in this desert region for more than 500 years. From the warrior sect of Rajasthan, a man named Jambaji Bhagavan founded the Bishnois community in 1451. He laid down twenty-nine principles (*Bish* is 20 and *noi* is 9) which included vegetarianism, compassion, cleanliness, truthfulness, and a religious sensibility. The community is so caring towards animals that women have been known to suckle motherless deer. The Bishnois live close to water which they drink after it has been filtered through a cloth. They do not cut green trees, but wait for the tree to die. Wood is not used for funeral pyres so they bury the dead. They are perhaps the earliest environmentalists in India.

Watermelon Curry

On a scorching summer day if you are wandering in the desert looking for vibrant handicrafts, stop at a nearby village and taste this signature dish of Rajasthan. Watermelons, called *darbuj,* are available all through summer. Eat the curry with rice. Sweet, spicy, and cooling.

SERVES 4

1 large watermelon	Salt
1½ teaspoons red chili powder	2 tablespoons oil
¼ teaspoon ground turmeric	¼ teaspoon cumin seeds
½ teaspoon ground coriander	2 teaspoons sugar
1 teaspoon garlic paste	3 teaspoons lime juice

Cut watermelon and remove pulp from rind and cut pulp into cubes. Put 1 cup of watermelon cubes in a blender and puree into a juice. Add the chili powder, turmeric, coriander, garlic paste, and some salt to taste.

Heat oil in a frying pan and add cumin seeds and cook for 20 seconds. Add the seasoned watermelon juice and simmer until spices are well blended. Add sugar and lime juice. Cook for 1 minute.

Add the watermelon cubes and simmer over low heat for about 7 minutes or until softened.

Badam Sherbet

Almond Drink

It was a warm day in Jaipur, Rajasthan, and we were very hot because we had been dancing in the streets during the marriage procession of our cousin Arun Kathuria who was marrying the beautiful Anu from Jaipur. As the procession went down the road we, the bridegroom's family, danced in front of the bedecked horse on which sat the bridegroom covered with garlands of flowers. After the dancing we were offered almond sherbet in a tall steel tumbler—delicious, perfect for cooling off.

SERVES 2

2 cups ground almonds	**10 cardamom pods**
4½ cups sugar	**Almond extract to taste**

Place almonds, sugar, and 1 cup of water in pan. Simmer gently, stirring constantly, until the sugar dissolves. Grind the cardamom pods with 1 tablespoon of water; add to the almond mixture. Continue to cook about 15 minutes, until thickened. Remove from heat and strain. Add almond extract and serve over crushed ice.

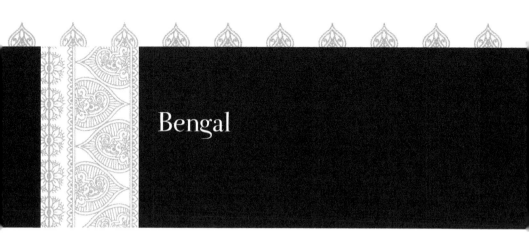

Bengal

The eastern part of India, which is West Bengal, is an extraordinarily fertile land with an abundance of canals, lakes, ponds, and rivers that tempt Bengalis to eat the plentiful fresh fish, prawns, and crabs from the rich coastal waters. Famed for cooking fish in diverse ways (stewed, grilled, fried, or stuffed), a Bengali does not throw any part of the fish away. Two major rivers, the Padma and the Ganges, have been the sources for a beloved fish called the *hilsa*. An excellent start to the day is to go to the market and bargain for the best fish—the *hilsa*, of course. The *hilsa* fish is perhaps the signature fish of Bengal with a unique identity. The softness of the flesh and an extraordinary flavor mark this specimen in the Bengal rivers. Mention *hilsa* to a Bengali and a strange emotion of nostalgia and longing sweeps over them.

Fish, the food so dear to a Bengali's heart, is also a symbol of prosperity and fertility and plays a major role in ceremonies. On the morning of a wedding, a big, prize carp (*rui*) is cleaned and the head decorated with oil and turmeric. Rich silks and garlands of jasmine flowers are wrapped around the fish which is placed on a silver tray decorated with fruits and flowers and taken to the bridegroom's house through the bustling streets accompanied by live musicians.

A typical Bengali menu could start with a steaming curry made of *neem*, bitter gourd, and spices, then rice flavored with ghee, next lentils and cooked vegetables, followed by fish and chutneys, and ending with a dessert of sweet curds and dried fruits. On a special occasion you would be offered a pilaf. A fish stew made with potatoes, gourd, and eggplant is a delectable item on any given day's menu. A Bengali dish becomes distinctive with the use of *panchphoron*—a five-spice mix which includes cumin, nigella, fennel, fenugreek, and mustard. It is interesting to note that though vegetarianism was advocated during the Bhakti Movement (a devotional movement), many Bengali Hindus eat meat.

With mustard growing profusely in the regions, mustard oil extracted from the seeds is used in cooking. *Choler dal* (Bengal gram with coconut), *mocha ghanto* (banana flowers), and *hilsa* fish cooked in mustard are popular. Green gram with vegetables is also dear to any Bengali's heart. *Golguppas,* made of fried dough and stuffed with spicy potato, are dipped in tamarind water and popped deftly in the mouth. *Shukto* is made with a bitter melon called *karela* accompanied by green banana, radish, eggplant, potato, and green papaya—making it a dish with surprising flavors. *Churmur* (the name itself is lighthearted) is a mix of crushed chickpeas and spicy potatoes mixed with tamarind water, crumbled fried dough, and brushed with mustard oil.

Indians have an addiction to desserts that are very rich, extremely sweet, and require a lot of patience to make. Try watching milk boil slowly. Sweets in Bengal range from setting-your-teeth-on-edge sweetness to madly creative dishes made from vegetables, lentils, nuts, or fruits. Unlike dessert which is served at the end of the meal in the West, in India you can start the day with a sweet dish and steadily eat sweets throughout the day. In any city in India, everyone has their own favorite sweet shop where large quantities are bought, especially at festival times, to be eaten and distributed to family and friends. The best sweets, in my opinion, come from West Bengal where there is a sweet shop on every corner. Made of milk and cheese, they are legendary for their variety. The special traditional sweet dishes include *sandesh*, made of melted cheese and jaggery flavored with mango saffron or orange and put into clay molds and shaped into fruits, flowers, or birds; and *rassagollas*, spongy white balls made from cottage cheese and syrup that are sold in shops on every street corner and made with recipes that are closely guarded secrets.

Rasagolla
Milk Sweet

Rasagolla is a traditional Bengali confection and, along with other Bengali sweets like *karapaker sandesh*, is remembered for its lush sweetness. Bengali sweets are rightly called "desserts fit for the gods."

MAKES 12 BALLS

4 cups milk
¼ cup lemon juice
1 teaspoon corn flour

3 cups water
2 cups sugar

Bring the milk to a boil and then slowly add lemon juice. Shut off the heat and set aside for 15 minutes (the milk will start to separate). Line a strainer with cheesecloth and put over a bowl. Pour the milk mixture into the strainer and allow to drain for 1 hour.

Remove the cheese/paneer that has formed in the strainer and squeeze out all the water and put it on a plate. Knead in the corn flour until the cheese forms into a soft dough. Roll cheese into small ½-inch balls, making 12 of them.

Mix the water and sugar and put in a pressure cooker on medium heat and when it boils turn off the heat and gently place balls in syrup. Close cooker. Bring to a boil on medium heat and cook for 7 minutes.

Turn off heat and wait for a few minutes. The syrupy balls will have increased in size. Remove the balls carefully with a large spoon and put them in a bowl with enough syrup to cover. Refrigerate until chilled and serve cold. (The balls will lose spongy texture, be deliciously soft and will be a little smaller in size.)

Singharas
Lamb Pastries

This is the Bengali version of the *samosa* and is offered at festivals and weddings. You may find yourself spending a long while in the kitchen but the result is a wonderful snack.

SERVES 3

FILLING:
3 ripe tomatoes
2 tablespoons ghee or oil
2 cinnamon sticks
5 cloves
1 cardamom pod
4 green chilies, chopped
1 large onion, minced
4 curry leaves
4 garlic cloves, crushed
1 teaspoon ground turmeric
2-inch piece fresh ginger, grated
1 pound ground lamb
1 cup peas
1 teaspoon garam masala (page 69)

PASTRY:
2 cups maida or all-purpose flour
½ teaspoon salt
2 tablespoons ghee

To make the pastry, mix flour and salt in a bowl. Slowly mix in ghee until the mixture is dry. Add half a cup of warm water a little at a time and knead the dough so that it is smooth. Set aside for half an hour.

Scald tomatoes in boiling water for 20 seconds, drain, and peel. Finely chop, discarding seeds.

Heat ghee or oil in large pan on low heat and fry the cinnamon sticks, cloves, cardamom pod, and chilies for a few minutes. Add the onion, curry leaves, garlic, turmeric, and ginger. Fry for 5 minutes. Add the lamb and fry until the meat becomes brown. Add the chopped tomatoes and cover.

Cook for 10 minutes, stirring often. Add the peas, cover, and cook for another 5 minutes. If there is any liquid left, turn up the heat to cook it off. Remove the whole spices and season with salt and garam masala.

Divide the dough into 12 portions. Roll out each to a small circle about 1-inch in diameter and cut each circle in half. Take one half, form a cone, and seal the edges of the cut sides together. Fill the cone three-quarters with filling and seal top edges. Repeat with remaining dough and filling.

Deep-fry the *singharas* in a pan of hot oil in batches until they are browned. Drain.

Machili aur Kela Patha

Fresh Fish in Banana Leaves

You need a steamer for this dish and a deep saucepan. Mustard oil is used in Bengali cooking giving the dish an interesting flavor. If this is not available, any vegetable oil can be substituted.

SERVES 8

5 pounds fish (mahi-mahi or
   catfish), skin removed
1½ teaspoons ground turmeric
2 tablespoons lemon juice
½ teaspoon salt
3 tablespoons brown mustard seeds
2-inch piece fresh ginger, peeled
   and chopped

5 green chilies, chopped
4 teaspoons mustard oil or
   vegetable oil
1 teaspoon red chili powder
4 pieces of banana leaf, if
   available, or parchment paper

Mix 1 teaspoon of the turmeric with some water and use this mixture to wash the fish. Pat dry with paper towels. Mix lemon juice and salt; rub mixture into fish.

Grind mustard seeds and blend with remaining ½ teaspoon turmeric, ginger, chilies, mustard oil, and chili powder into a paste. Baste fish with spice paste.

If using, make banana leaves soft by dipping in hot water and wiping dry. Grease leaves or parchment paper. Place fish and some marinade in center of each leaf and loosely fold the leaf over it to enclose. Tie with string and put in a steamer over a saucepan of hot water. Cover. Steam for 12 minutes or less depending on the kind of fish. Check one to see if fish is cooked.

Gujarat

Gujarat in Western India evokes images of Jain temples, diamonds, enterprise, crafts, superb vegetarian food, and the Gujarati *thali* (platter). Ninety percent of Hindu Gujaratis are vegetarians. Light nutritious meals consist of rice, rotis, salads, shredded coconut, dry or curried vegetables, *kadhi* (a dish made of sour curd and *besan*), crunchy snacks, pickles, and a sweet dish, which might be an ice cream stuffed with cashews, raisins, and saffron, and flecked with pistachio. Walk down any street in Gujarat and you will find snack vendors sitting before mountains of deep-fried snacks and savories inspiring countless orders from customers. Spongy squares of steamed *besan* called *dhokla*, garnished with cilantro and accompanied by a sweet chutney, and *khandvi besan*, paste rolls, often form part of the daily diet. Right through the day you can munch on *patrel* (steamed *neem* leaves and a spicy *besan* paste), potato chips, cashew nuts, fried chickpeas, peanuts, and sticks of fried *besan* (*gathia fafda*). In the rural areas villagers place dal, beans, yams, and eggplant in earthenware pots and bake them under the earth. In the west and northern parts of Gujarat, the women are excellent pickle makers; the bottles of Gujarati pickles in the Indian groceries in Los Angeles are always in great demand. There is a variety of fruits and vegetables to choose from. I've tasted potato, beet, bitter *karela*, and pear pickle, but my all-time favorite is the mango pickle. Here in Los Angeles, my friend Prema Raj Mohan makes pickles from lemons gathered from her trees, and using salt, chili, and mustard liberally, she marinates the lemons and then stores large bottles of the mouthwatering pickle. She then generously shares it with her friends and family.

Order a Gujarati *thali* (platter) anywhere in India and you will be presented with rotis enriched with ghee, five different vegetable delicacies, *khandvi* (rolls of cooked chickpea paste), *kadhi* (a yogurt curry laced with vegetables), *rabri* (a milky dessert), and a rich *halvah* made from semolina and sugar. In certain restaurants you may be presented with a plate made of an alloy of five metals considered good for memory and purifying the blood.

The Jain community observes vegetarianism with great discipline. Many Jains undertake fasting during festivals and survive on water or eat only restricted foods. Honey is forbidden and any vegetable with roots underground, like onions, potatoes, and garlic are avoided. The belief being that in the uprooting of the vegetables, insects may perish. There are only certain fruits and vegetables that Jains eat but these dietary choices together with rice, millet, wheat, corn, barley, and dairy products with spices result in a tasty and nutritious diet. A banana can become a simple dish to enjoy. The skin is lightly fried with spices after being coated with a batter of chickpea flour. To add more richness, they split ripe bananas, place within them a filling of chickpea flour that has been seasoned with cumin powder, cilantro, green chilies, and a dab of sugar, and fry the bananas over low heat.

The Muslim community in Gujarat, the Bohris, are disciples of Abdullah, a prophet of the 11th century AD. They like rich meat gravies, *kababs*, and the superb gelatinious stew *siri paya* made of goat's head, trotters, and beef kebabs (*malai kebab*) that have been marinated in thick cream. The *Pattar Gosh kabab* is a tongue-burning kebab named because it is still cooked on a heated stone. The scalding stone is said to release certain minerals when heated, which the meat absorbs and therefore exudes a spectacular flavor. Another choice dish is the *Lageena sheekh,* which is ground meat topped with a beaten egg and baked.

Another Gujarati community, the Parsis, are today small in number but they have retained their culture with pride; and their culinary traditions are creative and far ranging. Hardly anyone is a vegetarian. Eggs are a favorite with Parsis who eat them scrambled, omelet fashion, poached with tomatoes, or seasoned with vinegar, a pinch of salt, a sprinkling of sugar, or cooked with chips. I have even heard of eggs cooked with bananas.

A non-vegetarian dish called *dhansak* is a traditional dish of the Parsis and is made from chicken or lamb cooked in a puree of up to six kinds of dal, herbs, greens like spinach, tamarind juice, and vegetables. Lush pilafs are studded with nuts and raisins. Fish smothered in coconut, meat, and vegetables cooked in vinegar and thick dals is another signature dish. One of the most exotic dishes described to me by a Parsi is the *oomberiu*. In this preparation lamb or partridge, eggs, spices, potatoes, eggplant, and onions are placed inside an earthenware pot that is then sealed with banana leaves. A hole is dug in the ground and twigs are placed in it and set on fire with a large potato in the center. The sealed pot is placed over the potato and cooked for two hours.

The British colonial influence is seen in the preparation of sweets in the presentation of flans, soufflés, cakes, and rice puddings, while the Indian evaporated milk sweets like *peda* splashed with rose petals or rose syrup are delectable.

Dahi Kahdi
Okra in Yogurt

This dish has a sour sweet flavor and is made with *besan* (gram flour) and yogurt. Okra is my favorite vegetable, but you can substitute any other vegetable.

SERVES 5

2 cups plain yogurt

4 tablespoons *besan* (gram flour)

3 teaspoons chopped fresh ginger

1 teaspoon chopped green chilies

2 tablespoons sugar

Salt

20 small okra, washed and stems trimmed

2 tablespoons ghee or oil

7 cloves

1 teaspoon fenugreek seeds

1 teaspoon cumin seeds

Pinch of asafetida

10 curry leaves

Beat the yogurt and add the besan. Mix with 3½ cups of water. Blend the ginger and green chilies to make a paste.

Bring yogurt mixture to a boil and add ginger-chili paste, sugar, salt, and okra.

Heat ghee or oil; fry cloves, fenugreek seeds, and cumin seeds for a few seconds. Remove from heat and add asafetida. Add to okra mixture with curry leaves. Cook for 15 minutes, until okras are soft.

Ghosh aur Zard Aloo
Lamb with Apricots

This is a popular Parsi dish with a taste of sweet and sour. Dried apricots often find their way into Parsi and Muslim dishes and can be used in chicken and vegetable curries as well. The fruit absorbs the cooking juices and becomes plump and juicy. If you like, sauté the apricots as a garnish. You can also substitute raisins for the apricots. This dish can be eaten with rice or rotis.

SERVES 4

½ cup dried apricots
¼ cup oil
2 medium onions, minced
½-inch piece fresh ginger, peeled and chopped
2 garlic cloves, chopped
1 teaspoon ground cinnamon
1 teaspoon ground cardamom
½ teaspoon ground cumin

½ teaspoon black peppercorns
2 tomatoes, chopped
1½ pounds lamb, cut in small cubes
¾ teaspoon garam masala (page 69)
Salt to taste
1 teaspoon vinegar or lime juice
1 teaspoon sugar

Soak dried apricots in ½ cup water for 2 hours.

Heat oil in pan and fry onions until golden brown. Add ginger and garlic and fry 2 minutes. Add cinnamon and cardamom and after 1 minute add ground cumin and stir. Add peppercorns and tomatoes and cook for 5 minutes.

Add lamb and garam masala. Stir fry for 5 minutes. Add salt to taste and cook over low heat, adding water if all liquid evaporates. When the meat is cooked, add vinegar or lime juice, sugar, and drained apricots. Cook for 10 more minutes stirring constantly.

Dhansak
Lamb, Lentils and Vegetables

Served on special occasions, *Dhansak* (*dhan* meaning rice or grain and lentil; *sak* or *shak* meaning vegetables), a Parsi dish, is inundated with flavor and made with lamb or chicken, lentils, and vegetables. It is typically served with rice.

SERVES 6

½ cup *toor dal*
1 tablespoon *moong dal*
1 tablespoon dried chickpeas
¼ cup *urad dal*
1 eggplant
1 small pumpkin
2 cups spinach leaves
3 tomatoes
3 green chilies
3 tablespoons ghee or oil
1 onion, minced

3 garlic cloves, crushed
1-inch piece fresh ginger, grated
2 pounds boneless lamb, cut into cubes
1-inch piece cinnamon stick
4 cardamom pods
3 cloves
1 tablespoon ground coriander
1 teaspoon ground turmeric
1 tablespoon chili powder
3 tablespoons lime juice

Soak dals in water for 3 hours. Drain. In a large pot, put dals in 5 cups of water, cover, and boil, stirring until soft. Drain and mash.

Cook eggplant and pumpkin in boiling water until soft. Peel eggplant and cut into small pieces. Scoop out pumpkin flesh and cut into pieces. Cut spinach leaves into small pieces. Halve tomatoes and split chilies.

Heat ghee or oil in deep pan; fry onion, garlic, and ginger for 5 minutes. Add lamb and brown for 10 minutes. Add cinnamon stick, cardamom pods, cloves, coriander, turmeric, and chili powder; fry for 5 minutes. Add ¾ cup water and simmer until the lamb is tender.

Add mashed dals and all the prepared vegetables; season with lime juice, salt, and pepper. Simmer for 15 minutes and stir and serve.

Sevai

Vermicelli Milk Pudding

This sweet Parsi dish can be eaten as a snack or at the end of a meal. The vermicelli is thin and delicate and makes a simple dessert.

SERVES 6

1 pound almonds
1 pound pistachios
¼ cup raisins
½ cup ghee
1 cup rice vermicelli, broken into
    1-inch pieces

6 cups milk
1 cup sugar
4 cardamom pods, ground

Soak the nuts in warm water and then drain, peel, and chop. Soak raisins in warm water separately for about 10 minutes.

Heat the ghee, and fry the vermicelli stirring all the time over low heat. When the vermicelli turns golden brown, add nuts and fry for a few seconds. Set aside.

Boil the milk until reduced to half the original quantity. Add sugar, cardamom, vermicelli and nuts, and raisins; cook on low heat for 10 minutes. Remove from heat. Serve warm.

Maharashtra

Flaunting unique Gothic architecture, Mumbai (originally known as Bombay) is the "gateway of India" and the capital of Maharashtra. Mumbai is the largest industrial, commercial, and cosmopolitan city in India. The financial capital of India, it is bordered by beaches and prides itself on not just Bollywood but a diversity of neighborhoods and a flamboyant cuisine that embraces all regional delights. It all began in 1534 when a treaty between the Indian ruler Bahadur Shah and Viceroy Nuno da Cunha resulted in seven small islands being placed in Portuguese possession. They called it Bom Bahia which means "Good Bay." Later in 1662, Charles II of England received the islands as part of a dowry when he wed a Portuguese princess, Catherine of Braganza. He in turn leased it to the British East India Company, who named it Bombay.

The Konkan coast is generous with its offerings of fish and seafood. *Bombil* is the favorite fish of Mumbaiites. It is known as "Bombay duck," but has nothing to do with duck—it is actually a fish known to dart and snatch food like a duck. Fish is the staple of the non-vegetarian. A thick curry of ground coconut, red chilies, fried garlic, and ginger is the base of a fish recipe. *Kala masala,* made with distinctive powdered spices as well as cloves, cardamom, cinnamon, and star anise is a great spice blend that lends its flavors to many Maharashtra specialties.

Roadside vendors are synonymous with Mumbai cuisine. Mumbai's Chowpatty and Juhu beaches are crowded not just with surf and sea lovers but with vendors who hawk *bhelpuri,* a chaotic mix of sweet, sour, and salty dough mixed with puffed rice, onions, and potatoes laced with tamarind juice; *pani puri,* delicate balls of fried dough intensely garnished with raw onions, chickpeas, raw tomatoes, mint sauce, and tamarind chutney; *chakli,* crunchy sticks made from gram flour, onion, and potato fritters (*bhajjis*); and *chevda,* beaten rice deep-fried to a crisp and mixed with almonds, raisins, peanuts, salt, and curry leaves and spiced delicately. You can also nibble on the soft, spongy *dhokla* made with *chana dal* and curds, then fermented and steamed leaving you with a subtle flavor.

The Marathi community in Maharashtra pride themselves on being descendants of Shivaji Bhonsle, a warrior known for his valor and heroism who had been a constant threat to the mighty Mughul empire in AD 1670. Once in a daring exploit, Shivaji escaped from Agra in a basket of sweets. Today in Mumbai and Pune, a city nearby, the Marathis are known for their nutritious healthy vegetarian diet which includes *khichdi* (rice and lentil dish), bean sprouts, rice, roti, sago, and a variety of vegetables often garnished with coconut; while the non-vegetarian food features *kaalvaan*, a fish cooked in a gravy of coconut and red chilies with lashings of garlic. Vegetarian dishes, spicy meat and fish curries, seasonal greens, dal, and rice are favorites here.

Dahi Aloo
Potatoes in Spiced Yogurt

When frying spices, you can substitute a teaspoon of *chana* or *urad dal* for the coconut.

SERVES 4

1 pound potatoes	2 teaspoons ground coriander
1 teaspoon ground turmeric	1 teaspoon ground cumin
2 medium onions	1 teaspoon black peppercorns
¼ cup freshly grated coconut	2 tablespoons oil
4 green chilies	½ teaspoon mustard seeds
3 garlic cloves	Few curry leaves
1-inch piece fresh ginger, peeled	1 tablespoon cilantro leaves
1 teaspoon garlic paste	2 tablespoons plain yogurt, whisked

Peel potatoes and cut into round slices. Boil potatoes with ½ teaspoon of the turmeric and some salt. When potatoes are almost done, drain and cool.

In a blender, blend remaining ½ teaspoon of turmeric, onions, coconut, green chilies, garlic cloves, ginger, garlic paste, coriander, cumin, and peppercorns with 3 tablespoons water to make a paste.

Heat oil in pan and add mustard seeds. When they pop, put in the curry leaves and cilantro leaves. Add spice paste and fry for 10 minutes. Add yogurt and mix. Add ½ cup of water and season with salt if needed. Add potatoes and cook over low heat for 15 minutes or until well done.

Shrikand

Sweet Yogurt

A delicious sweet—simple to make. Served on special days in Maharashtra and loved by young and old alike.

SERVES 4

2 pints plain yogurt
4 teaspoons milk
3 tablespoons sugar

¼ teaspoon ground cardamom
1 tablespoon ground almonds
Few raisins

Place yogurt in a piece of cheesecloth over a bowl or in a colander for 3 hours to drain off the whey.

Put the milk into a bowl and mix with drained yogurt. Add sugar. Blend well with ground cardamom and ground almonds. Garnish with raisins.

Parsi Patra ni Machi

Fish Fillets in Banana Leaves

The Parsis who live in Mumbai and in Gujarat have made a great contribution to the arts, commerce, and cuisine of India. A favorite recipe is *Patra ni Machi*, a fish marinated in coconut and cilantro chutney, wrapped in banana leaves, and steamed.

SERVES 4

4 pounds mackerel fish
3 tablespoons lemon juice
Salt to taste
2 banana leaves or 2 pieces of
    parchment paper
Oil

COCONUT AND CILANTRO CHUTNEY:
4 ounces grated coconut
5 green chilies
5 garlic cloves
1-inch piece fresh ginger
Small bunch of cilantro
6 mint leaves
1 teaspoon ground cumin
½ teaspoon chili powder

Clean the fish and cut into large pieces. Marinate with lemon juice and salt for about 30 minutes.

Grind all the ingredients for the chutney together to form a paste. Coat the fish well with the chutney paste.

Place the 2 banana leaves on counter. Brush them with some oil. Place half of the fish on top of each. Fold sides of leaves in to enclose the fish and tie with thread to secure.

Steam the fish until it is cooked, about 20 minutes.

Transfer fish to plates and open the packets. Serve with sliced cucumber.

Sind Siyala Gosh

Classic Sindhi Lamb Dish

After the Partition, many Sindhis from the province of Sind in Pakistan settled around Gujerat and other cities in India and brought with them their own flavors of Sind cooking. *Siyala* means "layered and slow-cooked" in the Sindhi language. This is a simple dish, but it will be memorable. It has few ingredients but the flavor of the meat is distinguishing.

SERVES 5

1 pound lamb, cut into 1-inch cubes
¾ cup plain yogurt
4 tablespoons oil
3 onions, chopped
1-inch piece fresh ginger, peeled and chopped
6 garlic cloves, chopped

4 green chilies, chopped
2 teaspoons ground coriander
2 teaspoons ground cumin
1 teaspoon red chili powder
4 tomatoes, chopped
Salt to taste
1 teaspoon chopped cilantro

Soak lamb in yogurt mixed with some salt for 30 minutes.

Heat oil in heavy pan and fry onions, ginger, garlic, and green chilies until onions are golden brown.

Add meat and yogurt. Cook until it is a rich brown color. Add ground coriander, ground cumin, and chili powder, and cook for a few minutes.

Add tomatoes, 4 cups water, and salt to taste. Simmer for 30 minutes until lamb is tender. Garnish with chopped cilantro.

Sai Bhaji

Spinach and Seasoned Lentils

This dish is usually served with yogurt, *papad* (lentil wafers), and *khichadi* (rice dish).

SERVES 2

Oil
½ teaspoon cumin seeds
2 garlic cloves, minced
½ teaspoon ground turmeric
½ teaspoon red chili powder
1 small piece fresh ginger, minced
1 small potato, grated

2 carrots, grated
1 small onion, grated
2 tomatoes, minced
10 ounces spinach, chopped
¼ cup *chana dal* (yellow split peas)
Salt to taste

Heat a small amount of oil in a wok. Add cumin seeds and when they pop, add garlic. Cook for a minute or two. Add turmeric, red chili powder, and ginger and stir.

Add potato, carrots, onion, tomatoes, spinach, and dal and 2 cups water. Cook on low heat until dal becomes soft, about 20 minutes. Add salt and serve hot.

Besan Curry

.... Chickpea Flour Curry ....

The many ingredients make this dish rich and flavorful. This dish is ideal for serving vegetarians and can be served with rice or even as soup.

SERVES 6

4 tablespoons oil
1 teaspoon fenugreek seeds
1 teaspoon cumin seeds
2 teaspoons chopped fresh ginger
4 green chilies, chopped, plus 2 whole green chilies
10 curry leaves
½ teaspoon asafetida
⅓ cup *besan* (chickpea flour) or whole-wheat flour
1 teaspoon black peppercorns
1 teaspoon turmeric powder
12 thin green beans

3 medium potatoes, diced
12 okras, chopped into small pieces
1 small carrot, cut into thin strips
4 small eggplants, diced
3 small yams, cubed
Salt to taste
1 teaspoon sugar
1 teaspoon tamarind paste
8 mint leaves, minced
1 tablespoon chopped cilantro leaves

Heat 3 tablespoons of oil and add fenugreek seeds followed by cumin seeds. After 30 seconds add ginger, the chopped green chilies, and curry leaves and fry for 1 minute; add asafetida, *besan*, and peppercorns and stir for 5 minutes until a paste forms.

Add turmeric and remaining tablespoon oil; sauté for 3 minutes. Add 8 cups of hot water and stir and simmer for 10 minutes until paste dissolves.

Add 2 whole green chilies, all the vegetables, some salt, sugar, and tamarind paste. Boil until vegetables are cooked. Add mint and cilantro leaves and cook until curry thickens.

Suji Jo Seero
Semolina Sweet Dish

A Sindhi sweet dish eaten year round this is light and fluffy and easy to make for unexpected guests.

SERVES 3

1 cup ghee
1¼ cups semolina (*rava*), sifted
3 tablespoons wheat flour
2 cups sugar

8 to 10 green cardamom pods, ground
10 to 12 strands saffron
10 almonds, sliced, for garnish

Heat the ghee and fry the semolina and wheat flour over a very low flame until the semolina is aromatic and a shade darker than golden brown.

Dissolve the sugar, ground cardamoms, and saffron in 4 cups of warm water; add this syrup to the semolina and cook over a low flame, stirring continuously until the semolina dries up.

Place mixture on a pre-heated *tawa* (*griddle*) and let it simmer for 5 to 7 minutes. Serve hot, garnished with chopped almonds.

Goa

Before the arrival of the Portuguese, the first European power in India, in 1510 AD, Hindu and Muslim kings reigned in the rich and fertile land of Goa crisscrossed with canals, streams, and rivers. Four hundred and fifty years of Portuguese rule left this palm-fringed coastline of western India with a fascinating legacy of churches, basilicas, Indo-Portuguese architecture, music, vinegar, and red chilies.

Fueled by the memorable food stories of Goa told by my cherished Goan friend Denis Lobo, who lives in Mumbai but still has family connections in Goa, I traveled there with my husband. To my delight I discovered that Goan food is a unique cuisine celebrating saints days, weddings, carnivals, and food itself. At least 177 varieties of fresh and saltwater fish can be found in the waters of Goa! One Goan acquaintance insisted he had personally read these statistics in the *Gazetteer* of Goa. There is even a poem he said, where Yama the God of Death arrives and the poet cries out pleading:

"Do not make it my turn today
There's fish curry for dinner."

I still remember a meal made from *xacutti* lamb marinated in a green spice paste of green chilies, cilantro, and ginger, and cooked with coconut, spices, onions, and tomatoes. Then came the roe of the kingfish which was salted and fried, a harbinger of good things to come. The *pao*, small square-shaped bread made from rice flour and molasses, was leavened with toddy and glazed with egg yolks before baking. It was baked to form four sections so that when it was taken out of the oven it could be broken apart.

Pork is very popular among Goan Christians. One reason I am told is that there is very little pasture land for sheep or goats, and since the pig is very resourceful when it comes to foraging for food, pig livestock is encouraged. And thus appeared the pork dish *sorpotel*. They say in Goa that this dish should be eaten several days after it is made to enjoy the intense flavors. This amazing dish often has pork meat, liver, heart, and even a dash of pig's blood added to kick it up a notch! Other spices like tamarind, turmeric, cumin, ginger, cardamom, chilies, peppercorns, cloves, and vinegar are added. Goan sausages pickled in red chilies and vinegar are as everyone confesses a "died-and-gone-to-heaven good." I concur.

And then there is the fiery taste of the *vindaloo,* cooked with diverse spices and lashings of vinegar. *Vindaloo* took its name from a Portuguese dish. When the Portuguese first arrived in 1510 and landed on Goan shores they brought meat cooked in wine and garlic called *vinho de alho.* The popularity of *vindaloo* is so widespread in England that it inspired a football song in 1998 called "Vindaloo."

I found the local spirit *feni,* or *sol kadhi,* a cold coconut drink laced with dried mango rind, at every celebration where there is much feasting and drinking. The *feni* comes from the juice of the cashew apple which is fermented in vats and then distilled and it is quite potent. It is imbibed with much gusto, and we did not hesitate to follow this local custom.

Goan Hindus maintain a vegetarian diet with a lot of vegetables and fruits. All Goans use coconut milk generously in their dishes. An interesting fable was told to me about the bountiful coconut tree. In this Biblical story Joseph and Mary traveled through the harsh land and became exhausted. One night they stayed for shelter under a banana tree, but the tree refused to protect them from the rigors of the cold night. They walked around wearily until they found a coconut tree and asked for shelter. The coconut tree immediately spread its enveloping fronds over them. Mary showered blessings on this tree and said every part of the tree would be useful to mankind. So that is why the leaves of the coconut tree are used to thatch homes, the thick woody stems to make brooms, the trunk is used as timber, and the fruit is partaken throughout the year. The banana tree was punished by dying every time it bore fruit.

Goans are renowned for fancy and elaborate puddings, cakes, and desserts. And as for the luscious *bebinca*, a rich cake that is made of sixteen layers (one layer at a time), there are no words to describe that distinctive dessert made with egg yolk, coconut milk, and flour. I ate forkful after forkful of the *bebinca* in Salcette on a drowsy afternoon under the somnolent sun on an *abalcao* (balcony) with the mandatory stone seats of a house that had a mix of Spanish and Portuguese architecture, surrounded by bougainvillea, mango, jackfruit, papaya, chickoo trees, and listening to the birds as a kingfisher flashed by. On another twilight drenched evening sailing down the Mandvi river, serenaded by Goan balladeers, I was offered the luscious *dodol*, a black cake made with jaggery, rice flour, and coconut cream, and the *leitria*, a sweet made of egg yolks, tender coconut, and sugar syrup. And if I wanted to nostalgically remember the Indo-European connection, I had merely to sample a pastry decorated with mango strips dipped in melted sugar.

When reluctantly leaving this blessed plot of land I was gifted prawn *balachao*, prawns in a bottle steeped in vinegar and chunks of onion to give them a sweet and sour flavor, and a tape of Remo Fernandez's Goan songs to bliss me out. I fell so much in love with Goa that when I left I carried with me a large red stone from the Goan earth and kept it at the threshold of my home until I left for America.

Pork Vindaloo

This is a Portuguese-based dish since Goa had been colonized briefly by the Portuguese after they arrived in AD 1500. The word *vindaloo* comes from the Portuguese *vin* for vinegar and *alho* for garlic. You can substitute lamb or beef for the pork, but you must marinate for 3 hours or more. For best results, cook the *vindaloo* and serve after reheating the next day. De-seed the chilies if you prefer it less spicy.

SERVES 4 TO 5

8 whole dried red chilies
1 teaspoon cumin seeds
6 cloves
2-inch piece cinnamon stick
10 peppercorns
1 teaspoon poppy seeds
1-inch piece fresh ginger
6 garlic cloves
1 tablespoon tamarind paste

4 teaspoons cider vinegar
2-pound leg of pork, cut into small cubes
⅓ cup oil
3 medium onions, chopped
Salt to taste
10 curry leaves
½ teaspoon jaggery

Soak chilies in a little water for 10 minutes.

Grind cumin seeds, cloves, cinnamon stick, peppercorns, poppy seeds, ginger, and garlic with tamarind paste and vinegar to make a paste.

Rub a little paste on the pork and marinate for 15 minutes.

Heat oil in a pot and fry onions and chilies until brown. Add remaining spice paste and fry for 5 minutes, adding a little water if necessary.

Add pork and sauté for a few minutes. Add 2 cups water and salt. Cook over low heat until pork is tender, about 20 minutes.

Stir in curry leaves and jaggery. Simmer for 5 minutes.

Kenkda Curry
Crab Curry

This recipe can also be used for fish or prawns. Scrub the shells of the crabs thoroughly and snip off any serrated edges on the shells.

SERVES 4

4 pounds crabs	1 teaspoon poppy seeds, crushed
10 red chilies, seeds removed	1 teaspoon ground coriander
6 green chilies	1 teaspoon cumin seeds
2 onions, minced	1 teaspoon tamarind paste
½ teaspoon ground turmeric	8 tablespoons oil
6 garlic cloves	1 can (12 ounces) coconut milk
1-inch piece fresh ginger	Salt

Wash the crabs and cut into pieces. Remove the sac attached to the shells and the claws. Remove brown meat from the top of the crabs and wash the shells; set all aside.

Grind chilies, onions, turmeric, garlic, ginger, poppy seeds, coriander, and cumin seeds to make a paste. Add tamarind paste.

Heat oil in pan and add spice paste. Cook over low heat for 15 minutes.

Add coconut milk and simmer for a few minutes. Add crab claws and main shell and some salt and simmer for 15 minutes. Add brown meat and heat thoroughly.

Goan Beef Curry

Essential flavors, hearty, hot, spicy and delicious. You can either add potatoes, or serve with rice to make a complete meal.

SERVES 4

9 cardamom pods
1 teaspoon fennel seeds
7 cloves
3-inch piece cinnamon stick
½ teaspoon black peppercorns
3 teaspoons coriander seeds
3 teaspoons cumin seeds
¼ cup oil

3 onions, minced
1 teaspoon garlic paste
2 teaspoons ginger paste
½ teaspoon ground turmeric
2 teaspoons red chili powder
2 pounds beef, cubed
1¼ cups coconut milk
Salt to taste

Remove cardamom seeds from pods and fry in a little oil along with fennel seeds, cloves, cinnamon stick, peppercorns, coriander seeds, and cumin seeds for a few minutes until roasted. Grind well.

In a separate pan, heat the ¼ cup oil and fry onions, garlic paste, ginger paste, turmeric, and chili powder until slightly brown. Add beef and fry until brown. Add roasted spices and fry for 1 minute.

Add coconut milk and bring to a boil. Cover, reduce heat, and simmer for 1 hour. Add a small amount of boiling water if too much liquid evaporates to make a thick sauce. Season with salt.

Tamil Nadu

It is easy to label South Indian food as a rice, vegetable, and lentils menu. And yet each rice and lentil or vegetable dish in the four main states is made differently. A unique mix of ingredients lures with varied flavors but there is a cohesion that reflects the distinctive South Indian flavor. Culture, identity, and traditions demarcate the states of Tamil Nadu, Andhra Pradesh, Kerala, and Karnataka. The borders have merged, separated, and extended under different ruling powers, but the popularity of South Indian food is rooted in centuries of history. I begin my culinary journey in the south in Tamil Nadu.

Tamil Nadu, the land of the Tamils, has a rich tradition of culture, literature, mythology, arts, and cuisine. The official language of Tamil has been in use in literature for the past two thousand years. Vegetarian food dominates in Tamil Nadu as it is firmly believed that this kind of food has a balance of nourishment, proteins, fats, fiber, and carbohydrates. Every festival is associated with a particular dish. The basics are rice, lentils, and vegetables, with lots of sour dishes that offset the hot chilies, curry leaves, coriander, mustard seeds, and asafetida creating the typical subtle finesse of a South Indian flavor wherever you go.

One of the most interesting meals I have eaten in the capital city of Tamil Nadu, Chennai, was in Dakshinachitra, a resource center for architecture, crafts, and folk and performing arts of all four southern states. A project of the Madras Craft Foundation, Dakshinachitra is thirty kilometers from Chennai and retains the traditions and culture of the four states by constructing residences linked to the environment of an 18th-century period. Traditional houses of various communities in South India have been transported brick by brick and reconstructed at this site. I walked through a merchant's house of the Nattukottai Chettiar community where the front and central portion of the house was originally a Tamil silk weaver's house of the 19th century, a Muslim house in Kozhikode, or a craftsman's house from Sringeri. The emphasis is to make people realize how our ancestors lived, and eating a delicious vegetarian meal of rice, dals, and fresh vegetables among swaying palms while watching a potter use his hands sinuously around clay was a symbiotic experience.

Tamilians are a rice-eating people. Rice was cultivated three thousand years ago and is still the staple food of most South Indians. Travel across Tamil Nadu and you will always see lush paddy fields. A baby's first solid meal is a small ball of cooked rice and ghee. A special ceremony marks this event with friends and relatives invited for the occasion. Rice symbolizes purity and fertility in wedding ceremonies and *pujas*. Rice is used in all meals of the day, starting with *idlis* (steamed rice cakes) and *dosas* (pancakes made from rice batter) in the morning, rice in the afternoon accompanied by lentils, *tiffin* (early evening snack), and rice at night with an assortment of vegetable or meat dishes.

Since Tamil Nadu is on the coast, fish is plentiful and non-vegetarians relish the fresh catch every day. Despite mechanized boats, fishermen still set out on the Coromandel Coast into the Bay of Bengal at dawn in their *kattamarams* (tied logs) for their daily catch ranging from catfish, ray, white bait, silver belly, perch, mullet, and grouper to prawn, pomfret, mackerel, and shark. In the summertime my mother would rouse me at dawn and we would walk briskly through the deserted, silent streets to the seashore to watch the sun rise and see the fishermen setting out to sea in the frail catamarans. It was a thrilling sight to see the fishermen clad in just loincloths on a piece of wood take on the mighty ocean with pure faith in their fishing skills. Only when the fish baskets are full in the late evening does the craft return to shore. Many an evening we returned to the beach to see the fish auctioned off by the wives of the fishermen. The last auction of the day is a special one, when it is most generous and the extra money goes towards community festivals and rituals. The remaining baskets that were unsold were quickly hoisted on the heads of the women, and off they went running across the sand, on the roads to the nearby markets where customers were eagerly waiting. Meanwhile each weary fisherman took a handful of fish from his basket to take home. In later years, when visiting the fish markets of Mumbai, I was to see the hardworking Koli fisherwomen in brightly colored sarees worn like tight trousers with elaborate ornaments worn on their ears, neck, and nose and neatly combed hairstyles sit with their baskets of fish and haggle with their customers with wit and aggressive selling.

South Indians insist the best vegetarian food is cooked in Tamil Nadu. Tamarind is used in South Indian dishes for its distinctive tartness; while pepper, chilies, garlic, and ginger make the food hot. Spices like cumin and mustard seeds are used for seasoning.

A South Indian vegetarian meal consists of rice, *sambar* (lentil soup), two or three vegetables cooked with grated coconut, yogurt, *rasam* (a hot soup made from tamarind juice and pepper), crisp *papads* or *appalams* (lentil wafers), mango or lime pickles, buttermilk, and a sweet dish.

The *dosa* and *idli* are icons of South Indian food. A *dosa* is a large pancake made of fermented ground rice and lentils. There are ninety kinds of *dosas*, Tamilians assure me. And the number is still growing. They are often a breakfast specialty but can be eaten during any part of the day. My favorite is the special golden *masala dosa* that can be six feet in length, perfectly crisp, and stuffed with a delicious filling of potatoes and spices. The *paper dosa* is true to its name, as thin a paper; and the *butter dosa* is saturated with butter and filled with several spices. *Pessarettu* (batter made with lentils) *rava dosa* is made with semolina, *addai* is made with several lentils, rice, red chilies, and ginger, and then there is *utthapam,* another type of *dosa* that uses minced vegetables in the batter giving it a piquant taste.

Idlis are steamed rice cakes low in calories, highly nutritious, made of fermented batter, rice, and lentils, that are dipped in *sambar* or various chutneys. A particular favorite accompaniment for *idlis* is *mulaga podi*, a powdered mix of several dried lentils and chili powder eaten with generous helpings of oil or melted ghee. *Idlis* and *dosas* make a hearty breakfast after which you are ready to take on the day.

The traditional brothy *sambar,* a lentil and tamarind curry (varying from state to state) is usually cooked with a vegetable. Eggplant, carrots, beans, cauliflower, squash, and spinach can be added to the cooked dal. The *sambar* is then tempered: With a little oil heated in a small pan, fenugreek seeds, mustard seeds, cumin seeds, and red peppers are added until they sizzle; the mixture is then poured into the vessel with the dal, and the lid is firmly closed.

Rasam, a thin, peppery tamarind and lentil soup eaten with rice twice a day, is said to be responsible for the mathematical prodigies in the South. *Sambar* and *rasam* are mandatory dishes cooked every day in South Indian households.

Vadas are like doughnuts with a hole in the center and are made of black *urad dal*, crispy on the outside and soft and spongy on the inside. They can be made with chickpea flour, chilies, and onions, and fried—perfect for snacks. Order some of these items and you can enjoy a leisurely feast.

Sabzi Chaval
Vegetable Rice

Of all the varieties of rice, basmati (queen of fragrance) is sold around the world. The grains are long and white, and the unique aroma sets it apart from other rice. If you want some crunch to this dish, put in the raw vegetables just before the rice is fully cooked. Otherwise, cook the vegetables before adding to the rice.

SERVES 4

2 cups basmati rice
4 medium tomatoes
5 black peppercorns
2 tablespoons ginger paste
2 tablespoons garlic paste
3 tablespoons ghee
2-inch piece cinnamon stick
6 whole cloves

2 cardamom pods
½ teaspoon ground turmeric
1 teaspoon salt
2 cups vegetables (peas, carrots, cauliflower, beans, corn, zucchini, peppers), cubed if large
Lime juice
Mint leaves or cilantro for garnish

Wash and drain rice twice until water runs clear.

In a pan combine 2 cups of water, tomatoes, peppercorns, ginger paste, and garlic paste and bring to a boil. Boil for 10 minutes. Reduce heat and simmer for 5 minutes. Remove from heat and mash mixture.

Heat ghee in a heavy-bottomed pan and fry cinnamon stick, cloves, and cardamom pods for a few seconds. Add rice and stir-fry for 2 minutes. Pour in tomato mixture and add turmeric and salt. Bring to a boil. Reduce heat and simmer until rice is tender.

If you want crisp vegetables, just before the rice is fully cooked, stir in vegetables and allow to steam for a few minutes. If you want softer vegetables, in a separate pot steam the vegetables to desired doneness and then add to the rice when it is finished cooking.

Squeeze in a little lime juice and garnish with mint leaves or cilantro before serving.

Idlis

.... Fluffy Steamed Cakes ....

Idlis are a South Indian specialty that has become popular all over India. To make them, you need to have a special *idli* steamer which is sold in Indian stores. It is a deep stainless steel vessel with five or four layered molds.

Kanchipuram was an academic center and a religious destination in Tamil Nadu. Centuries ago when scholars from this city traveled to other centers of pilgrimage, they would take with them *idlis* because they lasted for weeks without spoiling and losing taste or flavor. The *idlis* made of fermented rice batter in this recipe are easy to make and must be served hot.

MAKES 20

⅓ cup *chana dal*

1-inch piece fresh ginger, peeled and minced

1 cup plain yogurt

2 tablespoons oil

½ teaspoon mustard seeds

10 curry leaves

1 green chili, minced

2½ cups semolina

½ cup grated coconut

¼ teaspoon baking soda

2 teaspoons salt

In a deep bowl, soak dal in water for at least 5 hours. Overnight soaking will give best results.

Drain dal and blend with ginger, yogurt, and 2 cups water until it makes a paste.

Heat oil in pan and fry mustard seeds, curry leaves, and chili for one minute. Add semolina and coconut and fry until the semolina becomes brown.

Mix together the dal paste and the semolina mixture and stir in baking soda and salt. Let sit for 1 hour.

Gradually add up to 2½ cups of water to the mixture until you have a thick batter.

Pour some of the batter into greased *idli* steamer molds three-quarters full. Close lid of steamer and steam over simmering water for 10 minutes until the *idlis* are puffed and soft. Repeat with rest of batter.

Murukus

Crispy Snack

You can make these crispy spiral snacks with rice, corn flour, or *chana* flour, but you do need a special *muruku* press, a small press with a nozzle. My friend Prema, a cook of great skill and imagination, has three kinds of *muruku* presses that she has carried through Europe, Canada, and the U.S. for the past 45 years as she traveled with her husband, Rajkumar. But you can make the *murukus* by hand if you are adept in rolling them into tubular form, then rolling into circles making two circles next to each other and pressing the ends into the circle to make it secure.

MAKES 10 TO 12

¼ cup *urad dal* (black gram)
2 cups rice flour
½ teaspoon crushed cumin seeds
½ tablespoon sesame seeds
1 teaspoon red chili powder
1 tablespoon lemon juice

¼ teaspoon asafetida
½ teaspoon salt
¼ cup butter
2 tablespoons oil, plus more for deep frying

Fry the dal to a light brown color. Cool and grind to a fine powder.

Sieve rice flour and dal flour together to remove impurities and mix thoroughly.

Add cumin seeds, sesame seeds, chili powder, and lemon juice. Dissolve asafetida and salt in ¼ cup water and mix with flours.

Make a dough with the flour by rubbing in butter and 2 tablespoons oil and knead well.

Using the press make round spiraled circles. Fry dough circles in hot oil until golden brown. Do not turn them over as they will break. Remove and drain on paper towels. Allow to cool and store *murukus* in an airtight container to keep crispness.

Dosas ~ *Rice Pancakes*

South India is the home of the *dosa*—the preparation of which is a little time consuming, but they can be eaten with pleasure any time of the day or night. *Dosas* can be made from rice flour, wheat flour, cream of wheat, or maize flour and can be made plain or spiced or with various fillings. They store well and can be used days later if well preserved in a refrigerator. A flat, heavy-bottomed griddle called a *karahi* or a *tawa* are ideal for cooking them.

Wipe the surface of the griddle with a cut onion to prevent sticking of the batter. If you have no time to deal with the batter preparation you can buy a ready-made packet of the batter in Indian grocery stores. *Dosas* can be served with *sambar*, chutneys, vegetable curries, or stuffed with mashed potatoes and roasted spices. Note that the first two *dosa* in your batch may come out scorched or crumble—but don't worry, the next *dosa* will be perfect.

Sada Dosa
.... Plain Dosa ....

Instead of rice you can also use rice flour in this recipe. These *dosas* can be served accompanied by *sambar*, lentil curry, or a chutney. Remember—making *dosas* requires patience.

SERVES 4

1 cup *urad dal* (black gram or
   lentils)
2 cups rice

1 teaspoon salt
½ cup vegetable oil

Soak the *urad dal* and rice separately in lots of water for 6 hours. Drain the water and put the dal in a blender with ½ cup of water. Blend to a smooth paste. Remove. In the same blender, grind the rice with ½ cup of water to make a coarse paste. Add rice paste to dal paste and mix thoroughly. Set the batter aside and allow to ferment overnight. The room temperature should be warm, otherwise the batter will not ferment. The batter will have risen in the morning.

Add salt to the batter and mix well. Add enough water until it has a thick consistency.

Put a large non-stick or iron skillet on the stove. Heat the pan with a teaspoon of oil. Rub the cut side of an onion on the skillet. (This prevents batter from sticking to the surface.) Add a thin coating of oil. Pour a ladle of batter in the center of the pan and slowly use the ladle to make a large thin circle of the batter moving outward to the edges of the pan in a circular motion. Cover the pan and cook the *dosa* for 2 minutes on low heat. Open the lid, the edges should be slightly brown. Increase the heat and drizzle a teaspoon of oil around the edges. Fry for 20 seconds and then carefully ease the *dosa* out of the pan. Repeat with remaining batter.

Masala Dosa

Dosa with Spicy Stuffing

Anuradha Ganpati, my younger daughter, having lived many years in India when growing up, has her favorite iconic South Indian vegetarian foods. "The diverse flavors and textures are so refreshing," she says. "A vegetable can be the main entrée, an appetizer, or a part of a classic dish and each one inherits its own flair for seasonings and a delicacy of taste"—her ode to vegetarian cooking. This is a richer and more flavorful *dosa* that does not need any accompaniment like a chutney. Make the *dosa* in previous recipe. Then make this filling.

SERVES 4

4 tablespoons oil	½ onion, finely chopped
1 teaspoon mustard seeds	¼ cup green peas
1 teaspoon *urad dal*	¼ teaspoon ground turmeric
2 green chilies, chopped	Salt
1 sprig curry leaves	2½ cups boiled, mashed potatoes
½ teaspoon ground ginger	*Dosa* batter (page 148)

Heat oil in a griddle and season with mustard seeds, *urad dal*, green chilies, curry leaves, and ginger.

Add onions and fry for 5 minutes. Add green peas, turmeric, and salt. Cook until peas are tender. Add mashed potatoes and stir. Cook until well heated.

Prepare *dosas* as directed in recipe. Spoon about 3 tablespoons of filling onto each *dosa* and fold over to eat.

Coconut Chutney

The ebullient couple Prakash and Sudha have entertained us with euphoric coffee and a palette of enticing South Indian dishes for a long while. It's all about celebrating the possibilities of a simple dish. This is a delicious perfect blend, eaten with *idli* or *dosa*.

SERVES 4

1 teaspoon *chana dal*
1 teaspoon *urad dal*
1½ cups grated coconut
2 green chilies, minced
½ teaspoon salt

1 tablespoon oil
1 teaspoon black mustard seeds
5 curry leaves
1 teaspoon tamarind paste

Soak dals in cold water for 3 hours and drain.

Blend in a blender the grated coconut, chilies, and salt.

Heat oil in pan and add mustard seeds and dals. When the mustard seeds pops, add curry leaves and fry until dal browns.

Add dal mixture to coconut mixture and add tamarind paste and mix well. Store in a glass dish covered tightly.

Avial

········ Vegetarian Medley ········

A dish with mixed vegetables, coconut, and spices that accompanies plain rice very well. All vegetables must be sliced very thin. Easy to prepare and healthy, too!

SERVES 6

2 tablespoons oil
1 teaspoon fenugreek seeds
1 teaspoon mustard seeds
½ teaspoon cumin seeds
2 onions, thinly sliced
4 green chilies, minced
6 curry leaves
½ teaspoon ground turmeric
4 small whole dry red chilies
1 teaspoon ground coriander
1 carrot, cut into thin sticks
8 green beans, thinly sliced

2 potatoes, peeled and cut into thin sticks
2 green bell peppers, cut into thin strips
½ head cauliflower, cut into small pieces
Salt to taste
1 cup plain yogurt
½ cup grated coconut
1 pinch asafetida
1 teaspoon chopped cilantro

Heat deep pan over high heat. Add oil. When oil is hot, add fenugreek seeds, mustard seeds, cumin seeds. When it splutters add onions, chilies, and curry leaves. Cook stirring until onions are crisp.

Add turmeric, whole red chilies, and coriander and sauté for 5 minutes. Add all vegetables and stir-fry over high heat for a few minutes. Add salt to taste.

Blend yogurt with coconut and add to vegetables. Cover and cook for 20 minutes until vegetables are cooked. Add asafetida. Garnish with cilantro.

Manga Paruppu

Mango Lentils

The mango has been mentioned in writings as far back as 1000 BC and its virtues have been praised for thousands of years. Mango blossoms are considered sacred and are said to be the arrows of Manmatha, the Indian God of Love (Cupid). Many groves in India have mango trees well over a hundred years old.

SERVES 4

2 cups *tur dal*
2 tablespoons cooking oil
1 teaspoon mustard seeds
1 pinch asafetida
1 tablespoon *urad dal*
1 tablespoon *chana dal*
5 curry leaves
3 green chilies, minced

2-inch piece fresh ginger, peeled and minced
1 medium raw green mango, peeled and cut into small cubes
Salt to taste
1 teaspoon ground turmeric
1 teaspoon red chili powder
A few cilantro leaves

Cook *tur dal* in water to cover until tender. Drain and mash well.

Heat oil and temper with mustard seeds and asafetida for a few seconds. Add *urad dal* and *chana dal* and cook for 2 minutes. Add curry leaves, green chilies, ginger, and mango. Sauté over medium heat for 5 minutes.

Add some salt, the turmeric, and chili powder. Pour in mashed *tur dal*. Add enough water to make the sauce the consistency of a gravy. Garnish with cilantro. Serve with rice.

Baingan Sambar
Eggplant Sambar

Sambar is an everyday South Indian staple made with lentils. It has a distinctive taste and texture, and can be made colorful by using varied vegetables. Cauliflower, broccoli, beans, beetroot, and carrots are some of the flavorful and colorful vegetables found in *sambars*. It is interesting to note that all the six primary tastes identified in the Ayurvedic tradition—sweet, sour, salty, pungent, bitter, and astringent—are balanced in this dish. This is used as a side dish to *idli* and *dosa* too, as well as a curry for rice.

SERVES 4

3 cups *tur dal*, boiled until tender
½ cup cubed eggplant
2 teaspoons grated coconut
1 tablespoon *sambar* powder
2 teaspoons ground coriander
Pinch of ground black pepper
2 tomatoes, crushed

1½ tablespoons oil
½ teaspoon mustard seeds
10 curry leaves
¼ cup chopped onion
½ teaspoon ground turmeric
1 teaspoon tamarind paste

In a heavy-bottomed pan, place 3 cups of water, the boiled dal, and eggplant. Add coconut, *sambar* powder, coriander, pepper, and crushed tomatoes. Stir to mix. Bring the mixture to a boil and simmer for 10 minutes. Remove from heat.

In a small pan, heat the oil and add the mustard seeds. When it begins to sputter, toss in curry leaves. Stir in onion, turmeric, and tamarind paste. When the onion turns brown remove from heat and pour the mixture over the *sambar*. Stir gently.

Vermicelli Uppuma
Delicate Rice Noodles

My fascinating 100-year-old Aunt Beulah Souri in Olympia, Washington, still makes this dish with joy. Once when I was leaving for Los Angeles on an early morning flight, she quickly rustled up the delicate, feathery *uppuma* studded with curry leaves and coriander for my journey home.

SERVES 4

4 tablespoons vegetable oil
2 cups rice vermicelli, broken into
    1-inch pieces
¼ teaspoon mustard seeds
¼ teaspoon *urad dal*
2 onions, chopped
5 green chilies, finely chopped
1 teaspoon ground ginger

6 curry leaves
8 cashews, chopped
3 or 4 cauliflower florets, chopped
1 cup peas
2 teaspoons lemon juice
½ teaspoon ground turmeric
2 teaspoons chopped cilantro
Salt to taste

In a deep pan, heat 1 tablespoon oil and rice vermicelli and roast until golden brown. Remove from pan and set aside.

Add remaining 3 tablespoons oil to pan and when it is hot add mustard seeds. When they pop add *urad dal*, followed by onions, green chilies, ginger, curry leaves, and cashews. Stir-fry for 5 minutes. Add cauliflower and peas and stir-fry for a few minutes.

Add 4 cups of water and some salt and bring to a boil. Add vermicelli, stirring continuously. Add lemon juice, ground turmeric, and cilantro. Cook over a low flame until water is absorbed, about 8 minutes. Add salt to taste.

Adhrak Nimbu Rasam
Ginger Lemon Soup

This *rasam* is low in carbohydrates and high in proteins. This is a very nutritious and comforting soup when you are suffering from a cold. *Rasam* is also offered as a digestive after a meal.

SERVES 4

¾ cup *tur dal*
1 tablespoon oil
½ teaspoon mustard seeds
½ teaspoon cumin seeds
1 pinch asafetida
5 to 6 curry leaves
1 dry red chili, broken into 3 pieces
1 tablespoon minced fresh ginger

1 teaspoon ground turmeric
¼ cup diced tomatoes (fresh or canned)
Salt to taste
1 teaspoon *sambar* powder
Juice of 1 lemon
1 teaspoon chopped cilantro

Soak *tur dal* for 15 minutes. Rinse and cook on stove or in pressure cooker until tender.

Heat 1 tablespoon oil in deep pan. Add mustard seeds, cumin seeds, asafetida, curry leaves, and dry red chili pieces and stir. Add ginger and turmeric and stir. Add diced tomatoes and salt to taste.

Stir in *sambar* powder and cooked *tur dal*. Add 3 cups of water and bring to a boil. Simmer 5 minutes. Remove from heat and add lemon juice. Garnish with cilantro. Serve hot as a soup or with rice.

Payasam

Rich and Creamy Pudding

I met Professor David Gere at a South Indian wedding in Los Angeles. He has lived often in South India working on Aids projects and we found ourselves talking about *payasam*. His eyes lit up and he was in such a state of euphoria just thinking about it, I had to include the dish in this cookbook. This is the last item after *rasam* is served in a South Indian meal and there are hundreds of varieties of *payasam*, including jackfruit pulp, and adding ginger, jeera, bananas, rose water, rice, and wheat to this auspicious sweet dish.

SERVES 4

½ cup sago
3 tablespoons ghee
⅔ cup sliced almonds
½ cup raisins
¼ cup chopped cashews
¼ cup *seviyan* (very fine rice vermicelli), broken into 1-inch pieces

4 cups milk
1 cup light brown sugar
1 teaspoon ground cardamom
¼ teaspoon ground cloves
2 tablespoons coconut powder

Cook sago thoroughly in 4 cups water for 25 minutes. Drain twice.

Heat ghee over low heat and brown nuts and raisins. Remove.

In same pan, fry *seviyan* till light brown. Add most of the milk and simmer, while stirring. Add sago. Add sugar and more milk as payasam thickens. Add cardamom and cloves, and stir in most of the nuts and raisins. Garnish with coconut powder and remaining nuts and raisins. Serve hot, warm, or cold.

The Coffee Ceremony

While tea, or *chai,* is consumed in the North, South Indians travel everywhere with a coffee filter. A legend tells us that Baba Budan, a holy Muslim man from India, went on a pilgrimage to Mecca in the 16th century. There he discovered the wondrous aromatic brew and smuggled seven coffee beans wrapped around his belly out of the Yemen port. Returning to the Mysore State known as Karnataka, he settled on the gentle slopes of the Chandrgiri Hills and planted coffee. The hill range is now named after him as the Baba Budan Hills. Planting began around 1820. The British East India Company was the first to begin cultivating coffee for commercial purposes and India is today one of the world's largest coffee producers. South India is one of the major coffee-producing areas and the coffee beans are grown on the hills of Malabar in Kerala, in Chikmagalur in Karnataka, and in the blue mountain valleys of Niligiris in Tamil Nadu.

India Coffee Houses became a popular rendezvous for journalists and intellectuals like the coffee houses in Europe. The first India Coffee House opened on Churchgate Street in Bombay in 1936. Down South, the Madras Filter Coffee became an institution. Making filter coffee in South India is a ritual. All vessels must be thoroughly washed in hot water and then dried. A good brand of coffee powder is then placed in a filter vessel found in every South Indian household. You can buy it from any South Indian grocery store. It is a metal cup with a bottom that is porous. This fits neatly into another regular cup. Fresh coffee grounds are pressed into the bottom of the porous upper cup. Boiling water is poured into this cup so that the brewed coffee drips into the cup at the bottom. This is the *decoction*—a rich, thick syrupy brew. After being allowed to set for seven to ten minutes, freshly boiled milk and sugar are added for taste. A delicious, frothy, golden brown, creamy liquid with an exhilarating aroma is ready. Serving the coffee is a skilled art. A small stainless steel or brass vessel with a wide brim and a tumbler are used. Some of the coffee is placed in the wide vessel with lipped walls and gently spun around for cooling. The tumbler holds the rest of the scalding coffee. The tumbler is held high above the wide vessel, and the coffee is poured in one single stream into the waiting vessel. This vessel is lifted into the air, and the coffee is poured into the waiting tumbler held in the hand. The coffee thus gets aerated resulting in the perfect blend of coffee, milk, and sugar. The alternate pouring continues until the coffee is the right temperature. It should then be served immediately.

I often heard coffee being called *"degree coffee"* in India. I presumed that the coffee was of a pure quality, a high degree of purity perhaps. Years later I discovered that chicory beans were sometimes used to make coffee, and the South Indian pronunciation of chicory became *"chigory,"* and then mutated into *digory,* resulting in *degree.*

Chettinad

The Chettiars of Chettinad in the southern part of Tamil Nadu soon realized that their infertile region offered no opportunities, so in the nineteenth century, the adventurous Chettiar community migrated to Sri Lanka, Vietnam, Indonesia, Burma (Myanmar), Malaysia, and Singapore where their business skills brought them success throughout Southeast Asia. Many returned to India with their new money and invested in property and gold, building palatial homes that retained the splendid architecture of the past with intricate wood pillars and extensive courtyards. But they also brought back new cooking styles that they incorporated into their own methods of cooking. Chettinad cuisine is known for its repertoire of spicy hot fish, chicken, liver, brain, and meat curries suffused with generous amounts of peppercorns, cinnamon, bay leaves, cardamom, and green and red chilies.

On wet monsoon days my father would give the servant a big black umbrella and a huge tiffin carrier and ask her to run across to the Chettinad restaurant to bring home the spicy fare, a surefire remedy against any colds. In the deep southern region of Tamil Nadu there are hotels known as "military hotels." These "military," or non-vegetarian, hotels offer Chettiar specialities. Why "military?" Non-vegetarian food was supposedly filled with nutrients that would make the sinews of a warrior or soldier stronger. These hotels had a very colorful décor. Blue walls, green pillars, and red cement floors lit up by neon or tube lights giving the surroundings an exuberant kaleidoscopic effect.

My teenage years were spent in Chennai, and I found myself living with my parents on a street lined with Chettiar homes. It was like one huge communal family, except for the fact we were the only non-Chettiars. But we were highly respected since my mother was a teacher at Lady Willingdon Training School, a very prestigious educational institution and, what is more, she was an authority in English. From money orders to letters to legal documents, my mother was the one who dispensed advice and translated

English documents into Tamil. At festival times, I was part of the Chettiar households and celebrated every one of them with gusto, wearing silk skirts, blouses, heavy jewelry, plaiting my hair with flowers, and even taking the mandatory early morning oil bath. We exchanged food, plates of fruits and flowers, and small gifts. We attended weddings where I ate fish and prawn curry, pepper chicken, crab *masala*, and even shark *puttu*.

The Chettiars are also known for an astonishing assortment of delicious vegetarian dishes. My Chettiar neighbors often told me that back in their home town in Chettinad they owned homes with extensive halls and open courtyards and pillars and verandahs with everyone living as a joint family. There were sets of rooms for each family they said; when the rice was harvested the paddy was cleaned and distributed to family members who managed kitchens on their own, and all brides were given brass, copper, iron, enamel, and stainless steel vessels as part of their dowry.

When I visited a Chettiar friend's home recently in Chennai, I asked for Chettinad food and gorged on *kosamalli*, mashed, boiled eggplant cooked with green chili, onion, tamarind water, and salt. I then topped it with a mutton *kozhambu* (curry) and satiated myself with *kavani Arisi*, which is red rice cooked with grated beetroot, sugar, and coconut and laced with ghee. The dish is garnished with nuts and raisins. Another popular dry dish preparation is *varuval* made with dried fish and vegetables fried with onions and spices. Pickles, roasted powders and ground spices, and dry snacks like *appalam, vada,* and *papads* are sold in shops and often brought by nonresident Indians (NRI) back to their host countries. Rice is an important part of the diet. Chettinad food makes up a well-balanced meal and spices are always freshly ground. A fine *sambar* powder is made of asafetida, fennel seeds, cumin seeds, peppercorns, *toor dal*, ground coriander, chilies, and rice roasted in a little oil. Varied pickles, *sambar* powders, *appalams, papads, vada, murukus, paya* made of trotters, and pepper chicken in a gravy of coconut milk and heady spices are standards of Chettinad cuisine.

A Chettinad feast is a lavish affair with the numbers of dishes correlating to auspicious odd numbers (like 5, 7, 9, 11). But this ritual is reserved for only special occasions. Aromatic and spicy, the food is infused with nutmeg, peppercorn, green and red chilies, dried ginger, *kalpasi* (a dried flower), onions, fennel seeds, and other spices. These dishes accompany the regular *dosai, appam, uthappam,* and *idli.* Chettinad friends tell me that in the olden days at a wedding, the food was tested several times by the host and if something was found wanting, the dish was prepared again. No guest would be dishonored by a mediocre dish. Pepper chicken, crab *masala*, shark *puttu,* fish *masala,* and mutton *uppukari*, made with mutton, red chilies, onions, ginger, garlic, tomatoes, cashew nuts, and oil, are Chettinad favorites. Then they round off their meal and cool their bodies with buttermilk flavored with salt, green chili, ginger, and curry leaf.

Pondicherry

When Portuguese colonialism swept into Goa, Pondicherry, south of Chennai (a mere three hour drive), was influenced by the French who arrived in 1670 and stayed for four centuries. The town still prides itself on its delectable French breads, baguettes, and croissants while pâté is made with spices and pork liver laced with cognac. Steamed fish may well arrive with mayonnaise and garlic paste, and desserts are known for their elegant French flavor and appearance. Many there still speak French. Pondicherry is suffused with a tranquil state of being which is enhanced by stucco colonial buildings, gardens, parks, and the sea that borders its edges. If you plan a trip to Pondicherry, you must include visiting Aurobindo Ashram, an utopian agricultural community with meditation centers, forests, and beaches and populated by people from all over the world.

Nariyal Chili Chicken
Coconut Chili Chicken

Many Indian dishes are pepper-fried to give them a fiery taste. The coconut milk is a soothing ingredient and cuts the hotness of the dish. Use more or less according to taste. Serve with rice or rotis. Rotis will need a thicker gravy.

SERVES 4

- 1 teaspoon dried chilies, lightly pounded
- 1 tablespoon coriander seeds, lightly crushed
- 1 teaspoon black peppercorns, lightly crushed
- 6 teaspoons vegetable oil
- 3 onions, sliced
- 5 garlic cloves, crushed
- 2-inch piece fresh ginger, peeled and grated
- 4 green chilies, chopped
- 10 chicken pieces, patted dry
- 1 cup coconut milk
- 2 tablespoons lime juice
- Salt to taste
- Large bunch cilantro, chopped

Stir-fry dried chilies, coriander seeds, and peppercorns in a dry frying pan for 2 minutes. Set aside.

Heat 3 teaspoons of the oil in a deep pan. Add onions and sauté for 5 minutes. Add remaining 3 teaspoons oil, garlic, ginger, green chilies, and chicken; stir-fry for 10 minutes. Add 1 cup of water and coconut milk. Bring to boil, reduce heat and simmer until chicken is tender, about 30 minutes.

Stir in lime juice. Add some salt and increase heat until gravy thickens. Garnish with cilantro.

Anda Kurma
Egg Curry

Non-vegetarian cuisine is legendary among the Chettiars, a wealthy business community in Tamil Nadu. This cuisine embraces an egg curry spiced with red chilies, onions, curry leaves, and a host of spices. You can replace the eggs with spicy meatballs (page 188), if desired. Perfect for unexpected guests, in South India this curry is usually part of any meal in a non-vegetarian household.

SERVES 3

3 teaspoons ground coriander
1½ teaspoons black peppercorns
1 teaspoon fennel seeds
1 teaspoon cumin seeds
1 teaspoon ground turmeric
¼-inch piece fresh ginger, minced
2 garlic cloves, crushed
Vegetable oil
½ teaspoon fenugreek seeds
2-inch piece cinnamon stick,
    broken up

2 onions, minced
3 tomatoes, finely chopped
3 cups warm water
Salt to taste
1 cup grated coconut
Juice of ½ lime
6 hardboiled eggs, peeled and
    halved

Blend coriander, peppercorns, fennel seeds, cumin seeds, turmeric, ginger, and garlic with 2 tablespoons water to make a paste.

Heat a small amount of oil and fry fenugreek seeds and cinnamon sticks for 10 seconds. Add onions and fry until golden brown. Add spice paste and sauté for 7 minutes. Add tomatoes and sauté for 2 minutes, adding a little water if curry sticks to the pan.

Add 3 cups warm water and some salt and simmer for 10 minutes. Just before removing from heat, add coconut and bring to a boil.

Remove from heat. Stir in lime juice and lay egg halves in the curry with yolks facing up.

Manga Oorga
Mango Pickle

Pickles need to be preserved for at least 4 weeks before they can be used. Otherwise they will have a raw taste. Saturated in oil, drenched in spices and aromatic herbs—that's a mango pickle. Pulpy mangoes mashed with curd and seasoned can substitute for the pickle, but the recipe here is very simple.

4 pounds mangoes, cubed
3 tablespoons dry ground mustard
3 tablespoons crushed mustard
    seeds
3 tablespoons fenugreek seeds
½ cup red chili powder
1 tablespoon ground turmeric

20 curry leaves
2 tablespoons salt
½ cup white vinegar
½ cup chopped green chilies
1 cup oil
1 tablespoon garlic paste

Soak mangoes in salted water. Wash, wipe dry, and dry in sun for 2 hours.

Mix remaining ingredients and add to mangoes.

Store in clean, dry airtight jars for 3 to 4 weeks, shaking jars daily. Keep jars in sun for a few hours every day if possible.

Nimbu Pickle
Lemon Pickle

Pickling enhances flavor and is an ancient art of food preservation. Any vegetable can be pickled—chilies, carrots, cucumbers, tomatoes, peaches, pomegranate seeds, oranges, papaya, onions, peppers, grapes, garlic, and *brinjals*. Some pickles may even contain fish or prawns. The dish below is traditional and a perfect accompaniment to any meal. Lemons in season are the best to use in this dish.

1 pound lemons	**1 teaspoon mustard seeds**
½ teaspoon ground turmeric	**1½ teaspoons red chili powder**
2 tablespoons salt	**3 tablespoons oil**
½ teaspoon fenugreek seeds	

Wash lemons and boil in 2 cups of water with turmeric for 10 minutes, removing scum that forms on top. Drain. Cut each lemon into 8 sections and remove pips.

Sprinkle lemons with salt. Place in a glass jar that has been sterilized with hot water and dried thoroughly. Secure with tight lid and keep lemons in jar for a week, tilting the jar once a day.

In a pan, dry roast fenugreek seeds and mustard seeds. When they pop, remove and grind to a powder. Put lemons in a bowl and toss with ground spices and chili powder.

Clean jar and sterilize again. Put lemons back in jar and pour oil on top. Secure with a tight lid and store in cool place for 3 to 4 weeks, shaking jar daily.

Badam Kesari Halwa
Almond Dessert

A very rich dessert made of almonds, milk, and sugar.

SERVES 4

1 cup ghee plus 1 teaspoon	1¾ cups sugar
1½ cups semolina (*rava*), sifted	A few strands of saffron
3½ cups milk	12 almonds, minced

Heat 1 cup ghee in heavy-bottomed pan, add semolina and roast until golden brown.

Add milk and cook on low heat for 5 minutes. Stir in sugar and saffron. Cook until sugar is dissolved. Garnish with almonds. Add 1 teaspoon ghee and serve hot.

A Day of Sugarcane, Silks and Pakoras

On one of my journeys to the rural areas of South India, lush with rice paddy fields, winding rivers, and sugarcane fields, I visited the Chola Brihadeeswera temple in Thanjavur dedicated to Nandi the Bull, the mount of Lord Shiva. Two hundred miles south of Chennai, it was built in AD 1012 by Raja Raja Chola. It has a magnificent monolith cupola made of a single granite block weighing eighty tons. Inside I marveled at the eighty-one carvings of the classical Bharata Natyam dance poses. Around the temple, vendors sold everything—from deities in sandalwood and garlands of *kadambam* (brightly colored fragrant flowers), bronze icons, bell metal castings, ornamental fans, and musical instruments made from jack wood to handloom silk and cotton sarees and crisp fritters like *pakoras* and *murukus* (fried rice dough in the shape of curly rings). Restaurants catered to thousands of pilgrims who had traveled for hundreds of miles.

Returning to Chennai I stopped at Kancheepuram, a town with a thousand Hindu shrines, to watch silk weavers weave gold thread into yards of pure, heavy silk sarees, as they designed parrots, mango leaves, peacocks, and abstract designs.

The day ended with a plate of soft spongy *idlis*, a butter *dosa* smothered with vegetables, and *vadas*. I rounded it off with a tumbler of South Indian coffee. It's just that kind of place.

Andhra Pradesh

Andhra food is hot—the hottest food in India. Keep six glasses of water nearby as you enthusiastically tackle this food. Being an Andhras I revel in the tamarind-laced meat, fish, and chicken dishes to which red chilies are recklessly added. Guntur district is famous for its fiery red chilies. Dried vegetables called *veppudu* and *araselu*, fried dumplings with a sweet dal or rice filling, are my all-time favorites. A spicy Andhra *podi*, a combination of dals, red chilies, and spices, is the perfect accompaniment to *idlis* or *dosas*; many Andhras who have settled abroad return with a stash of the *podi* after a vacation in India. *Pesarattu*, a typical Andhra dish, is like a *dosa* but the batter is made of *moong dal*, onions, and green chilies. In the western region of Andhra Telengana, *Jonna Rotta*, a roti made of sorghum (a kind of wheat flour) and *gaare*, is a dough snack deep-fried and spiced in a yogurt sauce. Vegetables, curds, and hot pickle supplement red hot fish, chicken, or lamb curries topped off with fried dumplings with a sweet dal filling (*araselu*). Chutneys, sauces, and pickles are integral to an Andhra household.

Since this state is a melting pot of Hindu and Muslim cultures, the cuisine has a unique make-up of lentil, vegetable, meat, and fish preparations. Andhra Pradesh is also home to Banjaras, a nomadic tribe. Banjara women are known for holding steadfast to their ancient mode of dress, a colorful and elaborate full-length skirt called a *gagra*. The colors are usually blazing red embroidered in emerald and golden-yellow thread, teamed with a bright yellow blouse that is embellished with tiny mirrors. The *odhni*, a scarf that covers the head and falls down their back, is intricately embroidered and studded with little mirrors. Thick silver anklets, bangles made of animal bone (almost twenty on each arm going up from the wrist to the forearm), jewelry of gold, silver, and brass gleaming in their noses and ears complete their wardrobe. Patterned cowries decorate their long hair. Banjaras are said to be the original gypsies whose lineage goes back two thousand years when some of them migrated to Europe and were known as the Roma gypsies. The Banjaras, who are constantly moving from one construction job to the other, often carry with them plain rotis stuffed with minced mutton and baked in a pit called the *khad*. An interesting custom during weddings is the exchange of seven round balls made of rice, ghee, and sugar that the bride and groom eat before holding hands and circling a decorated courtyard seven times as they pound grain with pestles to complete the ceremony.

Nariyal

.... Lentils with Coconut ....

This dish can be made fiercely hot if red chili powder is added generously while cooking. But it could result in sniffing and tears rolling down your face! There is a fiery intensity about Andhra dishes; but if you blanch at the hot spicy food yet cannot resist the flavors, add dollops of yogurt. Or while cooking, temper it down by using a lot of coconut.

SERVES 6

2 cups *chana dal*
2 cups chopped tomatoes
1½ cups shredded coconut
1 tablespoon grated fresh ginger
½ teaspoon ground turmeric
1 teaspoon salt
3 tablespoons ghee or vegetable oil
1 bay leaf
5 cloves
3 cardamom pods, seeded and pods
    discarded
1 2-inch cinnamon stick

½ teaspoon cumin seeds
1½ teaspoons coriander seeds
2 whole dried red chilies
Red chili powder (optional)
1 teaspoon sugar
Pinch of asafetida
1 small onion, chopped
½ teaspoon ground coriander
½ teaspoon fenugreek seeds
3 curry leaves, chopped
6 tablespoons plain yogurt

Soak *chana dal* in warm water for 3 hours. Drain.

Place *chana dal* in a large pot with 6 cups water. Bring to a boil, lower heat and simmer for about 15 minutes, until dal is soft. Skim off top layer of foam. Add tomatoes, coconut, ginger, turmeric, and salt. Cover and cook over low heat for 25 minutes.

In a small skillet, heat ghee and fry bay leaf, cloves, cardamom seeds, cinnamon stick, cumin seeds, coriander seeds, and chilies. (You can add some red chili powder at this point if you want it to be more spicy and hot.) When it sputters pour onto dal and add sugar. Cook, stirring, until dal is thickened. Remove bay leaf.

Heat a small amount of oil in large saucepan and add asafetida. Sauté for a few minutes. Add onion and fry until onion is translucent. Add coriander, fenugreek seeds, and curry leaves. Add yogurt. Stir into dal mixture and simmer 15 minutes.

Garam Garam Aloo
Red Hot Chili Potatoes

You can drop a few curry leaves into this delicious, easy traditional potato dish for added flavor.

SERVES 3

1 pound small potatoes
5 tablespoons oil
2 tablespoons red chili powder
2 teaspoons garam masala (page 69)
2 teaspoons ground black pepper
2 teaspoons mustard seeds

1 teaspoon ground coriander
½ teaspoon tamarind paste
Juice of 1 lemon
Salt to taste
1 teaspoon minced cilantro

Boil potatoes and then peel and cut into quarters.

Heat oil in deep pan on low heat. Add chili powder, garam masala, pepper, mustard seeds, and ground coriander. Fry for few minutes being careful not to burn.

Add potatoes and coat well. Add tamarind paste and stir. Add lemon juice and some salt and garnish with cilantro leaves.

Tomato Yogurt Chutney

Cousin Mahadev Souri, a gracious witty host often invites us to his idyllic sanctuary on Puget Sound, Washington. When the family meets, the long dining table is filled with wonderful food. And always, the traditional Andhra tomato chutney adds a fiery zest.

SERVES 4

1 teaspoon oil	1 green chili, chopped
½ teaspoon mustard seeds	½ teaspoon ground turmeric
½ teaspoon split *urad* dal	Salt to taste
8 curry leaves	2 large tomatoes, chopped
2 red chilies, chopped	1¼ cups plain yogurt
1 onion, minced	1 tablespoon cilantro leaves

Heat oil in a pan. Add mustard seeds and sauté until they pop. Add the dal and let it turn red. Add curry leaves and red chilis. Stir for a few seconds.

Add the onion and green chili. Fry until transparent. Add turmeric and some salt. Add the chopped tomatoes and cook until they turn soft. Turn off heat and allow mixture to cool.

Beat the yogurt until smooth. Combine the tomato mixture with the yogurt and garnish with fresh cilantro leaves. Serve with white rice or rotis.

Gongura Mamsaam

Sorrel Leaves and Mutton

The nutritional value of the sorrel added to this dish makes it distinctive. You can also use spinach in place of the sorrel leaves.

SERVES 5

2 pounds mutton, cubed
1 cup plain yogurt
1½ teaspoons ginger-garlic paste
½ teaspoon ground turmeric
Salt to taste
1 tablespoon chopped red chilies
Juice of 1 lemon

½ cup oil
4 medium onions, chopped
1 teaspoon ground coriander
1 teaspoon cumin seeds
1 tablespoon garam masala (page 69)
2 cups shredded sorrel leaves

Place mutton in a bowl. Mix together yogurt, ginger-garlic paste, ground turmeric, salt, red chilies, and lemon juice. Add to mutton and toss to coat. Marinate for 30 minutes.

Cook mutton in pressure cooker until almost tender.

Heat oil and fry onions, coriander, cumin seeds, and garam masala. Add mutton and fry for a few minutes. Add 1 cup water and bring to a boil. Reduce heat and cook for 10 minutes.

Add shredded sorrel leaves and cook until leaves blend with gravy.

Hyderabad

I lived for eight years in Hyderabad, the capital of Andhra Pradesh, situated on the Deccan plateau known for its rich history, culture, and architecture. Images of clustering bazaars, fluttering pigeons, quiet lakes, the expressive tones of the Urdu language mixing with the mellifluous cadences of the Telugu language, perfumes, pearls, the brilliance of mirrored bangles, and glorious food jostle my mind even as I write. Built around 1580, the city of Hyderabad was called Bhagnagar after the beauteous Bhagmati, a Hindu girl who was the beloved of the fifth Quili Qutab Shahi ruler. She became a Muslim and took the name of Hyder Mahal. Overwhelmed by his wife's love, Qutab Shahi renamed the city Hyderabad.

This city ruled by Muslims is also home to the indigenous Telugu-speaking Andhras. Medieval Indian, Indo Saracenic (Mughal Gothic), and colonial architecture create a rich blending of Hindu and Muslim cultures in Hyderabad. A certain grandeur of the past still lingers despite the fact that Hyderabad has become a booming techno city. Medieval monuments and palaces of Muslim kingdoms founded by the Qutab Shahi dynasty that flourished over five centuries still remain.

The rich aromatic northern India cuisine has been inherited in the twin cities of Hyderabad and Secunderabad. Spicy kababs, fragrant *biryanis*, and *achar gosh*, pickle-like meat with *kulchas* or rotis, *double ka meetha*, a heavy cream and milk dish topped with nuts and a silver sheet of foil, were all Mughlai dishes. Then there is *lukmi*, a square of dough filled with a spicy lamb mixture, and *khubani ka meetha*, stewed apricots with cream and almonds—a legacy of the Muslim rulers.

In olden days when *nizams* (rulers) dined lavishly, palace cooks would often create dishes that bordered on fantasy. A palace cook once worked on a massive pie containing live birds that flew away when the pie crust was opened astonishing the British guests who probably knew the English nursery rhyme, "When the pie was opened, the birds begin to sing. Wasn't that a dainty dish to set before the king?"

I was told if the woman in the household had the energy and time and was exhilarated by the joy of cooking, she could cook a dish for two whole days. The dish was called *subdeg,* a meat dish that simmers gently overnight in a clay pot filled with garlic, ginger, chilies, tomato, egg, chickpea flour, onion, and an assortment of spices. After a day the thick gravy is home to turnips, fried brains, kidneys, and boiled eggs to result in an exotic flavor.

Our Muslim landlord who lived next door often sent us *nihari,* a rich soup made of lamb trotters swimming in ghee, and this was at breakfast time! We often enjoyed *haleem,* a nutritious, rich, and pleasantly fattened dish made from goat's trotters simmered overnight on low embers with milk, five kinds of dal, and pounded grains of wheat. This mixture is then fried in ghee with onions, coriander, cream, and hot peppers. It is particularly relished during Ramadan, the holy month of fasting.

The *Baghare baingan* has always been voted by foodies as the king of any eggplant recipe in the whole of India. This simple vegetable simmered with spices, a smidge of jaggery, dried coconut, tamarind, cashews, red chilies, and yogurt has titillated the taste buds of *nizams* and anyone who has visited Hyderabad in quest of a rich gastronomic experience.

Ashrafi is a sweet made in the shape of a coin from almond paste, saffron, and milk that has been boiled for a long while. A small ball of dough is formed and pressed between two gold coins so that the sweet bears an inscription. Thin sheets of silver as light as air often decorated the food and were edible too. In the final stages of cooking, scented rose water was added wafting a sensuous fragrance. Serving dishes and platters were elaborate and ornamented, inscribed with designs of arches, domes, flowers, and leaves.

The secret of the tempting, festive *biryanis* lay in experienced cooks selecting choice, delicate pieces of meats and tenderizing them thoroughly. The raw meat was added to the rice and cooked with delicious dripping juices. A stew or *salan* made of a spicy broth cooked in coriander, dried coconut, green chilies, tamarind, and brown sugar accompanied the *biryani.* The broth is made more exotic with fried coconut, coriander, cumin, peanuts, sesame seeds, roasted and powdered and added to the broth along with tamarind and brown sugar. It has a strong South India identity as opposed to the North Indian variety of *biryani.*

A novel dish, *pathar ki ghosh,* which literally means "stone meat," is thin slices of lamb marinated for many hours in the juice of green papaya, crushed green chilies, and garam masala, then grilled on a thick slab of stone over an open fire. The stone is never washed but wiped down after each session of cooking and is regarded as an heirloom and passed on to the daughter of the house when she gets married.

I remember with amusement ordering every week one particular dish that was popular with family and friends. It was called "Chicken 65" in restaurants and was allegedly made with 65 spices. Someone else tells me that the name came about because it was the 65th most popular item on a menu in a restaurant called Buhari in Chennai, and hence it was called "Chicken 65" across the country. Either way it is delicious.

Today Muslims live with the indigenous Telugu-speaking Andhras and their cuisine embraces Andhra pickles, chutneys, and spices, presenting an exquisite gastronomic experience. Meanwhile mustard seeds, curry leaves, *gong kura* (sorrel) leaves, and tamarind from the Andhra cuisine merged with the pilafs and meat dishes.

My cousin Indrani Souri who comes from Hyderabad makes a fish preparation that is a gastronomic delight. No one makes better fish curry. When she comes to my home in Los Angeles, her husband, my cousin Rajkumar, precedes her carrying a gargantuan vessel of fish curry while we applaud. Though she migrated to America thirty years ago, she still serves up a symphony of Andhra flavors and ingredients surrounding the salmon, her favorite fish. Interestingly, her fish curry varies every time she makes it, making it an adventure in taste. Is it the tamarind, the ginger, the curry leaf, the chilies that make the difference? She never will tell.

While living in Hyderabad, weekends often found us walking near the tombs of the Qutab Shahi kings, visiting the Salar Jung Museum, an awesome collection of antiques. Salar Jung was a former prime minister of the Nizam and his collection was reputed to be the world's largest owned by one man. In another part of the city, Charminar ("four minarets") is hailed as the Arc de Triumph of the East. It was built in 1591 by Sultan Mohammad Quli Qutub Shah as a talisman to ward off a dreaded epidemic. The arched four minaret gateway dominates shops selling perfume, attar, sandalwood, pearls, gold zari work sarees, delicate silver work, and glass and precious stone bangles of every conceivable color. Hot spicy kababs and sweet shops tempt the passerby, and when there was time we indulged in an oven-baked *biryani* dish brimming with meat, vegetables, boiled eggs, nuts, and spices. Whenever guests from another state arrived, we would set out for the Pearl Bazaar where we sipped the traditional *khada chamcha* (standing spoon) chai, sifting through glistening pearls thrown over a sapphire blue velvet cloth, listening to the muezzin's call while boisterous young boys outside the store flew vividly colored kites high in the skies in a spectacular sky battle.

Hyderabad is noted for sweets made with pure ghee. The names are hypnotic—*kalakand, jelebis, baadshah, gulab jamun, basundi, milk khova, peda, som papdi, banaras laddu.* Pulla Reddy sweets were very popular in the city when we lived there decades ago. They were famous for their variety and fresh ingredients. We gorged on *kaju burfi, kova puri,* and the irresistible *basundi.* I was thrilled to find they are still a thriving business because my cousins often, after a trip to Hyderabad, bring a box of superb Pulla Reddy sweets for our family. In Hyderabad on the 11th day of the Hindu Ganesh Chathurthi festival, the most popular *Balapur Ganesh laddu* is sold at an auction in the ancient Balapur Ganesh temple. This tradition began in 1994. At the last auction it sold for Rs 400,000/$10,000! It is believed that the *laddu* will bring good luck and prosperity to the person who outbids the others.

Shammi Kebabs
Spicy Lamb Patties

The cuisine of Hyderabad is a fusion of Hindu and Muslim cultures. The rich gastronomic culture of the Muslim emperors blended with Indian herbs and seasonings results in an elegant form of cuisine, rich and lavish.

MAKES 30 PIECES

2 pounds minced lamb
2 garlic cloves, chopped
1 onion, cubed
10 peppercorns
6 cloves
2-inch piece cinnamon stick
1-inch piece fresh ginger, peeled
3 cardamom pods
¼ teaspoon black cumin seeds
12 dried red chilies

1 bay leaf
1½ teaspoons salt
¾ cup *chana* dal
3 eggs
Oil

FILLING:
1 onion, minced
2 green chilies, minced
1 sprig mint, minced

Place minced lamb, garlic, onion cubes, peppercorns, cloves, cinnamon stick, ginger, cardamom pods, cumin seeds, red chilies, bay leaf, salt, and *chana dal,* and 2 cups water in a deep pot and bring to a boil. Simmer for 1 hour until lamb and dal are tender. Cool.

Remove cinnamon stick, cardamom pods, and bay leaf. Grind lamb mixture to a fine paste. Add eggs to mixture.

Make filling by mixing together the minced onion, green chilies, and mint leaves.

Make small flat rounds from lamb mixture. Put a teaspoon of filling onto each round. Close lamb over mixture and flatten.

Heat some oil in pan and fry kebabs until golden brown. Drain on paper towels.

Tamatar

Kofta in Tomato Sauce

Lamb is perfect for intense spices. You can add fried red bell pepper, broccoli, chopped green beans, or snow peas to the *kofta* sauce and serve garnished with cilantro or mint leaves. This curry tastes even better the next day.

SERVES 3

KOFTA:
2 onions
1 pound ground lamb
2-inch piece fresh ginger, grated
4 garlic cloves, minced
3 green chilies, minced
½ teaspoon salt
1 tablespoon lime juice
1 egg
Cilantro or mint leaves

SAUCE:
2 teaspoons coriander seeds
2 teaspoons cumin seeds
4 tablespoons oil
2-inch piece cinnamon stick
6 cloves
6 cardamom pods
1 onion, minced
½ teaspoon ground turmeric
1 teaspoon red chili powder
1 teaspoon garam masala (page 69)
½ teaspoon salt
5 small tomatoes, diced
½ cup plain yogurt

Make koftas: Grate onions and remove liquid by straining or use a spoon to press it out. Combine the onions with lamb, ginger, garlic, green chilies, salt, lime juice, and egg. Divide into 20 equal portions and shape each into an oval or round ball. Refrigerate for 2 hours.

Meanwhile make sauce: Roast coriander seeds and cumin seeds separately in a little oil. Grind together to a fine powder. Heat remaining oil in a pan and add cinnamon stick, cloves, cardamom pods, and onion. Fry until golden. Add ground seeds, turmeric, chili powder, garam masala, and salt. Fry for 20 seconds. Stir in tomatoes. Stir in yogurt and simmer over low heat.

Add chilled meatballs to sauce and bring to a boil. Simmer, uncovered, for 45 minutes over low heat until meatballs are cooked, adding a little water as needed.

Garnish with cilantro or mint leaves.

Hyderabadi Chicken Biryani

My two cousins from Hyderabad, sisters Indrani Souri and Meera, are cooking divas and when we met for a family reunion we feasted decadently on a mélange of banquets. Creativity, zest, and a vibrant spirit made each dish come alive, especially this lusciously rich *biryani* which they packed for me to take back to Los Angeles. One handy tip: They rinsed the rice twice, threw away water, and then soaked again for 20 minutes to make the rice separate and fluffy. Cinnamon and mint added a heady fragrance to this special dish, and a few drops of food coloring gave the rice a golden tinge.

SERVES 6

2 pounds chicken	1 teaspoon oil
3 tablespoons plain yogurt	Pinch of saffron
1 teaspoon garam masala (page 69)	Salt to taste
½ cup onion paste	2 or 3 onions, sliced
2 tablespoons ginger-garlic paste	½ cup ghee
5 peppercorns, crushed	½ teaspoon cumin seeds
Juice of 1 lemon	2 large tomatoes, chopped
4 cups basmati rice	3 teaspoons red chili powder
4 cloves	1 teaspoon mint leaves, minced
3 cardamom pods	½ cup flour
1-inch piece cinnamon stick, broken in half	

Clean and cut chicken into 8 to 10 pieces. Mix yogurt, garam masala, half of onion paste, half of ginger-garlic paste, peppercorns, lemon juice, and some salt and toss with chicken. Allow to marinate for 2 hours.

Soak rice in water for 30 minutes. Bring 8 cups water to a boil in a large pot and add one clove, one cardamom pod, and half of cinnamon stick. Add rice and simmer. When rice is half cooked add 1 teaspoon oil, saffron, and salt. Drain and set aside.

Fry sliced onions in 3 tablespoons of the ghee and set aside.

Heat rest of ghee in a deep pan and add cumin seeds, remaining 3 cloves, 2 cardamom pods, half cinnamon stick, and sauté for a few minutes. Add remaining ¼ cup onion paste and 1 tablespoon ginger-garlic paste. Add tomatoes and red chili powder and sauté until slightly cooked. Add marinated chicken and cook over low heat for 15 minutes.

Remove half the chicken curry from pan and spread half of the boiled rice over the curry still in pot. Garnish with half of mint leaves and fried onion. Place second layer of curry over rice and spread with remaining rice and add remaining garnishes.

Knead flour with enough water to make a smooth dough. Cover the pot and seal with dough so no steam escapes. Cook over low flame for 15 minutes. Carefully remove seal before serving.

Mirch ka Salan
Green Chili Curry

This curry is a traditional accompaniment to a sumptuous *biryani*. The spiciness and hot flavor can be reduced by using less green chilies.

SERVES 4

2 cups onions, fried
¼ cup roasted peanuts
1 teaspoon ginger paste
1 teaspoon garlic paste
1 teaspoon sesame seeds
Oil
5 whole green chilies

½ cup plain yogurt, beaten
2 tablespoons lemon juice
Salt
2 tablespoons tamarind paste
2 teaspoons grated coconut
Cilantro leaves

Grind fried onions, peanuts, ginger paste, garlic paste, and sesame seeds to form a paste.

Heat some oil in a pan and deep fry chilies. Set aside.

Fry ground paste in same oil for about 10 minutes, adding a little water now and then and stirring all the time. Add yogurt, lemon juice, and some salt. Add tamarind paste and coconut and stir.

Add fried chilies. Bring to boil and remove from heat. Garnish with chopped cilantro leaves and serve hot with *biryani*.

Baingan Bartha
Eggplant Chutney

This is lush purple eggplant roasted with spices, a traditional dish of Hyderabad known for its richness and flavor. Choose eggplants that are firm or even hard to the touch. Green leaves at the end of the stem should be fresh.

SERVES 6

2 large eggplants
4 tablespoons oil
4 tablespoons ghee
2 medium onions, chopped
1 tablespoon chopped fresh ginger
1 teaspoon cumin seeds
½ teaspoon *amchur* (dried mango powder)

1 teaspoon garam masala (page 69)
½ teaspoon ground turmeric
1 teaspoon black peppercorns
1½ teaspoons salt
1 large tomato, chopped
3 tablespoons chopped cilantro

Coat eggplants with oil and grill over open flame until they are roasted and interior is soft. Remove from heat and scrape off outer peel. Mash eggplants.

Heat ghee in pan and fry onions and ginger for 1 minute. Add cumin seeds, *amchur,* garam masala, turmeric, peppercorns, and salt. Add tomato and cook until mixture is soft.

Add mashed eggplant and cook for 10 minutes while stirring. Stir in cilantro.

Paya

Goat Trotters Special

Nasir Ahmad, my son-in-law, is passionate about traveling and cooking. In the kitchen, beef or goat trotters (*paya*), cooked by him with myriad spices, becomes a rich gelatinous stew of meat and crunchy melt in your mouth bones. Nasir the perfectionist honors authenticity and plans this meal with loving detail, tempting us further with *naan* to mop up this rich curry. A truly epicurean delight to lovers of exotic cuisine.

SERVES 4

8 to 10 goat trotters (feet)
1 tablespoon rice flour
Salt to taste
1 teaspoon ground turmeric
1 cup oil
2 onions, chopped
1 clove garlic, chopped
2 tablespoons ginger paste
1 2-inch cinnamon stick
1 teaspoon ground coriander

1 teaspoon garam masala (page 69)
6 cloves
1 tablespoon cumin seeds
1 teaspoon ground cumin
4 black cardamom pods
10 black peppercorns
2 cups plain yogurt
2 tablespoons lemon juice
2 tomatoes, cut into small pieces

Rub rice flour, salt, and turmeric on goat trotters and then wash well. Set aside.

Heat oil in deep pan. Add onions and trotters and fry until browned. Add sufficient water to cover and simmer for 2 hours.

In a small skillet, stir-fry the garlic, ginger paste, cinnamon stick, coriander, garam masala, cloves, cumin seeds, ground cumin, cardamom pods, and peppercorns for a few minutes. Set aside.

Add yogurt to the trotters. Stir for 5 minutes. When liquid starts to stick add 4 glasses of water and bring to a boil. Lower heat and simmer for 40 minutes.

Add fried spices, lemon juice, and tomatoes. Simmer for about 20 minutes.

Double ka Meeta

Bread Pudding with Nuts and Raisins

This is a rich and satisfying dessert.

SERVES 6

5 slices regular white bread, cut
    into squares
½ cup ghee
2 tablespoons chopped cashews,
    toasted
3 tablespoons sliced almonds,
    toasted

½ cup sugar
½ teaspoon ground cardamom
Few raisins
½ cup milk
½ cup heavy cream

Fry bread pieces in ghee until toasted. Place in a shallow casserole. Sprinkle with toasted cashews and almonds. Set aside.

Place sugar and ¼ cup water in a saucepan. Bring to boil, then cook over low heat for 10 minutes to make a syrup, stirring a number of times. Stir in cardamom and raisins. Then cook for a few more minutes. Spoon hot syrup evenly over nuts and bread.

Bring milk to a boil and pour over top of bread. Spoon cream over top. Cool for a couple of hours.

Kerala

On my first visit to Kerala, the memory that remains most vivid is sipping the heavenly coconut water from a coconut with the top sliced off. Cool, refreshing, delicious, pristine. Then I recall the tranquil beaches, rugged mountains, palm-fringed lagoons, diverse cultures of Hindus, Muslims, Christians, Arabs, and Jews, the wealth of legends as well as a cuisine deeply shaped by Ayurvedic beliefs. The word *Kerala* comes from *chera*, the name of the region's ruling dynasty in the 1st and 2nd centuries. Kerala has a literacy rate of 100 percent and the local language, Malayalam, is believed by linguists to be the fastest spoken language in the world. Kerala also follows a matrilineal tradition, making sure that women are empowered and valued.

There are many legends about the beginnings of Kerala. Here is one of the most popular. Parusuram, supposed to be an incarnation in human form of the God Vishnu, was a vengeful and murderous person who destroyed many members of his family. Deeply penitent after these horrific killings, he was given a piece of land by the God of the Ocean and the Goddess of the Earth. He took up residence and saw to it that future generations were faithful and true to the gods. That piece of land is believed to be Kerala.

Kerala was famous for the spice trade in the 1st century BC when spices were bartered between Kerala and the Roman Empire. Sanskrit texts mention the profitable trade in aromatic spices and even gold. Trade may have lasted from the 1st century BC to the 1st century AD or later. The Arabs, Chinese, and Portuguese (led by Vasco de Gama in 1498) discovered the rich spices of Kerala on the edge of the Indian Ocean. Pepper, cinnamom, cardamom, and vanilla grew in the Western ghats of Kerala in abundance. The Portuguese came for the region's black pepper and brought with them red chili peppers in exchange. Conversion was also on their agenda and they built many churches. Hot on their heels came the Dutch and the British, who became controllers of the spice trade.

Many ancient rituals still survive despite invaders and a blend of different cultures. It was thrilling one hot afternoon to drive deep into a forest to see *Kalari Payattu*, a ritualistic dance/martial art of the 2nd century and still taught today. During my visit to Kerala I saw a performance of the dance of the celestial enchantress Mohini. A fascinating legend of Mohini Attam is associated with this dance form.

In Hindu scriptures Brahma tells the other gods how to obtain the celestial ambrosia *(amrit)* that bestows immortality and power. This can be achieved, he says, by churning the ocean of milk. As this is a daunting task, the gods ask the help of the demons, who plot to keep the *amrit* for themselves. Lord Vishnu finds out the plot, takes on the form of a celestial nymph/dancer, and distracts the demons. The *amrit* is obtained by the gods and the world is saved from the demons. On my last night in Kerala, I attended a dramatic dance drama *Kathakali,* a compelling dance form narrating incidents in mythology. It lasts all night long and includes dancers, actors, vocalists, and percussionists. Even the performers' makeup takes four hours to complete, with artists placing crushed seeds under their eyes to make them red and dramatic and rice paste on the face in complex patterns.

The Kerala coast, lined with coconut palms, is a fertile and beautiful piece of land. The coconut is one of the state's primary agricultural products with every part of the tree used: oil for cooking; meat and pulp for food; the shell for making utensils; the trunk for furniture; the fiber for rope and stuffing; and the leaves for palm thatching. Kerala's dishes are always flavored with coconut and curry leaves. Coconut milk lends a soft silkiness to any dish. Fish or shrimp and coconut are an ideal combination.

A festive Kerala meal, typically served on a banana leaf, begins with *avail,* vegetables cooked with spices. More vegetables arrive prepared with coconut milk called *olan.* The next item, *kalam*, is made with raw banana and yogurt and a tuber, and then the chutneys arrive laced with tamarind water and jaggery in which okra and gourd are cooked. Finely cut ginger and green chilies spice up the dishes served on white rice. A small pot of ghee is placed on the left of the banana leaf. Most of the spices, like onions, chili, coriander, garlic, cardamom, clove, pepper, and cinnamon, can be found in the backyards of house in Kerala, including coconut to add piquant flavors.

Fish is bountiful. Fish is dried, salted, and preserved for use on a rainy day or cooked in savory gravies. A specialty, *Meen Veyuchadh,* is cooked in an iron pan with a special sauce made with tamarind, red chili, fennel seeds, garlic, and coriander. I always find fish curry tastes even better the next day.

Appam is a crepe made of rice flour, toddy (fermented palm juice), and coconut milk cooked in a special round-bottomed pan. The vessel is lifted and swirled around until a little batter sticks to the sides. It is then covered and cooked on a slow fire until the sides turn crisp and the center is soft. Finally the *appam* emerges, a spongy pancake with a thick base and a lacy, frilly crisp edging. It is served with spicy fish curry or sweetened coconut milk. Legend has it that the *appam* was brought to Kerala by the Syrian

Christians who came from Jerusalem to escape religious persecution. Due to the Christian influence some Hindus add fish and meat to their cusine. Seafood is a perennial favorite, with most foods cooked in coconut oil.

Christian roots are deep in Kerala. Saint Thomas, one of Jesus' twelve apostles, is said to have reached the Kerala coast in AD 52 and founded his mission. In the 17th century, the Portuguese arrived and converted a number of communities to Catholicism. Syrian Christians, one of the oldest Christian sects in India, came from Syria in the 4th century bringing with them their own cuisine and forming an integral part of the Christian community.

Beef and fish are pickled with vinegar, coconut oil, asafetida, chilies, ginger, garlic, fenugreek, and mustard. They can be preserved for long periods of time. Another preparation is fish with vinegar, sesame oil, and mustard seeds. Oils are flavored with cinnamon, cardamom, and cloves. Then the onions, ginger, garlic, and chilies are sautéed before the fish/meat is added and finally the fresh coconut milk creates a fabulous stew that can be eaten throughout the day.

There is a ritual during the austere season of the Christian Lent when no animal products are eaten and no vessels in which meat has been cooked are used. A unique bread made by the Syrian Christian community is popular at this time. It is made of black gram and decorated with a cross made out of a palm leaf. The bread is divided into thirteen pieces (representing the 12 apostles and Jesus Christ) and eaten by the family. Each person drinks a special drink of coconut milk, jaggery and plantains, symbolic of the wine at the Last Supper. Food is usually served on plantain leaves. An interesting Christian custom has the bride and groom eating their first meal out of the same plate on their wedding day to symbolize a shared union.

The Muslims of northern Kerala who speak Malayalam are known as Moplahs. Their roots go back to trading Arabs who visited Kerala for pepper and other spices. Many stayed behind and intermarried with the locals introducing an Arabic influence on the cuisine. They mostly live in the Malabar region of northern Kerala. *Aleesa*, a traditional Arabic dish served to the bridegroom and guests at weddings, consists of lamb cooked with wheat and eaten with sugar. Egg garland or *Mutta Mala* made from egg yolks is a fixture at weddings. It is egg yolk cooked in syrup which forms long yellow strands. This is removed and spread out on a plate in the form of a garland. *Neichoru* rice is served on the eve of the wedding. This is a simple staple dish made of rice, fried onions, cardamom, cloves, cinnamon, and lots of ghee. Stuffed fish, chicken, tapioca, and yam are all firm favorites of this community. An unusual way of cooking chicken is stuffing the bird with spices and a hard-boiled egg and then frying it over low heat in a deep pot. Interestingly, the Moplahs do not use basmati rice (used predominantly by the Muslim community) but use a short-grain variety instead.

Kerala is also home to a few Jews who fled Israel to the town of Cochin on the coast in 70 AD after the destruction of King Solomon's Temple by the Romans. Today, many have migrated back to Israel and only seven families remain. They do not eat pork and follow the kosher system of animal slaughter (the jugular vein of the animal is cut allowing the blood to drain out thoroughly as it is considered a part of life). Meat is not eaten alongside dairy products and fish without scales (like shellfish) is not a part of their diet. Apart from rituals like the Passover, when not one grain of cracked wheat is allowed to be used in cooking (the women spend hours in sifting), Cochin Jews have assimilated to local culinary techniques and use spices, coconut, and vinegar and eat fish, chicken, and vegetables, as well as yogurt and rice.

In the vegetarian world, many vegetables are common to all communities; Hindus, Christians, and Muslims serve a variety of savory delicacies. Vegetables are cooked with some onions and spices, and a paste of coconut, garlic, and cumin seeds is mixed in and the dish is usually tempered with coconut oil and curry leaves.

Bananas and banana leaves are popular in cooking. When ingredients are wrapped within them, banana leaves can add tremendous flavor to a dish. Palm syrup is often poured over ripe steamed bananas to make them more flavorful. A delicious and traditional Moplah fish dish requires placing a small banana leaf on a *tawa* with oil smeared on it. A piece of fish is covered with spice paste and then placed on the leaf and covered with three more banana leaves and cooked to perfection.

There are many varieties of bananas in Kerala—they come in many different shapes, textures, and tastes. *Nendraparram* is a succulent large orange-red banana grown in practically every backyard in Kerala. It can be made into a dessert, cooked as a vegetable, made as fritters, or candied or roasted for chips. Banana desserts are extravagant with jackfruit, rice, and sugar used generously. *Puttu* is a combination of rice flour and ground coconut steamed in a bamboo steamer which is then eaten with ripe banana and milk or with a sauce made of spices and peanuts. At the end of any meal, a slightly sour concentrated drink made out of the syrup of the palymra tree is usually offered to help with digestion.

Before I left Kerala, I was fortunate enough to be a spectator at the dramatic snakeboat races held on Punnamada Lake. They are held during the harvest festival and feature 120-foot-long canoes carrying 100 rowers, 4 helmsmen, and 25 singers who chant rhythmically. The boats move with the swift elegance of a snake through the water channels. A stunning water fiesta! Another awe-inspiring festival is the Pooram festival which is held at a temple in Trissur. Spectacularly decorated elephants, drawn from every region in Kerala, parade through the town. After the procession, some twenty or so elephants, gorgeously ornamented and caparisoned, congregate at the temple and stand in two lines. Atop each magnificent elephant sporting an elaborate gold headdress is an umbrella holder who holds a brightly colored canopy of an umbrella, a peacock fan carrier, and a fly whisk carrier. Percussion and wind instrumentalists stand between the elephants playing out dazzling syncopations of sound. The festival ends with a fireworks display.

Meen Varatharcha

Fish in Coconut Gravy

You can make this with snapper, pomfret, mullet, or mackerel. If you do not have tamarind paste, you can use more tomatoes.

SERVES 4

½ cup grated coconut
1 teaspoon anise seeds
2 tablespoons minced onion
4 green chilies, sliced
5 curry leaves
Oil
½ teaspoon fenugreek seeds
1 teaspoon ginger paste
2 teaspoons garlic paste
1 teaspoon tamarind paste

2 teaspoons red chili powder
1 teaspoon ground coriander
½ teaspoon ground turmeric
Salt to taste
1 pound fish fillets
2 large tomatoes, cut into large
 pieces
½ cup coconut milk
½ bunch cilantro leaves

In a small skillet, roast the coconut, anise seeds, half of the chopped onion, half of the chilies, and 3 curry leaves in 1 tablespoon of oil until golden brown. Grind well to a paste. Set aside.

Heat a little oil in a large skillet and fry fenugreek seeds until brown. Add remaining onions and chilies. Sauté. Add ginger paste and garlic paste. After a few minutes add tamarind paste, chili powder, ground coriander, ground turmeric, and salt. Boil for a few minutes.

Reduce heat and place fish gently in simmering curry and add tomatoes. Cook gently, taking care that the fish does not break up, until fish is almost cooked (time will vary depending on thickness of fillets). Add coconut milk, cilantro leaves, and remaining curry leaves being careful not to break up fillets. Continue to simmer until fish is cooked. Remove from heat.

Kofta
Spicy Meatballs

Easy to make, satisfying comfort food, ths dish can be frozen for a week. It is perfect as an accessory to rice and dal dishes and can be made with any kind of meat.

SERVES 4

2 pounds ground lamb or goat	1 tablespoon ginger paste
2 teaspoons red chili powder	6 curry leaves
1 teaspoon ground turmeric	Few cilantro leaves, chopped
4 tablespoons coconut powder	1 small cinnamon stick, crushed
1 tablespoon oil	3 cardamom pods, crushed
4 green chilies, chopped	1 teaspoon chili powder
½ teaspoon poppy seeds, ground into a powder	1 egg, beaten
½ teaspoon cloves, crushed	1 tablespoon lime juice
1 tablespoon garlic paste	1½ teaspoons salt
	Oil for frying

Cook meat with chili powder, ground turmeric, and salt until browned.

Roast coconut powder lightly in 1 tablespoon oil. Add chilies and fry lightly.

Mix poppy seeds, cloves, garlic paste, ginger paste, curry leaves, cilantro leaves, and roasted coconut powder and chilies. Mix in ground meat and cinnamon stick, crushed cardamoms, chili powder, beaten egg, and lime juice. Add salt. Mix well.

Shape meat mixture into balls and deep fry in oil.

Kala Mirchi Murg
Pepper Chicken Fry

A spicy fry full of flavor and easy to prepare, this dish can be eaten with rice or rotis. It is fairly hot so reduce pepper for a less robust flavor.

SERVES 6

2 teaspoons coriander seeds

2 teaspoons cumin seeds

½ teaspoon ground turmeric

1½ teaspoons ground black pepper

1 teaspoon salt

2 pounds skinless chicken thighs, cubed

5 tablespoons vegetable oil

2 cups sliced onion

1½ teaspoons garlic paste

1½ teaspoons ginger paste

1 teaspoon ground green chili

¾ cup coconut milk

1 tablespoon ghee

½ cup broken cashews

1 teaspoon lemon juice

Grind coriander seeds and cumin seeds. Mix with ground turmeric, ground pepper, and salt. Rub on chicken pieces and set aside for 1 hour.

Heat oil in deep pan and sauté onions until browned. Add garlic paste, ginger paste, and chili; fry for 1 minute. Add marinated chicken and fry, stirring frequently, until pieces are browned. Stir in ¼ cup of the coconut milk and ¼ cup water. Simmer for 30 minutes over low heat.

Heat ghee in a separate pan and sauté cashew nuts.

When chicken is cooked add remaining ½ cup coconut milk and simmer to heat through. Stir in lemon juice and garnish with cashew nuts.

Kathar Curry

Jackfruit Curry

Distinctively sweet and sour this curry is best eaten with rice as an accompaniment. Quick cooking enhances the flavor.

SERVES 4 TO 5

1 medium raw jackfruit
1 small onion, minced
4 green chilies
1 teaspoon cumin seeds
Salt to taste
3 cups grated fresh coconut, ground

1 teaspoon ground turmeric
2 tablespoons oil
1 teaspoon mustard seeds
1 teaspoon *urad dal*
Few curry leaves
Salt to taste

Peel jackfruit. Oil your hands and separate the fruit. Remove seeds and cut into pieces.

Grind onion, chilies, and cumin seeds together into a paste. Set aside.

Put jackfruit in a pan with a little salt, the ground coconut, turmeric, and a little water. Simmer over low heat until fruit is cooked and starts shredding. Remove from heat.

In a small skillet, heat 2 tablespoons of oil and add mustard seeds, *urad dal*, and curry leaves. When the seeds pop, add reserved onion mixture.

Add this mixture to fruit curry, simmer for 1 minute and serve with hot rice.

Karnataka

Visiting Mysore, the capital of Karnataka, is like stepping back into history and evoking the splendid opulent pageantry of the kings of yesterday. Today most of the palaces have been converted into luxurious hotels, but the palace where the present Maharajah belonging to the Wodayar Dynasty lives still dominates the city, a significant synthesis of Hindu-Muslim, Gothic, and Rajput architecture. Extensive artwork on walls, doors, and ceilings, bronze lamps imported from France, stained-glass domes, exquisite bird and floral motifs, oil paintings, and sculptures adorn hundreds of rooms. Be sure to book a tour when you visit before splurging on the famous Mysore silks, sandalwood, and incense.

The cuisine of Karnataka, like the other southern states' cuisines, has changed little over thousands of years. The food is mild with a tinge of sweetness and contains protein-based lentils, fresh vegetables, salads, rice, and the traditional *sambhar*. When I was a child growing up in Bangalore, Karnataka, my grandmother would give me a ball of *ragi* every day—a Kannadiga custom. I hated it. It was a dirty greyish black lump with no taste or smell, but it had to be downed every day as everyone said it was good for the body. *Ragi* (finger millet) is high in minerals and calcium and *ragi* flour is steamed to make the balls called *mudde*. The ball is usually soaked in a meat or fish curry, coconut milk, or *sambhar*, but in my case, my grandmother would pinch my nostrils shut with her firm fingers, demand my mouth to be opened, and pop it in forcibly with no accompaniments.

The cuisine of the western Konkan coast does resemble Goan dishes. Brahmins do eat fish, while non-Brahmin Hindus eat fish, chicken, and mutton. Grated coconut is lavishly used. Rice *dosas* and rice rotis accompany many a fish and meat curry. My sister-in-law Pushpa makes a tasty *gojju*, a vegetable spiced with red chilies, sesame seeds, coriander seeds, and tamarind, giving the dish a hot, sweet, and sour taste. Chilies fried in yogurt give a zesty flavor to any meat. The most popular dish is *bise bellle huli anna,* a mixture of rice, lentils, potatoes, beans, peppers, peas, and rice cooked in ghee and spices and embellished with fried peanuts and curry leaves. At breakfast you will be served *uppitu,* roasted semolina garnished with some spices and curry leaf. *Mysore pak,* a tempting sweet made of gram flour boiled in sugar and ghee, is offered after a meal. Fish and meat are eaten by a majority of the people of Karnataka.

The capital city of Karnataka, Bangalore (the Silicon Valley of India), was originally called *Benda Kaal Ooru*, or "the town of boiled beans." According to stories retold, a king who had lost his way asked for food in this region and was offered boiled beans. In gratitude he blessed the city and called it Benda Kaal Ooru. Today the city has a spectacular software industry priding itself on IT venture capitalists, homegrown software, and technology parks.

Mangalore is a seaport on the cusp of Karnataka and Kerala, also called the Konkan Coast. Food there resembles Goan fare with many Mangalore Christians eating pork. Mangalore Christian history dates back to the 16th century with trade contacts with the Roman Empire and the Portuguese influence from nearby Goa. With the arrival of the Muslim ruler Tipu Sultan, who fought against the British and suppressed Christianity, Mangalorean Christians were persecuted. But Tipu fell in battle, the British returned victoriously, and pork began to appear on the Mangalorian menu already famed for vegetarian dishes. Coconut is also a common ingredient and *akki roti* (rice roti) as well as *bari akki* (rice dosa) are eaten with relish when dipped in spicy meat and fish curries.

Coorg, a little bountiful region in Karnataka, 120 km from Mysore, welcomes with lush, verdant valleys, coffee, honey, and cardamom plantations, streams, teakwood, rosewood, silver oak forests, and waterfalls. It is called the "Kashmir of the South." We vacationed in Coorg one summer and traveled through the mountainous region by bus and car as there is no plane or train service. This is the home of my son-in-law Chetan Ganpati and his family, the Kambirandas, who have lived here for generations planting coffee. Weddings here are solemnized with elders' blessings and a shower of rice grains as there is no formal worship service, Vedic chanting, or priests. My daughter Anuradha, who married Chetan, took part in a special ceremony that evening, memories of which still evokes the hilarity and fun we had ten years ago. There she was in her wedding finery, carrying a brass pitcher of water on her head, balancing it and trying to walk towards her husband who was a hundred yards away. Nothing to it right? She took almost an hour to get to him, even though her friends and family behind her tried to keep her going, because the bridegroom's family and friends would not let her take one step forward. They danced with abandon to the beating of drums and would not allow her to proceed. Eventually, she did! This ceremony was devised years ago to test the stamina of the new member of the family and the mother of the next generation.

While in Coorg we trekked to Talacauvery, the birthplace of the River Goddess Cauvery. The river is known as the Ganges of the South and is revered and worshiped. On Tula Sankaramana day in the middle of October, the most sacred day for the Coorgs, thousands of pilgrims flock to the river's origin to witness a miraculous sudden upsurge of water. Legend has it that the Goddess Parvati appears on that day at that spot. Devout Coorgs take a holy dip and take home the holy water to perform worship on the day of Cauvery Sankramana.

Our days in Coorg were spent trying to climb the 5,700 foot Tadiandamole peak, watching elephants nuzzling their offspring, walking across meadows, verdant valleys, undulating hills, and cooling off at a 40-foot waterfall, while spotting the sloth bear, spotted deer, and bison. The Iruppu temple is in a mountain village which prides itself on a beautiful legend. There is a cleft on the mountain side through which a 40-foot high waterfall springs. The story goes that it was punctured by an arrow shot by Lakshmana, the brother of Lord Rama in the Ramayana. When Rama, after abdicating the throne, and his wife Sita traveled through the forest, they became thirsty and asked Lakshmana, an excellent archer, to find water. He shot an arrow into a cleft in the mountain and immediately a waterfall gushed forth.

The earliest mention of Coorg (also known as Kodagu) dates to the 9th century AD when the community of Kodavas claimed ownership of the land and kept away invaders as this formidable mountain region has always been remote and inaccessible. Some say they are descendants of migrating Persians, Kurds, or Greeks brought over by Alexander the Great. The Kodava people resisted invasions from warlords Tipu Sultan, Hyder Ali, and the Deccan sultanates, and exulted in their freedom. But in 1830, they surrendered to the British due to the weakness of a despot King Chikaveera Rajendra. The British surprisingly asked the people to choose their own governor and gave them nominal independence. The small well-knit community in this bountiful land is known for their martial traditions, so much so that at one time practically every family had a son in the armed forces. Many heroic generals have originated from this land of the coffee, cardamom, and pepper estates.

In the first week of September, *Kailpodhu* is celebrated—the worship of weapons. During the months when the men are busy in the fields the guns in the family are kept in the *puja* room. On the day which marks the transplantation of the crops, the weapons are taken out of the *puja* room, and there is much food, primarily spicy pork dishes and drink, shooting skills are tested, and from this day, the men will use the guns to guard their fields from wild boars and other animals.

Temples are few as the Kodavas revere their ancestors and rituals center around the remembrance of departed souls and celebration of nature. The harvest festival, *huthri* (new rice crop), is celebrated in November or December. On a full moon night the head of the household, accompanied by blazing torches made out of banana stumps carried by members of the family and laborers, makes his way to the new paddy crop. The lady of the house carrying a *thali* (platter) with rice, betel leaves, and betel nuts placed around a *diya* (lamp) joins the procession. The head of the household pours milk and honey on the first sheaf to be cut and a single gunshot reverberates through the still night to summon Lord Iguthappa while the chants of *"Poli, Poli, Deva"* (Increase, increase, O God) resound. The sheaf is cut and taken back home and placed in the *puja* room or hung on the door handles, bed posts, or pillars. Meanwhile small balls of dough made of bitter gourd peels, bananas, milk, honey, grated coconut, rice, flour, and water are placed on leaves. The balls are thrown up at the ceiling and the name of an ancestor is called out each time. If the dough sticks it means the ancestors are pleased with the descendants.

Coorg cuisine is very distinctive, as are their customs, clothing, and festivals. The most delectable items in their foods are the *Pandi* curry (succulent pork) and *kaddumbuttu* (rice puddings). *Pandi* (pork) is the favorite of non-vegetarians. The pork is boiled with mustard, ginger, garlic, coriander, a special tamarind, vinegar, and garam masala and then fried in pork fat. Pork can be preserved by pickling, salting, smoking, and drying.

Meat, chicken, and fish are cooked in a variety of ways—fried, roasted, grilled, stewed. Vegetarian dishes are also popular, like the *baimbale* curry made from tender bamboo shoots, *kemb* curry from the leaves of the colcosia plant, *mange paji* made from mangoes with yogurt, coconut, and *mudure kanni*, a gravy rich with spices and the juices of boiled horse gram. Rice is used in traditional dishes. *Akki roti*, rice rotis made from rice flour and cooked rice, various *puttus* (steam cooked dishes) made of rice flour or wheat are traditional dishes. Special steamers are used for the *puttus*. *Paaputtu* is cooked with milk and shredded coconut, while *Koovale puttu* is made with ripe jackfruit or bananas and steamed in banana leaves. Pickles are made from pork, mushrooms, tender bamboo, plums, gooseberries, citrus fruits, and even fish.

Coorg Pandi
Pork Curry

An all-time favorite, this is a hearty classic Coorg dish enhanced by numerous spices. When Kim and Prabha Kambiranda, my daughter's in-laws, visited Los Angeles, Prabha cooked this signature *pandi* curry full of intense aromatic flavors and the special pork *masala* and tamarind she had brought all the way from Coorg.

SERVES 6 TO 8

2 pounds pork chops
Salt to taste
2 teaspoons ground turmeric
6 red chilies, ground
4 garlic cloves, chopped
2 large onions, chopped
1 large piece fresh ginger, chopped

6 curry leaves
8 black peppercorns
1 teaspoon cumin seeds
Small bunch of cilantro
1 2-inch cinnamon stick
5 teaspoons concentrated tamarind
   juice or vinegar

Wash pork chops thoroughly and marinate in mixture of salt, turmeric, and ground chilies for 2 hours.

Fry the garlic, onion, ginger, curry leaves, peppercorns, cumin seeds, and cilantro.

Fry the pork chops in oil for 5 minutes. Add spice mixture and cinnamon stick and fry. Add concentrated tamarind juice and 3 cups of water and cook and stir until you make a rich gravy.

Sprinkle with some roasted curry leaves and cilantro leaves before serving.

Bell Pepper and Potato Sukke

This dish is from Mangalore, a seaport on the Konkan Coast of Karnataka. A quick and versatile stir-fry with fresh vegetables, it has a delicious combination of peppers and potatoes and lots of nutritional value.

SERVES 4

4 teaspoons oil
1½ teaspoons mustard seeds
1 medium onion, sliced
2 bell peppers, sliced lengthwise
1 large potato, cut in cubes
Salt to taste

2 roasted red chilies
¾ cup grated coconut
½ teaspoon tamarind paste
½ teaspoon sugar
¼ teaspoon fenugreek seeds
2 teaspoons coriander seeds

Heat some of the oil in a deep skillet and add mustard seeds. After they pop, add onion and fry until slightly brown. Add bell peppers and sauté until beginning to soften. Add potato and fry for 2 minutes. Add some salt. Cover and cook until vegetables are tender.

Grind red chilies, coconut, tamarind paste, sugar, and a little salt with enough water to make a smooth paste. Set aside.

Roast fenugreek seeds and coriander seeds in a little oil. Add to coconut paste and blend. Add this mixture to cooked vegetables. Mix and heat well. Lower heat and cook uncovered for 5 minutes.

Mysore Pak

Chickpea Flaky Dessert

This sweet dish comes from the seaport town of Mangalore. A traditional dessert served at festivals and rituals, it is a treat at the end of a meal and has a distinct character all its own as well a crumbly appearance.

MAKES 12 PIECES

1½ cups sugar
1¾ cups water

1 cup *besan* (chickpea flour)
2 cups ghee

In a saucepan, dissolve sugar in water and heat, stirring until you can pull the syrup into a thread.

Add *besan* to syrup a little at a time to avoid lumps.

Reduce heat and add 2 tablespoons of ghee. Stir well and continue adding ghee 1 teaspoon at a time until the mixture becomes porous.

Transfer onto a greased dish and press mixture down to about 2 inches thick. Cool for 10 minutes. Cut into square shapes and allow to cool more. Can be stored in an air-tight container in a dry place.

Bise Bele Baath

Rice with Lentils

My sister-in-law Pushpa Gambhir is the real deal when it comes to authentic South Indian food. From Karnataka, she now lives in Las Vegas with her husband Ratan, children and grandchildren. When we visit, it's always a sure bet there will be great food and hospitality. A signature dish of the Kannadigas, the people of Karnataka, this makes a very rich, nutritious, and satisfying meal. In Indian stores you can get a ready-made mix of the spice powders used in this recipe.

SERVES 4

½ cup *tur dal*
1½ cups rice
1 teaspoon ground turmeric
2 medium onions, chopped
2 small eggplants, chopped
1 carrot, chopped
3 tablespoons oil
12 red chilies
1 teaspoon fenugreek seeds
1 teaspoon coriander seeds
2 cloves
2 tablespoons grated coconut

1 cardamom pod
1 small cinnamon stick
4 tablespoons chopped cashews plus 2 teaspoons whole
2 teaspoons mustard seeds
2 or 3 curry leaves
2 green chilies, chopped
1 teaspoon tamarind paste
Salt to taste
2 tablespoons ghee
1 tablespoon chopped cilantro leaves

Wash *tur dal* and rice and place in a pot with 4 cups water, turmeric, onions, eggplants, and carrot. Cook till tender.

In a skillet, fry the red chilies, fenugreek seeds, coriander seeds, cloves, and grated coconut in 1 tablespoon oil until browned. Grind to a powder and set aside.

Heat 1 tablespoon of oil and fry cardamom pod, cinnamon stick, and chopped cashews. Grind to a powder and set aside.

Heat 1 tablespoon of oil and fry mustard seeds, curry leaves, and green chilies. When mustard seeds crackle, add to cooked rice and mix well. Add tamarind paste and some salt.

Fry whole cashews in ghee and add to rice along with cilantro leaves and powdered ingredients. Mix thoroughly.

Pork Bafath

Robust Spiced Pork Curry

Although food in South India is primarily vegetarian, the Portuguese influence in Mangalore remains. Here is an excellent recipe for an aromatic pork dish infused with spices. It can be eaten with rice, *puris*, or *chapatis*. Substitute beef or lamb for the pork if desired.

SERVES 6

25 red Kashmiri chilies, seeded
3 teaspoons coriander seeds
1 teaspoon cumin seeds
½ teaspoon ground turmeric
12 black peppercorns
2 tablespoons tamarind paste
2 pounds boneless pork leg, cut into cubes
2 tablespoons oil
2 onions, cut into small pieces

2-inch piece fresh ginger, peeled and minced
8 green chilies, slit
8 cloves
1-inch piece cinnamon stick, pounded
3 garlic cloves, chopped
2 tablespoons vinegar
Sprig of cilantro leaves

Dry roast red chilies, coriander seeds, cumin seeds, ground turmeric, and peppercorns in pan over low heat. Grind into a fine powder. Mix these roasted spices with tamarind paste and pork. Marinate for 3 hours.

Heat oil in deep pan on high heat and add meat mixture and cook until brown. Add onions, ginger, chilies, cloves, and cinnamon stick. Mix and cook for 20 minutes on low heat until there is a thick sauce.

Add garlic, vinegar, and 1 cup water. Simmer for 1½ hours on low heat.

Season with salt and garnish with cilantro leaves.

Prawn Curry

A bachelor friend of mine, Vivek Coona, is always in pursuit of passion in the kitchen whether he makes *appams* (crepes) or a succulent tangy prawn curry. With precise and focused detail, he brings his own cast-iron skillets, star power knives, masses of curry leaves, and a heady mix of spices to make fresh, easy food in our home. He never uses tomatoes though!

SERVES 4 TO 5

2 pounds prawns
4 large onions, chopped
6 tablespoons oil
2 teaspoons ground coriander
1 piece cinnamon stick
3 cloves
2 teaspoons black peppercorns
3 cups grated coconut
½ teaspoon cumin seeds

3 red chilies
½ teaspoon ground turmeric
1 tablespoon tamarind paste
Small piece fresh ginger
4 green chilies, chopped
Curry leaves
2 or 3 cilantro leaves, chopped
    fine, plus a sprig

Devein prawns and remove tails.

Fry the onions in oil until golden brown. Set aside.

Dry roast the ground coriander, cinnamon stick, cloves, peppercorns, coconut, cumin seeds, red chilies, ground turmeric, and tamarind paste. Grind together.

Sauté the ginger, green chilies, curry leaves and cilantro leaves for a few minutes. Add browned onions. Mix with roasted mixture.

Fry prawns in a little oil until just cooked. Add spice mixture and a little water. Bring to boil. Garnish with cilantro leaves. Serve with plain rice.

Street Fare

Pushcarts abound in street food areas, spilling over with spicy foods, vegetable fritters, an assortment of snacks and sandwiches, so delicious that you know you will return again and again. Traditional foods, as well as noodles and pizzas, favorite ice creams, and dried fruits offer reasons for casual socializing. Varying regionally, this is a feast for the senses with enticing smells, sights, and flavors at every street corner. Deep-fried puffs of bread (*golguppa*), peeled pineapples cut into chunks and wrapped in banana leaves, tandoori paneer (cubes of cheese threaded on skewers with mixed vegetables and cooked in a tandoor oven), peanut *bhujiya* (peanuts coated in chickpea batter and fried), corn roasted on red hot charcoal, chickpeas cooked with spices and garnished with onions and tomatoes and cilantro, peeled cucumbers dipped in salt or sold as a drink ... eating is a way of life among street vendors. But be sure to use common sense when eating on the street and be alert about hygiene. If there is a long line at one vendor, you can be sure that you will find the tastiest snack right there. For street food is part of the culture of India and the diversity of freshly made snacks is not only tantalizing but astounding as snacks are consumed by those on the way to work, at lunchtime, and again in the evenings on the way back from work or later at night when families arrive.

Aloo ki Tikki
Potato Patties

This dish is popular all over North India. Street vendors sell many variations and serve it with a variety of chutneys like mint, cilantro, and tamarind. These snacks are so appealing and fortunately they are as easy to make as they are irresistible.

MAKES 25

1 pound potatoes
1 cup peas
5 tablespoons oil
3 green chilies, minced
½ medium onion, minced
½-inch piece fresh ginger, grated
1 teaspoon ground turmeric

1 teaspoon ground cumin
1 teaspoon ground coriander
½ teaspoon garam masala (page 69)
2 tablespoons *besan* flour
1 tablespoon lemon juice
Salt to taste

Boil potatoes until very tender. Add peas for a few minutes until soft. Drain, peel potatoes, and mash the potatoes and peas.

Put 1 tablespoon oil in a medium saucepan and fry chilies, onion, ginger, and remaining spices for 1 minute. Set chutney aside.

Add the *besan* flour to potato mixture and mix. Add lemon juice and some salt. Divide mixture into 25 balls and flatten into patties.

Heat remaining 4 tablespoons oil in a heavy pan and add patties a few at a time. Fry on each side until crisp. Serve with the chutney.

Samosas

Vegetable Pastries

Samosas are a deep-fried crispy pastry with a savory filling of spiced vegetables served and enjoyed on the streets of India any time of the day or night. Perfect for unexpected guests at home, if you have frozen samosas they can be quickly thawed and you are ready for company. You can also spike them with a meat mixture or even paneer cheese. Samosas should be eaten piping hot.

SERVES 6

2 cups all-purpose flour
1 teaspoon salt
5 tablespoons ghee
2 teaspoons ground coriander
Pinch of asafetida
½ teaspoon mango powder
½ teaspoon red chili powder

1 teaspoon cumin seeds, roasted and ground to a powder
1 tablespoon oil
1 cup cooked peas
½ pound potatoes, boiled
Oil for deep frying

Sift flour and salt together. Make a well in center, add ghee, and knead to a firm dough.

Roast ground coriander, asafetida, mango powder, red chili powder, and ground cumin with 1 tablespoon oil on low heat for 1 minute. Add peas and potatoes, and cook on low heat. Stir and mash well. Remove from heat.

Make small balls with dough 1 inch in diameter and roll into small circles. Cut each circle in half and shape each half into a cone. Fill the cones with 1 tablespoon of vegetable mixture. Overlap edges to cover filling and seal all around by applying a little water. Deep fry until golden. Serve hot.

Sev Puri

Cracker Snack

Popular as street food, snacks, or an appetizer, *puris* are flat or puffed. The *puris* and *bhel* mix can be bought ready-made at Indian grocery stores.

MAKES 24

24 small *puris*
½ cup plain yogurt
2 teaspoons water
3 white potatoes, peeled, boiled, and cubed

¼ cup tamarind chutney
½ cup *bhel* mix
¼ cup mint or cilantro chutney

Place *puris* on platter. Beat yogurt with water. Top each *puri* with some yogurt and a few potato cubes. Drizzle each puri with ½ teaspoon tamarind chutney. Place some *bhel* mix on top of each. Add ½ teaspoon mint or cilantro chutney to each.

Onion Pakoras

Crispy Fritter Snack

Onion *pakoras* are welcome any time as they make a crispy snack. *Pakoras* can also be made with shrimp, vegetables, or fish pieces and go well with a mint chutney (see page 209). The *besan* flour gives them a light flavor.

SERVES 12

¾ cup *besan* flour
½ cup minced onions
3 tablespoons vegetable oil
½ teaspoon salt

Pinch ground black pepper
Pinch baking soda
Oil for frying

Mix *besan*, onion, oil, salt, pepper, and baking soda in bowl. Add ⅓ cup water to make a dough. Knead out any lumps. Divide dough to make 12 balls.

Heat oil for frying. Place dough balls gently into hot oil and fry until golden. Drain on paper towels.

Soan Papdi

.... Flaky Sweet Squares ....

Come Divali time you find millions of *Soan Papdi* boxed in Indian stores as it is a delectable flaky sweet to be given as a gift at festival time.

1¼ cups gram flour	1½ cups water
1¼ cups *maida* (fine white flour)	2 tablespoons milk
½ pound ghee	½ teaspoon ground cardamom
2½ cups sugar	

Sift flours together. Heat ghee in deep pan. Add flour mixture and roast on low heat until golden brown. Set aside, stirring occasionally.

Mix sugar, water, and milk together in a saucepan and cook over low heat, stirring constantly, until it forms a syrup, about 10 minutes.

Pour syrup onto flour mixture. Beat well with fork until you get threadlike flakes. Pour onto greased surface and roll to one-inch thickness.

Sprinkle ground cardamom on top and press down with palm. Cool and cut into one-inch squares.

Quick Takes

So you don't have time for elaborate traditional recipes and varied ingredients. If you want to rustle up a spontaneous recipe with minimum fuss here are some quick fixes to whip up and leave you time for conversation and relaxation with your guests.

Cucumber Raita

Cucumber with Yogurt

Who does not love a cool, refreshing cucumber? This vegetable claims a storied history—it was even mentioned in the Rig Veda (Hymns of Praise written in 1000 BC). Cucumbers can be green, yellow, thick, smooth, or bumpy. Since lettuce salads are not typically served in India, cucumbers often serve as the "salad" of the meal, simply seasoned with a squirt of lime or salt, or chopped into yogurt for *raita*. Shredded mint, slivers of peanuts, grated beetroot, or carrots can be used as a substitute for the cucumber in this recipe.

SERVES 4

1 cucumber
1 cup plain yogurt
½ teaspoon salt

Ground black pepper
¼ teaspoon ground cumin

Peel and grate cucumber and place in a bowl. Add yogurt, salt, dash of pepper, and cumin. Mix well. Store in refrigerator.

Mint Chutney

This aromatic and refreshing mint chutney can be served with any savory snack like *samosas* or *singharas*. South Indians serve it with any meal.

1½ cups fresh mint leaves	½ teaspoon salt
1 cup cilantro leaves	1½ teaspoons sugar
2 green chilies	4 tablespoons plain yogurt
1 tablespoon tamarind paste	

Wash mint and cilantro thoroughly. Throw away tough stems.

Blend all ingredients except yogurt in a blender, or chop finely and pound. Add more salt if needed.

Stir in yogurt for a thick, rich effect.

Kachumber

Garbanzo Salad

Light and refreshing in summer, this salad can be made ahead and kept in the refrigerator before serving.

1 cup chickpeas, dried or canned
Salt to taste
1 cup chopped red onions
1 large tomato, chopped
½ cucumber, peeled and chopped
2 tablespoons lemon juice

¼ cup chopped cilantro, plus some for garnish
1 tablespoon chopped fenugreek leaves
Ground black pepper to taste
1 green chili, chopped

If using dried chickpeas, rinse thoroughly and boil in water with ¼ teaspoon salt until tender. Do not overcook. Drain. If using canned chickpeas, simply rinse with cold water and drain.

Put chickpeas in a bowl. Add remaining ingredients and toss. Add some salt to taste. Add a little more lemon juice if needed. Garnish with some cilantro.

Appalam *or* Poppadam
Rice Wafers

These wafers are called *appalam* in South India and *poppadam* in the North. Dough made from *lentils* is seasoned and flattened into circular shapes and dried in the sun. You can also deep fry or roast the *appalam* directly over heat. They can be served with drinks or with a meal. *Appalam* can also be purchased ready-to-cook in Indian groceries. But if you enjoy making things from scratch go ahead and enjoy working on this recipe.

MAKES 8 TO 10

2 cups rice	¼ teaspoon asafetida
¼ cup sago	½ teaspoon salt
8 green chilies	3 tablespoons ghee

Grind rice and sago into a powder. Set aside.

Grind chilies with asafetida and salt. Put in a pot, add 2 cups of water and bring to a boil. Add the ground rice mixture and cook for 1 minute while stirring. Remove from heat.

Make small balls from the dough by rolling with your hands. Baste the balls with ghee and knead until soft. Roll them out into a thin round shape.

The *appalams* can be cooked in any of the following ways:

To sun dry: Dip the top of the appalams in dry flour, lay in one layer on a white cotton sheet and dry under full sun or in front of a fan. Once they are dry, store in tins.

To fry: Put a little oil in the pan (just use 1 teaspoon oil—you don't want the *appalams* to be greasy) and heat. Put in a few *appalam*; they will sizzle and expand. Turn over and cook other side. Remove with a slotted spoon and place on a paper towel.

To roast: You can roast *appalams* directly on top of a low flame on a stove. Take a pair of tongs and hold one half an inch above the flame. When the *appalam* turns light brown in color, turn it quickly upside down until it is roasted on the other side.

To grill: Place *appalams* on a grill at least 2 inches away from flames and wait until bubbles appear on surface; turn over and grill other side.

Carrot Sherbet

Carrot-Laced Drink

A scrumptious drink filled with goodness—simple, quick, and refreshing. Serve cold.

SERVES 2

2 medium carrots, scraped and
   diced
¼ cup celery leaves
2 spinach leaves
4 lettuce leaves

¼ teaspoon salt
⅛ teaspoon ground coriander
1 teaspoon crushed mint leaves

Combine all ingredients in a blender and process for 30 seconds. Add ½ cup water. Blend for 10 more seconds. Pour over ice.

Kela Kheer

Banana Drink

A rich and nutritious drink filled with a lush sweet flavor. Makes a refreshing treat at the end of a meal or a pick-me-up on a hot day. Serve cold or warm.

SERVES 3 TO 4

3 teaspoons ghee
2 tablespoons wheat flour
1 can (12 ounces) coconut milk
6 ripe bananas, mashed

4 teaspoons sugar
½ teaspoon ground cardamom
1 teaspoon ground nutmeg

Heat ghee and fry wheat flour over low heat until brown. Gradually add coconut milk, stirring all the time. When smooth, add mashed bananas and sugar. Cook until slightly thick. Sprinkle in cardamom and nutmeg. Remove and serve when slightly warm.

Honey Dew

Almond-Rich Dessert

The name evokes a fragrant spring morning and the drink reflects the memories of an idyllic time of life. Deliciously sweet and has a nutty texture.

SERVES 3

12 almonds	3 cups chilled milk
12 cashews	1 teaspoon ground cardamom
1 tablespoon poppy seeds	Honey, according to taste
12 pistachios	2 tablespoons cream

Grind all nuts and seeds to smooth paste.

Stir in milk and cardamom. Mix well and strain through a fine cloth.

Stir in honey and chill. Add cream before serving and mix well. Serve in 3 glasses.

Masala Chai

Spiced Tea

The chai guru in our home is Bobby Kishore, my husband, who is known to brew forty to fifty cups of *chai* throughout the evening for family, guests, and even strangers. He believes in slow heating of water, the auspicious moment for blending milk and sugar, and an intuitive eye and hand for the perfect *chai*. Accompanied by his dazzling wit and humor the *chai* connections make for a memorable get together. But I always urge him to accept that a little spice goes a long way when making tea Indian style! So here is my version of Masala Chai.

SERVES 4

½ cup water
6 whole cardamom pods

2 cups milk
2 teabags, black tea preferable

Combine water and cardamom pods in a pot and bring to a boil. When liquid is boiling, add milk and teabags. When the liquid reaches the boiling point again, turn the heat off and let sit for 5 minutes.

Pour *chai* into teacups through a sieve to remove cardamom pods.

Lassi

Yogurt Drink

Perhaps the most popular drink in India, this is easy to prepare at a moments notice. It can be salted or sweetened with the addition of sugar. Add a litlle rose essence to make it more enticing.

SERVES 4

2½ cups plain yogurt

1⅓ cups water

Sugar

8 ice cubes

Blend ingredients except ice cubes and chill. Serve over ice in glasses.

Thank you to my Food Network

My editor Priti Gress, the meticulous Barbara Keane-Pigeon, and their team for incredible support, superb feedback, patient editing, and reassurance.

To Lily Dong, my adventuresome world traveler and photographer, with deep gratitude for sharing some of your amazing pictures.

Prem (Bobby) Kishore, who shares my first name and the rich possibilities of life, love, and family. A truly blithe spirit who quotes my favorite poetry.

My grandmother Grace and grandfather Charles, parents Mabel and Jeevanah Souri, Aunt Dora Venkatesulu, and mother-in-law Besant Gambeer, who blessed me with rich memories to write this book.

Nasir Ahmad, seasoned traveler, who gave us splendid vacations in distant lands. A connoisseur of barbecue grilling, he taught me to embellish gourmet fare with special nuances and flavors.

Nasir Ahmad's gracious mother, Ammi, who brought an aesthetic art and skill to cooking whether she was making a favorite dish or slicing a green chili. A perfect companion while watching glitzy Indian TV soap operas drenched with emotion on warm late nights in Zurich.

Chetan Ganpati, who retrieves my lost files, the bedrock of my writing.

Taha, Aleenah, Aneeq, Uddanta, and Tavasya for giving me joy, joy, joy, joy, joy.

Kim and Prabha for the spectacular food we have always delighted in in your Chennai garden home.

Sundar and Rani for hosting us in regal style in India and constantly advising us on dietary concerns and the gift of faith.

Vivek Coona, a favorite friend, addicted to pepper and curry leaves –he even gifted me with a lush plant. For coming over with iron skillets and appam woks, preparing delicious meals, and spiking up the evenings with eloquence and humor.

The Narang family—Mummyji Satwant, Harbir, Sushil, and Sonia—for many meals and planning the fantasy wedding feasts of Nisha and Amar.

Sunny and Rashmi Narang for fun parties ranging from famed food trucks to home swirled pizzas.

Fun loving Dolly Bhutani, who invited our family often for robust Punjabi *rajma* and rotis, topped with a Bollywood film.

Ratan, Pushpa Gambhir, Nitin, Ashika, Kiran, and Akhil, who delight us with South Indian, North Indian and Fiji dishes.

Balbir and Pammi Narang, Dr Binesh Batra, Upaasna, Sneha, Gulu, Pushpa Gulati, Chand and Preeti Gulati, and all 120 of the in-laws in Orange County, California, for the festive food gatherings.

The Zurich Connection—Global dishes and deep friendship with the families of the Habibs, Zuby Aunty, Fatima, Usha, Maya, Rehana, Uma, Padmaja, Anna, and many more.

Cousin Mahadev of Seattle, for your warm generosity and deep affection in hosting us many a time on the waters of the Puget Sound. The children, Immanuel and Aruna, for many laughs and family time.

Rajkumar and Indira, for memorable meals, the legendary fish curry, and exciting car journeys.

Christy and Sheela Thiagarajan, Ahalya Alfred, Hem and Larry Parsons, Meera, Pratap and Asha Souri, and Nimmi for splendid food fests in Chennai, Ohio, Los Angeles, and Seattle.

David and Pratima Pandian, for relaxed weekends in their San Diego home spiced up with authentic South Indian cooking.

Om and Bimla Bhatla, Sunil, Chintu and Murali for delighting our family with superb hospitality and cuisine over the decades.

The Dream Team in Chennai: Suresh Thommandram, Ashi Kapadia, Kunju Bhaiya, and Suri for the profusion of shared meals and witticisms. Babu Prasad, the eternal raconteur, and Balu, who wrote recipes for me on the kitchen wall. Vinod and Raj Grover, who entertain always with fine dining and good conversation.

Sagar and Kaveri Sethi, for myriad cups of tea, conversation, and togetherness.

Raj and Prema Mohan, Nalini, Ian, Rupa, and Kevin for a sumptuous table at Thanksgiving, impromptu meals, and a warm friendship.

Chatura and Ravi Vavulli for their inventive spice combinations.

Kay Talwar, Judy Mitoma, Marcia Argolo, Jorge Vismara, Sabrina Motley, Karen Ito, Etsu Garfias, Lily Bulhoes, Steve Williams, and Danilo, Lillian Wu, Shana Mathur, and countless others who nurtured our family with diverse foods during a difficult illness and shared much laughter and stories.

Vijay and Titoo Krishnan, for festive parties and authentic Goan pork dishes.

Jimmy Charles, the fun loving, gregarious uncle who was magical in a London kitchen, whipping up gourmet meals for me when I was homesick for Indian food. His wife, Noreen, living now in the beauteous Isle of Wight, can still serve up a flavorsome Indian meal and lace it with Irish humor.

Uncle Major Joshua Charles, who introduced me to my first grown-up dinner at the Military Officers Club in Bangalore, his wife Binky, and daughter Shalini, who serve out-of-this-world baked goods.

Mohan and Felicia, for pristine vegetarian fare topped with scintillating humor and *appalams*.

Mohan and Jessica Gnanadickam, for the legendary late night boisterous dinners in Chennai.

Rupert and Jayanti Benjamin, who left behind a legacy of deep friendship and will always be remembered.

Lionel and Sreeni Perera, for the good times and sharing joy and peace in our home for special get-togethers.

In Dubai, Balan and Christine Raj, for motivation sessions and loving hospitality when we first arrived in that fascinating city.

Martha D. Souza, my endearing friend with whom I discovered interesting eating places and relished a Friday night Middle Eastern fish fry from a roadside stall.

Our helpers in the kitchen, Govindamma and Lakshmiamma, who served faithfully over many years.

To innumerable food bloggers for their delightful, fascinating, rich-in-detail anecdotes, recipes, and personal writings.

Index

About the Author

Prem Souri Kishore is an author, lecturer, and broadcaster who has traveled extensively in search of stories about food. Born in Chennai, India, she has also lived in England, the Middle East, and the United States. She is author of *India: An Illustrated History* (Hippocrene Books, 2003). She currently resides in Los Angeles, California.

Prem Souri Kishore as a child in Bangalore

CPSIA information can be obtained
at www.ICGtesting.com
Printed in the USA
LVHW02s1540170818
587124LV00001B/1/P